Canada

ENGLISH CANADA PROVINCE

Builders *of a* Nation

Builders *of a* Nation

A HISTORY OF JESUITS IN ENGLISH CANADA 1842–2013

VOLUME 2
IN THE JESUIT HISTORY SERIES

Jacques Monet, s.j.
Executive Editor

NOVALIS

Cover design: Martin Gould
Photographs and illustrations provided by the Jesuits in English Canada, The Archive of the Jesuits in Canada, and other sources. Copyright and attribution provided where the photographs or illustrations appear.
Map on endpapers: © Archives of the Jesuits in Canada
Layout: Audrey Wells

Published by Novalis

Publishing Office
10 Lower Spadina Avenue, Suite 400
Toronto, Ontario, Canada
M5V 2Z2

Head Office
4475 Frontenac Street
Montréal, Québec, Canada
H2H 2S2

www.novalis.ca

Library and Archives Canada Cataloguing in Publication

A history of Jesuits in English Canada, 1842-2013.

(Jesuit history series)
Includes bibliographical references and indexes.
Contents: Volume 1. Teachers of a nation / Joseph B. Gavin, S.J.
-- Volume 2. Builders of a nation / Jacques Monet, s.j., executive editor.

Issued in print and electronic formats.
ISBN 978-2-89688-124-6 (v. 1 : bound).--ISBN 978-2-89688-128-4 (v. 2 : bound).-- ISBN 978-2-89688-125-3 (v. 1 : mobi).--ISBN 978-2-89688-126-0 (v. 1 : epub).-- ISBN 978-2-89688-127-7 (v.1 : pdf).--ISBN 978-2-89688-129-1 (v. 2 : mobi).-- ISBN 978-2-89688-130-7 (v. 2 : epub).--ISBN 978-2-89688-131-4 (v. 2 : pdf)

1. Jesuits--Canada--History.

BX3711.A1H58 2015   271'.53071   C2015-900018-1

Printed in Canada.

We acknowledge the financial support of the Government of Canada through the Canada Book Fund for business development activities.

5 4 3 2 1   19 18 17 16 15

Contributors

Dr. Peter Baltutis

Michael Knox, S.J.

Jacques Monet, s.j.

John D. O'Brien, S.J.

J. Winston Rye, S.J.

Michael M. Stogre, S.J.

About the Contributors

Dr. Peter Baltutis graduated from the University of St. Michael's College with a thesis on the development of Catholic Social Thought in Canada. He is currently Assistant Professor of History and Catholic Studies at St. Mary's University in Calgary. He published a number of articles while teaching at the University of Toronto and at Corpus Christi College in Vancouver.

Joseph B. Gavin, S.J., was ordained a Jesuit priest in 1968. A graduate of Columbia and McGill Universities, he has published widely in Canadian and Church history. He served as President of Campion College, University of Regina, and as founding Director of the Loyola Peace Institute at Concordia University in Montreal.

Michael Legros Knox, S.J., was born in Quebec City in 1978 and was ordained a Jesuit priest in 2011. He served on the training staff at Sainte-Marie among the Hurons from 2002 to 2013. After graduating in history from the University of Toronto and from Memorial University in St. John's, he is a Doctoral Candidate at the University of Oxford.

John Meehan, S.J., studied in France, England, and the United States before publishing two major works in the history of Canadian Foreign Affairs. He entered the Society of Jesus in 2000 and was ordained in 2010. He is currently the President of Campion College in the University of Regina.

Jacques Monet, s.j., entered the Society of Jesus in 1949 and was ordained a priest in 1966. His degree in Canadian History is from the University of Toronto and his research and writing have been consistently in Canadian, Church, and Jesuit history. He was elected to The Royal Society of Canada in 1978.

John D. O'Brien, S.J., worked in freelance journalism, television, and other media between his graduations in Communications from the University of Ottawa in 2000 and in Philosophy from the Gregorian University in Rome in 2008. He entered the Society of Jesus in 2008.

J. Winston Rye, S.J. entered the Jesuit Order in 1960 and was ordained in 1973. A graduate in History from Gonzaga University, in Spokane, Washington, he taught in Jesuit high schools in Toronto, Montreal, and St. John's. He served as Director of the Canadian Martyrs' Shrine in Midland, Ontario, before appointments as Principal at Brebeuf High School in Toronto, Gonzaga High School in St. John's, and St. Bonaventure's College in that same city. He is currently Secretary General of the Jesuits in English Canada.

Michael Stogre, S.J., became a Jesuit in 1962 and was ordained a priest in 1974. In 1978 he graduated as a medical doctor from McMaster University. Most of his practice has been with native people, their main health and welfare issues, as well as their health-care delivery system. His book *The Development of Papal Social Thought on Aboriginal Rights* was published in 1992.

This book is dedicated to the memory of all the Jesuits who worked in various ministries in English-speaking Canada.

CONTENTS

Acknowledgements 9

Abbreviations 10

Glossary of Jesuit Terms 11

Introduction by Jacques Monet, s.j 21

I The Jesuits' Ministry to the Native People in Canada since 1842
Michael J. Stogre, S.J. 27

II The Witness of Jean de Brébeuf and His Companions Through the History of the Jesuits in Canada
Michael L. Knox, S.J. 73

III Communities of Sacrament and Prayer Committed to Justice: Jesuit Parishes in English Canada since 1842
J. Winston Rye, S.J. 103

IV "Do Justice. Love Kindness": A Faith that Does Justice: Jesuit Social Apostolate in English Canada, 1842–2014
Dr. Peter Baltutis 157

V The Ministry of Communications in the Jesuit Province of English Canada,1842–2013
John D. O'Brien, S.J. 189

Chronology of Jesuit Events 235

Index 269

ACKNOWLEDGEMENTS

The Jesuit History Series has been initiated and supported by the Canadian Institute of Jesuit Studies.

Our special thanks is owed to the Provincial Superiors of the Canadian English-speaking Jesuits, Jean-Marc Laporte, s.j., James Freeman Webb, S.J., and J. Peter Bisson, S.J., for their financial and personal encouragement in the preparation and publication of this book; to the Jesuits at Maison Bellarmin, and particularly to the Superior, Michel LeFebvre, s.j., our thanks for their friendly hospitality and interest; to the staff of the Archive of the Jesuits in Canada, Montreal, especially to Céline Widmer, Bruce Henry, and Theresa Rowat, for their ready assistance; to Erica Zlomislic, for her careful research; to Anne Louise Mahoney, who made the preparation of this book such a pleasure; and to Prescy Alumaga, Mahal Yu-Daquiado, and Arthur White, S.J., for their obliging secretarial help. For Anne M. Delicaet, who died before this book went to the printer, we reserve a very fond and special thank you for her generous help and assistance.

Jacques Monet, s.j. for the Committee of Authors

ABBREVIATIONS

AJC	Archive of the Jesuits in Canada
CCCB	Canadian Conference of Catholic Bishops
CCHA	Canadian Catholic Historical Association
DCB	*Dictionary of Canadian Biography*
DJB	*Dictionary of Jesuit Biography: Ministry to English Canada, 1842–1987* (Toronto: Canadian Institute of Jesuit Studies, 1991), vol. 1; *Dictionary of Jesuit Biography: Ministry to English Canada, 1988–2006* (Toronto: Canadian Institute of Jesuit Studies, 2007), vol. 2
GIAN	Global Ignatian Advocacy Network
JESEDES	The Jesuit Secretariat for Social and Economic Development
Jesuit Relations	Reuben Gold Thwaites, *Jesuit Relations and Allied Documents*
Lecompte	Édouard Lecompte, *Les Jésuites du Canada au XIX siècle* (Montréal: Imprimerie du Messager, 1920)
The Messenger	*The Canadian Messenger of the Sacred Heart*
SJES	Social Justice and Ecology Secretariat

GLOSSARY OF JESUIT TERMS

As do many institutions, the Society of Jesus has developed its own terminology and vocabulary. Some of these were taken from the traditional language of the Church and of other Religious Orders; some were based on the writings of the Jesuits' founder, Ignatius Loyola, on the Constitutions of the Society of Jesus and their "complementary norms", or on the decrees of the Jesuits' General Congregations. Others were improvised in Canada. A glossary of Jesuit terms used in this book therefore might be useful.

Assistant A senior Jesuit administrator in Rome who advises and assists the Superior General in the governance of the Society of Jesus, either Regional (e.g., Assistant for India) or General (one of four who assists the Superior General in the governance of the Society of Jesus). See also below, "Minister" and "Socius."

Biretta Originally, a head-piece for monks and priests to protect their heads from the elements; a stiff, square unadorned black cap with three ridges across the crown, once worn by Jesuits after first vows. The biretta disappeared from use between the late 1950s and late 1960s.

Brother A man who has taken the three vows of religion and is a member within a Religious Congregation or Order but who is not in Holy Orders; traditionally, in the Society of Jesus, referred to as a Coadjutor Brother.

although this terminology has gradually gone out of use since the 1960s.

Bursar The treasurer of a Jesuit Province, Community, school, or college.

Cassock A long black robe worn by Jesuits, without buttons and secured at the waist with a woollen cincture. In Canada, the term "Blackrobe" was used to refer to a Jesuit during the seventeenth century; it went out of use during the late 1960s to early 1970s.

Community An ecclesiastically approved house for members of a Religious Order; a group of Jesuits living together under the authority of a designated Rector or Superior; sometimes referred to as "local Community." According to Canon (Church) Law, there had to be three or more Jesuits living together to form a Religious Community, although more recently only two Jesuits can be declared to form a Community.

Consultors Jesuits appointed in each Community by the Provincial Superior, at the suggestion of the Superior or Rector, to advise him; Jesuits appointed by the Superior General from the Province to advise a Provincial Superior. The number of Consultors in local Communities varies according to the Community's size; the number of Consultors for a Provincial Superior is set at four.

Cura Personalis Latin meaning "care for the individual person"; a significant responsibility of a Provincial Superior towards the individual members in the Province, and of a Rector or Superior towards the members of his Community.

Curia A Latin term originating in ancient Rome, now used to describe the central administrative office in the universal Society of Jesus (Rome) or in a Jesuit Province; hence the term "curial."

Dean of Studies One responsible for an academic program of an educational institution; in modern North American Jesuit high schools, this is the principal. For a time, the term designated the one appointed by the Provincial Superior to assist in the educational formation of Jesuits.

Formation The period beginning with the Novitiate for the training and educating of Jesuits, and ending with Final Vows. See below, "Vows."

General Congregation The supreme legislative body of the Society of Jesus that elects the Superior General; an official meeting of delegates of the whole Society of Jesus; the Jesuit equivalent of a monastic General Chapter; there have been thirty-five General Congregations since 1558.

Instructor of Tertians The Jesuit priest who directs Jesuit priests and Brothers in their final year of formation; sometimes referred to as Tertian Master or Master of Tertians. See below, "Tertianship."

Jesuit As a noun, a member of the Society of Jesus; as an adjective, pertaining to the Society of Jesus; adapted from the Latin word *Jesuita* (a follower of Jesus), and in common use today, even officially.

Junior The term formerly used for a Jesuit Scholastic and Brother in the period of formation known as the Juniorate. See below, "Juniorate."

Juniorate The term formerly used for the house and for the period of classical and humanistic studies, usually for a two-year period for Jesuit Scholastics immediately following the Novitiate; also used for Brothers in their technical training after the Novitiate.

Master of Novices The Jesuit priest who directs Jesuit novices in their first two years of formation; also referred to as "director" of novices. See below, "Novitiate."

Minister A term for the assistant to a Rector or Superior; one who is responsible for the practical and material needs of a Jesuit Community; also, traditionally, the one who assigns pastoral ministry for members of a Community.

Ministry The term used by Jesuits to refer to their works by which they render aid and service to others; often referred to as "apostolate."

Mission Usually an area or centre where the Gospel is preached, often in foreign lands, hence the term "missionary"; may also be referred to as a regional administrative unit of Jesuits. The term is often applied to an assigned task, and is sometimes used for popular preaching in a parish.

Novice The term used for someone in the first period of spiritual formation in religious life, usually referred to as the Novitiate. For the Jesuits, the term refers to the individual during the first two years of Jesuit formation in the Novitiate.

Novitiate A house for novices, and a place for their spiritual discernment, training, and testing, which includes the Spiritual Exercises of Ignatius Loyola; the first two years in the course of Jesuit formation. At the end of this period, the first vows in the Society of Jesus are pronounced; also known as the Second Probation. See below, "Vows."

Ordination The conferring of the holy orders of sub-deaconate, deaconate, and priesthood; traditionally, and unlike other Religious or diocesan candidates to the priesthood, Jesuits received the sub-deaconate and deaconate during their third year of theological studies and the priesthood followed shortly afterwards that same year. Since the 1980s, the sub-deaconate has been abolished while the deaconate is conferred at the end of the third year of theological studies, followed a year later by the ordination to the priesthood.

Philosophy Usually a three-year period for the pursuit of philosophical studies and related disciplines; hence terms such as "philosopher" (for the student who studies philosophy) and "philosophate." Traditionally, for the Jesuit, this period followed four years after his Novitiate years and two years after finishing his Juniorate studies. In more recent years, the taking of a Jesuit's philosophical studies depends on his previous studies and with what graduate degrees he entered the Novitiate.

Prefect The traditional term for certain administrative officers in a Jesuit institution (e.g., prefect of studies, prefect of discipline).

Province The common division of the Society of Jesus for administrative and jurisdictional purposes. There can be more than one Jesuit Province in a country: for example, in Canada, the Province of French Canada and the Province of Upper Canada. The use of the word dates back to Roman times and to the beginnings of the Society of Jesus in the sixteenth century; hence the terms Provincial Superior and Provincialate.

Provincial Superior The major Superior in charge of a Jesuit Province, appointed by the Superior General for three years, and usually renewed once only.

Ratio Studiorum A Latin term meaning "plan of studies"; the document outlining the program of studies for all Jesuit educational institutions; basis of the Jesuits' classical college system of education (classical course). First published in 1599, it has been modified several times since.

Rector The Superior of a Jesuit Community or institution, such as a college, university, or school, appointed by the Superior General for a three-year term (renewable usually only once); hence the term "rectorship."

Refectory A traditional term signifying the dining room of a monastery or university college and used since the sixteenth century for the dining room of a Jesuit Community; hence a refectorian would be the one in charge of the refectory. It is rarely used today except in very large Jesuit houses.

Regency A term used to refer traditionally to the teaching years of a Jesuit Scholastic between his studies of philosophy and of theology; hence the term "Regent"; more recently, the term is used for the years of a Jesuit Scholastic between his studies of philosophy and of theology, whether he is teaching or not.

Religious An ecclesiastical term used for a man or woman in a Religious Order or Congregation under vows. See below, "Religious Order" and "Vows."

Religious Order Ecclesiastical term to denote a community of men or women bound by common customs and rules of life, and who pronounce the three vows of religion. Orders are distinguished from Congregations by their solemn as opposed to simple vows; Jesuits alone pronounce perpetual vows after the Novitiate. See below, "Vows."

Retreat The term referring to a specific period of spiritual exercises and prayer such as three days, eight days, or thirty days; retreats may be directed, preached, or made privately. See below, "The Spiritual Exercises."

Retreat House A place or centre for lay retreats (see "The Spiritual Exercises"), reflection, and spiritual renewal programs.

Scholastic The traditional term used to designate a Jesuit student during his formation between the Novitiate and final vows; it is used to distinguish Jesuit students from Jesuit Brothers in formation: a Scholastic was formerly addressed as "Mister" until ordination.

Scholasticate The term used for Jesuit houses of formation following the Novitiate.

Society of Jesus From the Latin *Societas Jesu*; the official title of the Jesuits as a Religious Order, abbreviated as S.J. (English language) or s.j. or S.I. (most other languages); equivalent to the term "Jesuit Order" or to the "Jesuits." In most languages, except English, the Latin term has usually been translated as "Company of Jesus."

Socius A Latin word meaning "ally" or "companion"; used formally in the Society of Jesus to designate the assistant to the Provincial Superior, who is appointed by the Superior General; also used for the assistant to the Master of Novices; an alter ego of the Provincial Superior.

Sodality of Our Lady An association founded by the Jesuits in 1563 at their Collegio Romano, Rome, to foster a devout Christian life of prayer and social action for lay people, under the patronage of Mary, the Mother of God.

The Spiritual Exercises A manual composed by Ignatius Loyola, the founder of the Society of Jesus, reflecting his spiritual conversion, and based on his methods of prayer and personal decision making; used during Jesuit retreats (see above, "Retreat"), either personal or those retreats given to others. See above, "Retreat House."

Superior The one designated to administer a Jesuit Community and appointed by the Provincial Superior with the approval of the Superior General.

Superior General The major Superior of the Society of Jesus, usually referred to by Jesuits as "the General" or "Father General"; chosen for life by a General Congregation to direct the Jesuits between Congregations; sometimes referred to as "The Black Pope."

Tertian The term for a Jesuit priest or Brother in the final year of spiritual formation.

Tertianship The final year of Jesuit formation, also known as the Third Probation: the First being postulancy and the Second being the Novitiate. It is a synthesis of spiritual, intellectual or technical, and pastoral formation and is sometimes referred to as "spiritual theology."

Theology The period set aside for the study of Church doctrine, scripture, Church history, liturgy, and pastoral practices; usually of a four-year duration; hence, terms such as "theologian" (for the student who studies theology) and "theologate" (for the house where these studies take place).

Upper Canada Province The name given to the English-speaking Canadian Jesuits in 1924 when the Province of Canada was divided into the English-speaking Vice Province of Upper Canada (in 1939, the Province of Upper Canada) and the French-speaking Province of Lower Canada; in theory, the area served for each Province was set according to the two national language groups; in 2006, the name for the "Province of Upper Canada" became "The Jesuits in English Canada."

Vicar General A Jesuit empowered to act as the Superior General of the Order during the grave illness or death of the Superior General, or when the Superior General is especially occupied.

Vice Province An administrative unit of the Society of Jesus that, due to its insufficient number of members and finances, has not yet attained the status of a Province (see above, "Province" and "Upper Canada Province"); rarely used today for distinguishing local Jesuit administrative units.

Vice Rector The Superior of a Jesuit Community or institution, such as a college, university, or school, appointed by the Provincial Superior with the approval of the Superior General for a three-year term (renewable usually only once).

Visitor A Jesuit appointed by the Superior General to visit a Province on his behalf; usually designated to investigate the governance, finances, and state of religious life in a Province, sometimes with the full authority of the Superior General, and at other times with limited authority. The office was abolished in the 1960s.

Vows The three vows of religion—poverty, chastity, and obedience—are common to all Religious Orders and Congregations. These are perpetual in the Society of Jesus: that is, the Jesuits' first vows are simple and perpetual, and are pronounced at the end of their Novitiate of two years. After a specified time of formation ultimately determined by the Superior General, and after the Jesuits' Tertianship, the Jesuit priests and Brothers are approved by the Superior General to pronounce their final vows. A Jesuit must ask the Provincial Superior in writing to pronounce his final vows; traditionally, some pronounced simple vows (Spiritual and Temporal Coadjutors), while others pronounced solemn vows (Solemnly Professed), which included their special fourth vow of obedience to the Sovereign Pontiff with regard to missions. Since the 1960s, most Jesuit priests are invited to pronounce the four vows.

INTRODUCTION

The Jesuit Framework and Context II

Next to the energy and time devoted to higher education by the Jesuits working in anglophone Canada, it was the ministry among the native peoples that mostly occupied the devotion and zeal of the newly arrived Jesuits in 1842. Within months of their return, Dominique du Ranquet and Joseph Jennesseaux were in Oka studying the Ojibway language; less than a year later, Pierre Point was the first to renew contact with native people in Sandwich (now Windsor); and in 1844, Jean-Pierre Choné was inaugurating the mission at Wikwemikong, where the Jesuits have remained ever since. Their inspiration was the epic tragedy of Huronia and, as Michael J. Strogre, S.J., and Michael L. Knox, S.J., highlight in their chapters, the exemplarity of the lives, writings, and deaths as represented in such missionary models as Jean de Brébeuf, Antoine Daniel, Isaac Jogues, Jacques Marquette, Paul Ragueneau, and so many others.

Yet the nineteenth-century Jesuits were not the same kind of men as their illustrious predecessors. Those latter came to Canada in the early 1600s, riding (if not having provoked) the crest of the Catholic Reformation wave that created both an educated Catholic urban middle class in Europe as well as a new missiology that included traditional Chinese and Malabar rites in Asia and prosperous native self-governing "reductions" in Latin America. In that context, the

Jesuits of the *ancien régime* were powerful in the numbers of their alumni. In 1750, for example, there were 700 Jesuit colleges and 200 Jesuit Seminaries throughout the world. The Jesuits were powerful also through the influence of numerous benefactors in the royal courts of Europe, by their chaplaincies to the great aristocratic land-owning families, and even more, perhaps, by their role as the choice confessors to most of the Catholic kings. They brought to the preaching of the Catholic faith, therefore, a definite self-assurance and the vigour of a correspondingly strong social order.

Were the Jesuits too powerful? By the 1750s, many Catholics began to think so, especially those, many of them Jesuit alumni, influenced by the "new ideas" of the Enlightenment, such as the primacy of reason over faith, and ideals of tolerance and material welfare. Many came to consider the Jesuits as enemies of progress. In many circles, the word "Jesuit" came to mean deceptive, devious, and manipulative. By the 1750s, strong, energetic, and forceful "enlightened" royal ministers in Portugal, then Spain and France, suspected the Jesuits of plotting to overthrow these nations' governments. A failed assassination attempt on King Joseph I of Portugal in 1758, then alleged Jesuit plots arising out of illegal fundraising deals in the Caribbean French Colonies, as well as deadly anti-tax riots in Madrid, all led to the expulsion of the Jesuit Order from those Catholic countries and from their allies throughout the Italian peninsula by 1768.

Pope Clement XIII resolutely and literally defended the Society of Jesus to his dying breath. However, his successor, Clement XIV, a timid and weak man, eventually gave in to the anti-Jesuit pressure, especially after the Empress Maria Theresa of Austria withdrew her support for the Jesuits to gain the consent, by 1770, of King Louis XV of France for the marriage of her daughter, Marie-Antoinette, to his grandson, the future Louis XVI.

The papal brief *Dominus ac Redemptor Noster* suppressed the Society of Jesus. Pope Clement XIV signed it on 21 July 1773 and made it public on the following 16 August. That was the first and only time since the suppression of the Knights Templar by Pope Clement V, in 1312, that a Catholic Religious Order or Congregation had been suppressed. The Grand Knight of the Templars, Jacques de Molay, was burned at the stake in Paris; Lorenzo Ricci, the Superior General of the Jesuits, was imprisoned in the Castel Sant'Angelo, where he died on 24 November 1775.

It was more than a quarter century later that the great Italian statesman Cardinal Ercole Consalvi is quoted as saying that he had long thought that the Catholic Church could do very well without the Jesuits, but that now he was convinced it could not do without them. He was reflecting, of course, a conviction he shared with his friend and mentor, Pope Pius VII. It would be more than a dozen years before they could fulfil their wish. For one thing, beginning in 1808, the Pope was a prisoner of the Emperor Napoleon. However, within hours of Napoleon's abdication in April 1814, Pius VII made himself ready to leave for Rome on what turned out to be a triumphal progress. He was acclaimed at every stop along the way by cheering and venerating crowds. On 24 May, he reached the outskirts of Rome, and very soon set the official proclamation of the restoration of the Jesuit Order for 7 August 1814 in the small Sodality chapel of the old Jesuit Collegio Romano in Rome.

There were a few elderly ex-Jesuit priests still alive to rejoice in the restoration, and more importantly, in Russia, there were several hundred who, after the suppression and under the protection of the Empress Catherine the Great and her successor Czar Alexander, had continued to recruit Jesuit novices. It was those latter who became the nucleus of the restored Society of Jesus. In Western Europe, applications to join the Jesuits began to multiply. Within a decade, the number of Jesuits worldwide had reached several thousand.

The new Jesuits were essentially the same as those Jesuits in the "old" Society of Jesus in their attitudes and spirituality. Yet they were also very different. They were men, after all, who were born and grew up between the 1770s and 1814 in one of the most tumultuous half-centuries in European history: civil and international wars, riots, bombings and massacres, ransacking and destruction of storied cathedrals and monuments, all accompanied by the most extraordinary movement of peoples: British officers occupied Rome, and their troops moved up the Spanish peninsula; the French took Vienna and reached the gates of Moscow; the Russians crossed the Rhine and eventually encamped in Normandy. Those turbulent years would make it difficult to bring to the Jesuits the self-assurance of the "old" Society of Jesus. Yet it probably did make them more available and flexible in their choice of ministries, at least after their second coming to Canada in 1842.

As J. Winston Rye, S.J., illustrates convincingly in his chapter, the first returning Canadian Jesuits became "parish priests", a ministry the Society of Jesus had only slightly occupied in New France. Beginning with La Prairie and Sandwich, they founded or took over an impressive number of parishes, especially in English-speaking Canada, where the flow of new settlers necessarily produced new small towns and the need for more Catholic churches. Rye's story will stand as the detailed authoritative reference work on Jesuit parochial ministry. It will also bring out another characteristic of the Jesuit identity, which is to respond to what is most urgent, or to take up a work for which no one else is available, and then leave it to others once the emergency is past or when others do become available. That is a vital element of Jesuit spirituality.

A good example of that Jesuit characteristic is the impressive Church of Our Lady Immaculate in Guelph. A miracle of Jesuit persistence over five decades in ensuring its completion, it stands as a remarkable, if not unique, example of Jesuit iconography. By the late 1920s, diocesan priests were available in greater numbers. Accordingly, on 6 September 1931, the Society of Jesus transferred the parish to the diocese of Hamilton. That Jesuit characteristic is apparent, too, as Joseph B. Gavin, S.J., illustrates in Volume 1, in the withdrawal of Jesuits in English-speaking Canada from the administration of almost all their institutions of higher education.

During the 1960s and early 1970s, the reforming Thirty-First and Thirty-Second General Congregations of the Society of Jesus drew attention to new priorities for the Jesuits. In addition to the traditional importance of intellectual ministry, the General Congregations encouraged greater involvement of the Jesuits in modern communications and, as a "priority of priorities", in the promotion of justice as an absolute requirement to the "service of the faith."

Dr. Peter Baltutis, an alumnus of the University of St. Michael's College, Toronto, and of the Toronto School of Theology, treats the Canadian Jesuits' involvement in social ministries, which includes their ministry in Jamaica. It was there that Martin Royackers, S.J., took up the defence of the land claims of the poor families in his parish at Annotto Bay. His life was threatened several times. On the night of 20 June 2001, he was murdered as he left his church; he became the first among the Jesuits of Upper Canada to be killed in a manner that has been interpreted as a martyr's death. Attention to communications as a priority was a less dangerous enterprise, as John D. O'Brien, S.J., writes in his minutely chronicled chapter.

There is much more to be recounted about the Jesuits' work in English Canada. The story of their high schools, of Jesuit formation, of the ministry of the Spiritual Exercises under the trail-blazing influence of the late John J. C. English, S.J., "foreign missions" and Jesuits International, ecology and the evolution of "Guelph": from parish to Novitiate to farm community to an internationally acclaimed Loyola House Retreat and Training Centre. Much also may be told about the life and lifetime influence of the renowned theologian Bernard Lonergan, not to mention the remarkable translation of his works by Michael Shields at The Lonergan Research Institute.

I very sincerely repeat what I wrote at the end of the preface to Volume 1, especially our appreciation for the generations of Jesuits who, a century ago, began their Religious life at St. Stanislaus Novitiate, Guelph, Ontario. Our team of authors has enjoyed working on this book and the previous volume, and hopes you will find pleasure in reading it. Meanwhile, some of us have begun the research and writing for another volume in the Jesuit History Series. God—and Novalis—willing, there will be a Volume 3. Meanwhile, I would like to express our continuing gratitude to our Jesuit Superiors for their support, and to Joseph Sinasac for his encouragement.

Jacques Monet, s.j.
7 August 2014

I

The Jesuits' Ministry to the Native People in Canada Since 1842

MICHAEL J. STOGRE, S.J.

How did it happen that French Jesuits destined for a mission in Madagascar ended up in Canada? Providence, it appears, intervened in the person of Montreal's bishop, Ignace Bourget. In 1841, he travelled to Rome for his *ad limina* visit, a canonically mandated visit every five years to report on diocesan affairs. He had been lobbying the Jesuit Curia for several years to have them return to the mission fields of Canada. On this occasion, he left a petition with the Jesuit Superior General, Jan Roothaan. This was his third attempt to recruit Jesuits to Canada. He stated clearly a two-fold ministry for the restored Order: "The undersigned [Bourget] has no doubt that the Reverend Jesuit Fathers will be persuaded to return to Canada, and assume the care of the Indian Missions, watered with the sweat and blood of their predecessors… . They will also find an ardent and studious youth to educate."[1]

1 Julian Paquin, s.j., *Modern Jesuit Indian Missions in Ontario*, unpublished manuscript, 21; Lecompte, 33–34.

Under the direction of the first Jesuit Superior of the Canadian mission, Pierre Chazelle, s.j., their educational ministry resumed in Montreal with the opening of Collège Sainte-Marie in 1848 under the guidance of Félix Martin, s.j.[2] Further to the west, in Upper Canada, the Jesuits for the most part evangelized and worked with the people of the "Three Fires Confederacy", a union of the Odawa, Ojibway, and Potawatomi First Nations. According to oral tradition, the precursors of these related peoples originally had lived in the Maritime region of Canada. Circa 1000, they had migrated up the St. Lawrence River and into the Great Lakes region. There they settled around what is now Sault Ste. Marie.[3] From that strategic meeting place, the tribes then spread out in the four directions. As a result, today they can be found in several provinces and states.

Of the Iroquoian-speaking peoples in southern Ontario, the best known were the Huron, who referred to themselves as the Wendat (Wyandot, in American usage). In the remote region west of Huronia, known to the French as the *pays d'en haut* ("the land higher up"), something new was forged among the First Nations and the predominantly French newcomers. There, in that unique setting on the fringe of the French empire, in territory that neither side could control fully, shared meaning and forms of accommodation developed.

The struggle to create a "middle ground", as Richard White, an historian of the period, has called it, had traumatic beginnings.[4] Disease and warfare on a scale unprecedented among northern native peoples became widespread. For survival, remnants of local tribes sought refuge further west in the region around Lake Superior. There they regrouped and realigned with their new allies, the French, fostering new cultural forms. To later commentators, such as noted Canadian essayist John Ralston Saul, this marked the beginning of Canada as a "Métis civilization". As Saul has argued in his provocative book *A Fair Country*, much of what lay at the heart of Canadian culture was

2 DJB, vol. 1, 55–58; DCB, vol. VII, 170–171; vol. XI, 587–589.

3 Eddie Benton-Banai, *The Mishomish Book: The Voice of the Ojibway* (Hayward, WI: Indian Country Communications Inc., 1988), 94–102.

4 Richard White, *The Middle Ground: Indians, Empires, and Republics in the Great Lakes Region, 1650–1815* (New York: Cambridge University Press, 1991), 50–94.

in fact aboriginal in origin.[5] In northern Ontario, this process began to occur in less than a century.

Sadly, however, the "middle ground" that developed over this period fell apart after the War of 1812, a conflict in which aboriginal warriors played a prominent role. Undoubtedly, Canada would not have survived that crisis had it not been for the contributions to its defence by the Three Fires and Iroquois Confederacy. The conflict helped shape the Canadian national identity, and also gave rise to peace on the continent for the next two centuries. At the same time, however, it dashed hopes for a native homeland. As Canadians recently marked the 200th anniversary of the war, it is a fitting occasion to honour such native contributions, particularly that of the celebrated Shawnee war-chief, Tecumseh.[6] As a commissioned officer in the British army with the rank of general, he arguably proved the best field general on either side of the conflict. After the war, regrettably, aboriginal peoples were shunted aside, and were no longer considered important partners in Canadian nation-building. In fact, a colonial government plan of the period called for the relocation of native people from this region of present-day southern Ontario to Manitoulin Island. In recent years, however, that period of irrelevancy has passed as aboriginal peoples experience self-revitalization and a greater participation in all aspects of Canadian life.[7]

This theme of "participation" has special meaning within traditional Catholic social teaching. As the heart of the quest for social justice, "participation" constitutes the main criterion for judging the relative state of justice in society. A key turning point in this regard was the world synod of Catholic bishops in 1971, whose published reflection entitled "Justice in the World" viewed "participation" as central.[8] As the bishops expressed it,

5 John Ralston Saul, *A Fair Country: Telling Truths about Canada* (Toronto: Viking Canada, 2008), 3–98.

6 DCB, vol. V, 795–800.

7 For a "periodization" of the relationship between First Nations peoples and Canada, see E. Palmer Patterson, *The Canadian Indian: A History Since 1500* (Don Mills: Collier-Macmillan Canada, 1972).

8 Synod of Bishops statement entitled "Justice in the World", in Austin Flannery, ed., *Vatican Council II: More Postconciliar Documents* (Boston: St. Paul Editions, 1982), 695–710.

> The chief threat to personal dignity in a world of rapid technological growth is that large segments of the population simply be excluded from any active participation in shaping the social patterns which provide the context of their lives.... Marginalization or lack of participation thus becomes a primary criterion for judging if human dignity is being violated. Lack of adequate nourishment, housing, education, and political self-determination are seen as a consequence of this lack of participation.[9]

In addition, lack of participation has serious effects on the spiritual and interior well-being of the human person. Low self-esteem and lack of respect for self and others have often led to social problems in First Nations and other communities. Obvious examples include alcoholism, drug abuse, compulsive gambling, and increased rates of suicide, to name only a few.[10] Strikingly, the bishops saw participation as the right that integrates all other basic human rights and that comprises the essence of what the Church means by "social justice". While encouraging responsibility for creating a more just world, the Catholic bishops called for a climate in which all human rights would be more fully realized. However, such a theology of social justice hardly existed when the Jesuits first arrived in Canada four centuries ago. The phrase itself was not introduced into Catholic social thinking until 1840, by the Italian Jesuit Luigi Taparelli D'Azeglio, just at the time when members of the Jesuit Order were returning to Canada.[11]

As a brief assessment of the Jesuits' mission to indigenous peoples of Canada since 1844, and especially to the province of Ontario, this chapter adopts a sense of "what was going forward", as outlined by the Canadian Jesuit theologian Bernard J. F. Lonergan.[12] This approach reflects an understanding of the Church and its mission that evolved

---

9 David Hollenbach, *Claims in Conflict: Retrieving and Renewing the Catholic Human Rights Tradition* (New York: Paulist Press, 1979), 86.

10 For a fuller treatment of native health issues, see Michael F. Czerny, S.J., and Michael J. Stogre, S.J., "Ancient Ways Made New: Health among the Chippewa of Rama", *Catholic Health Alliance of Canada Journal* 9, no. 3 (May/June 1981), 4–12.

11 Luigi Taparelli D'Azeglio, s.j., *Saggio Teoretico di diretto naturale, 2 vols.* (Palermo, 1840).

12 See Bernard J. F. Lonergan, S.J., *Method in Theology* (New York: Seabury Press, 1972), 128, and particularly chapters 8 and 9. Cf. also DJB, vol. 1, 188–192.

over the past 170 years among Jesuit missionaries. As the American Jesuit theologian Avery Cardinal Dulles has observed, every model of the Church entails a distinct approach to evangelization and to mission work.[13] First, however, it is necessary to review the relevant historical background from the earlier era of Jesuit missions to the First Nations peoples of Canada prior to the suppression of the Jesuits in 1773.

Pre-Suppression Jesuit Missions to the Native Peoples of Canada

The year 2011 marked the 400th anniversary of the arrival of the first Jesuits in Canada. From 1611 until the worldwide suppression of the Society of Jesus, Jesuits laboured among the Algonkian-speaking peoples in the maritime and central regions of Canada. They also worked among the Iroquoian linguistic groups in what are now the provinces of Quebec and Ontario. With the demise and dispersal of the Wendat Confederacy in Huronia in the mid 1600s, Jesuits served among its remnants at L'Ancienne-Lorette, near present-day Quebec City. In the Great Lakes region, Jesuits also laboured with members of the Three Fires Confederacy, many of whom kept in close relationship with remnants of the Huron, who had been their allies and trading partners. Jesuits also founded mission centres in other parts of the province of Quebec, including among the Mohawk at Kahnawake. With the recent canonization of Kateri Tekakwitha in October 2012, the latter site has regained its prominence in honour of the first aboriginal female saint, whose own bloodlines united the two great linguistic groups of eastern and central North America.[14]

In northern Ontario, the principal focus of this chapter, after the destruction of Sainte-Marie among the Hurons in 1649, there were no fixed settlements or long-established missions. Like the people they served, the Jesuit missionaries Charles Albanel, Claude-Jean Allouez, and others were, for the most part, nomadic.[15] This tension between *les missions volantes* ("flying missions"), which followed the migratory

13 For a discussion of this thesis, see Avery Dulles, S.J., *Models of the Church* (New York: Image Books, 1978).

14 Her mother was Algonquin from Quebec and her father was Mohawk from present-day New York State.

15 DCB, vol. I, 47–50; 57–58.

patterns of the newly Christianized, and the desire to gather them into settled communities, or reductions, remained a great challenge until recent times.

The Return of the Jesuits to Canada

Although the Jesuits officially returned to Montreal on 31 May 1842, Chazelle had been the first member of the restored Society of Jesus to visit Canada. Already working in Bardstown, Kentucky, since 1831, he was asked to come to Montreal in 1839 to give a retreat to local clergy.[16] Clearly, his presence had not provoked the "shock and awe" at the *Montreal Herald* that the Jesuits' arrival in 1842 later elicited. As Paquin has recounted, the return of the Jesuits that year was met with nothing short of sheer alarm:

> The terrified editor exclaimed: "There are Jesuits in Canada. They are in Montreal, these men whose records are written with blood, whose history is a series of deeds of violence and avarice, whose main ambition is to monopolize civil power for their profit, whose doctrine recognized no law human or divine when it interferes with their purpose. Yes, this society has been recalled to Montreal, to be, as heretofore, the most diabolical curse of the land, to fill it with carnage, to plunge it into superstitions, to corrupt its morals and stop its progress."[17]

Such accusations were soon countered in other papers by more sympathetic journalists, such as the young Irishman Matthew Ryan.[18] Needless to say, the development of Canada marched on despite the Jesuits' presence!

Nine Jesuits had comprised the first permanent group to arrive in Montreal. These included Dominique Chardon du Ranquet, s.j., the main protagonist in the opening scene of a drama that would later play out on Walpole Island near present-day Windsor, Ontario. Du Ranquet and Brother Joseph Jennesseaux, s.j., another of the first arrivals, headed first to the mission at Lake of Two Mountains at Oka,

16 Ibid., 56–57. Paquin, *Modern Jesuit,* 21.

17 Paquin, op. cit., 1.

18 Ibid.

west of the Island of Montreal.[19] There, La Compagnie des Prêtres de Saint-Sulpice (the Sulpician Fathers) had the care of both Algonquin and Iroquois-speaking native peoples. At the directive of Chazelle, his Superior, du Ranquet devoted himself to learning the Algonquin dialects and as much as possible about native culture. After further visits to native communities along the Ottawa River and the northern parts of the diocese of Montreal, he set out for Sandwich in present-day south-western Ontario to work with the Ojibways. He arrived there in October 1843.[20]

Jesuit Mission to Walpole Island

Walpole Island, also located in present-day south-western Ontario, was a fitting place for the first native mission of the restored Society of Jesus. As ethnologist James Morrison has noted, the mission had been its last in Canada before the Jesuits were suppressed.[21] However, since du Ranquet was new and inexperienced in native habits and culture, he made two fatal errors from which the mission never recovered. Because of the presence of four Catholic families on the island, he met the conditions for residency on native land. His first mistake was presuming permission to build a church on the highest point of land, a strategic location that also happened to be a burial site for the indigenous population. Second, he began a logging operation to furnish building materials for a church, a residence, and a school, an activity that displeased many of the local people. Not heeding requests for them to leave, the Jesuits carried on and completed their buildings. In April 1849, arson claimed their expanding complex, and the Jesuits were warned that if they tried to rebuild—which was their intention—any church buildings would be burned down again. Ordered by the government to leave the island, they soon withdrew to Sandwich. There they waited for an appeal from the bishop on behalf of the mission. It never came. Shortly thereafter, du Ranquet

19 DJB, vol. 1, 154–155.

20 Ibid., 101–102. See also the unpublished document by Leo J. Nelligan, S.J., entitled "Walpole Island Catholic Mission 1844–1860", date unknown, AJC, Box C-401.

21 James Morrison, "Upper Great Lakes Settlement: The Anishinabe-Jesuit Record", *Ontario History* 86, no. 1 (March 1994), 54.

and Jennesseaux were transferred further north to the mission of Wikwemikong on Manitoulin Island.[22]

In reflecting upon this early missionary experience, we can see echoes of earlier missiological strategies and thinking. In the period of Huronia, there had been two dominant views. On the one side, Jean de Brébeuf and others had opted for an "insertion" model, that is, one that meant spending long periods living among the people they sought to evangelize. On the other hand, missionaries like Paul Le Jeune promoted the "reduction" model, as actualized at Sillery, just outside Quebec City, and at Sainte-Marie among the Hurons, near present-day Midland, Ontario. According to the latter approach, the mission station became a sort of miniature *societas perfecta*, or perfect society. To a large extent, this reflected the dominant ecclesiology of the time, as championed by, among others, the well-known Jesuit theologian and cardinal Robert Bellarmine.[23] Within that model, the Church tried to replicate the structures of civil society, for example, in education and health care, areas in which it had become a pioneer. The Jesuits' reduction model, as established in Latin America, also had its influence on the Huron mission. Many thought that this approach would protect the flock from pagan influences, from the bad example of European settlers, and, in the case of the Latin American reductions, from slave traders as well.

Given the tenacious resistance to missionary efforts on Walpole Island, it is easy to see why the reduction model was attempted. In later years, the accompaniment model prevailed for a time, as it had done in the environs of Sillery in the seventeenth century, especially in northern settings where native people were predominantly hunter-gatherers and an integral part of the fur trade.[24] With the establishment of treaties and fixed native settlements on reserves, resident priests under diocesan direction became the norm where the availability of priests and sizable congregations warranted.

While the mission on Walpole Island was short-lived and, by all accounts, a failure, du Ranquet learned valuable cultural lessons in a

22 Lecompte, 183–192.

23 Dulles, *Models of Church,* 39–50.

24 Morrison, "Upper Great Lakes Record", 58.

native ministry that would span nearly sixty years. Indeed, he put such lessons to good use, participating, for instance, in a pipe ceremony when called before a council of elders to explain his actions.[25] He also learned to appreciate the aboriginals' rhetorical tradition.

Jesuit Mission to Manitoulin Island

During the second major phase of the restored Jesuits' native mission, both the itinerant missionary and the reduction strategies were employed. At Wikwemikong, a Catholic community under the direction of Jean-Baptiste Proulx already existed when the first Jesuits in over 150 years arrived in 1844.[26] Between 1836 and 1845, this zealous diocesan priest had ministered to the native people around Lake Huron, first from a base in Penetanguishene, then later from Wikwemikong. The first Jesuit priest there, Jean-Pierre Choné, was soon followed by Joseph-Urbain Hanipaux in 1845, Auguste Kohler in 1847, Nicolas Point in 1848, and du Ranquet in 1850.[27] In the early years of the mission, Jesuit Brothers also played an important role. For instance, Brothers Jean Veroneau, James Sweeney, Jennesseaux, and Martin Stoeklin all became indispensable assistants, and by taking up farming and skilled trades, provided great examples for the native community.[28]

When the Jesuits succeeded Proulx, they quickly adopted the "reduction" nomenclature. According to Morrison, the Wikwemikong Catholic enclave was referred to "for most of the nineteenth century … as the Holy Cross 'Indian Reduction.'"[29] In part, this stemmed from the fact that Point had worked with the Belgian Jesuit missionary Pierre-Jean De Smet in the western American missions, which were "consciously modelled on the Paraguayan reductions".[30] On the other hand, as noted above, there were many other native bands on the island and surrounding north shore of Lake Huron that were nearly

25 Ibid., 56.

26 DCB, vol. XI, 714–715; Lecompte, 192–216.

27 DJB, vol. 1, 59; 101–102; 129; 172–173; 283–286; DCB, vol. IX, 633.

28 Ibid., 337–338; 154–155.

29 Morrison, "Upper Great Lakes Record", 61.

30 Ibid.

always on the move, giving rise to what early missionaries called "flying missions".

While Jesuits had visited Manitoulin Island in the late 1600s, they had not established a permanent mission at that time. The island itself seems then to have been abandoned for a long period due to a massive forest fire. Some have speculated that the fire was started as a scorched-earth tactic to fend off attacking Iroquois. Others have claimed that it was set to drive out evil spirits. Still others have pointed out how such fires, especially those ignited by lightning, are natural phenomena, and are even a necessity for forest regeneration. In fact, large fires would continue to punctuate life on Manitoulin Island throughout the nineteenth century.

After Manitoulin Island had returned to its pristine state, it began to be repopulated once again, partially from the migration of native peoples from Michigan and elsewhere, including Quebec. Faced with the American government's removal policy, native people in Michigan were under pressure to vacate their land and relocate west of the Mississippi River and, ultimately, to the future state of Oklahoma. Some stayed behind and hid out, however, and eventually won the right to remain in Michigan. Others, too, were encouraged by the British colonial authorities to resettle in Ontario, in case they would be needed again as allies against the "long knives", as the native loyalists had called the Americans at the time of the War of 1812. In the same period of resettlement, with growing pressure for land in Ontario, the Crown, in the person of Sir Francis Bond Head, the lieutenant governor of Upper Canada (1835–1838), followed up on a plan to have all the tribes move to Manitoulin Island.[31] Since they were becoming fewer in number, he believed they were destined to die out. As he wrote to the colonial secretary, Lord Glenelg: "We have only to wait patiently with the [Indians] for a short Time, and with a few exceptions, principally the Half-castes, their unhappy Race, beyond our Power of Redemption, will be extinct."[32] On another occasion, he

31 DCB, vol. X, 342–343.

32 Cited in David Shanahan, "The Manitoulin Treaties, 1836 and 1862: The Indian Department and Indian Destiny", *Ontario History*, Vol. 86, No. 1 (March 1994), 20.

uttered a more memorable judgement: "They are vanishing like snow before the [April] sun."[33]

According to the treaty of 1836, Manitoulin Island became the sole possession of the remaining indigenous population of Upper Canada, provided they cede to the Crown all other lands. It was estimated at the time that approximately 9,300 indigenous people remained in Upper Canada.[34] While the signatories on Manitoulin Island may have agreed to the proposal, most of the remaining indigenous population were hesitant to give up good land where they lived for inferior land on Manitoulin Island; they continued to live across the length and breadth of northern Ontario. That necessitated further treaties, which resulted in fixed reserves and other rights on Crown land beyond the reserves. Later, the Crown wanted to allow non-native settlement on Manitoulin Island. That ultimately resulted in the treaty of 1862. The fact that all native people did not move to Manitoulin Island was used, in effect, as a pretext to abrogate the previous treaty, with the exception of the unceded reserve at Wikwemikong.

The 1836 treaty, in fact, did not stipulate such a requirement for numbers. According to the earlier treaty, the Crown would make no claim on Manitoulin Island and the nearby fishing islands as long as the present residents and owners agreed to receive indigenous people from across the province. However, that would have meant having to give up their exclusive rights to those territories.

It was into that rapidly changing landscape, during the time between the treaties, that the Jesuits took up their mission to Manitoulin Island and beyond. Proulx had spent some nine years labouring among the native people of Manitoulin Island and the North Shore, and had also preached the Gospel to thousands of First Nations who gathered yearly at Manitowaning for the annual distribution of gifts from the British government. He was remarkably successful as a missionary pastor. When he left there in 1846 to become vicar general of the diocese of Toronto, he left a register of the Holy Cross Mission in which were listed "327 Baptisms of children and 355 of pagan adults

33 Cited in R. J. Surtees, "Indian Reserve Policy in Upper Canada, 1830–1845", unpublished M.A. dissertation (Ottawa: Carleton University, 1966), 42, n. 56.

34 Shanahan, op cit., 27.

... seventy-one marriages and the erection of three crosses. ... He had gathered a congregation of about 500 Catholics."[35]

The Arrival of the Jesuits in Wikwemikong

In July 1844, Choné arrived in Wikwemikong by sailboat, accompanied by Proulx, their "donné" interpreter, Ferdinand Roque, and several native men who made up the sailing crew.[36] In the transition period, Proulx covered the outlying mission stations around Manitoulin Island and the North Shore, while Choné was resident at Wikwemikong. There he found a small wooden chapel and a rudimentary school but no priest's residence, as it had recently burned down.[37] For a time, he stayed with a native family, living on meagre rations and sometimes the largesse of the lake. The people themselves were in dire straits and at times sought the crumbs from his sparse table. Game was nearly absent from the island in those days, and the clearing of land was only just beginning.[38] The transition from a hunting, fishing, and gathering way of life to an agrarian one would be slow, and it was never completely successful.

The Manitowaning Establishment

Apart from the difficult living conditions on Manitoulin Island during this period, the Catholic mission base also faced a government-supported Anglican mission at Manitowaning. The latter had become the place where the British Crown continued to meet with Indian allies for the annual distribution of presents. At these gatherings, clergy from various denominations attempted to convert the native people who were not yet Christian, and ministered to those who were. The interdenominational rivalries between Catholics, Anglicans, and Methodists at this time were often fierce. Ecumenism was something far off in the future. One of the few things the Christian factions did agree upon was the evil of alcohol, especially its deleterious effect on

35 Paquin, *Modern Jesuit*, 39.

36 Ibid.

37 Ibid., 60–61.

38 The whitetail deer, which are now so plentiful on Manitoulin Island, had not yet arrived. The elk and woodland caribou of earlier times had been decimated, never to recover or return.

the native population. From time to time, however, touching stories of mutual hospitality occurred that presaged a more harmonious future.

By 1856, despite initial difficulties, the Jesuits had established a suitable rectory, two day schools, and the crown jewel of Nicolas Point's tenure, a stone church. During this period, the language of instruction in the schools was Ojibway. As Robert Carney noted, "This Indian language and instruction orientation was not well received by the colony's Indian administration or by school inspectors. There is evidence that the Jesuits' preference of Indian oriented, day-school programmes had repercussions in terms of the financial support given them by the Indian administration."[39] Thus, from the earliest years of the mission, the dual mandate to "evangelize and educate" that Bishop Bourget had requested of the Jesuit Order was being implemented even in this remote area. The initial missionary zeal spurred the Jesuits on to fulfil their responsibilities for mission work further north in Canada West. In 1838, after only four years at Wikwemikong, Choné was appointed Superior of a mission that began at Pigeon River, west of present-day Thunder Bay, on the American side of the border. Within a year, the mission base had been moved to Fort William. Already in 1845, independently of the Jesuits in the field, Chazelle had set out for Sault Ste. Marie to make plans for a third mission base in Canada West. Unfortunately, he fell ill. While not yet recovered, he made an ill-advised attempt to reach Sault Ste. Marie from Green Bay, Wisconsin, where he had been visiting an earlier Jesuit mission. Unable to complete the trip, he returned to Green Bay, where he died shortly thereafter. This mission was carried on for a time by Hanipaux, followed by Kohler in May of 1848. During this period, they ministered on both sides of the present-day Canadian-American border.

While these principal mission bases were being established in Sault Ste. Marie and Fort William, other mission stations on Manitoulin Island were being visited. These included Sheshegwaning at the western end of the island; Sheguiandah, about 10 miles south of Little Current, West Bay (then called Mitchikinatoning); and South Bay,

39 Robert Carney, "Aboriginal Residential Schools before Confederation: The Early Experience", CCHA, *Historical Studies* 61 (1995), 28.

a mission station on the Wikwemikong unceded reserve. In addition to Manitoulin Island and the North Shore, the Jesuits at Wikwemikong began to visit logging and mining camps, as well as other native settlements. Those flying missions took in Cape Croker on the Bruce peninsula, Dokis on the French River, and Garden Village on Lake Nipissing. The latter mission station formed the eastern boundary of the mission territory entrusted to the Jesuits. By this time, the Oblates of Mary Immaculate (Oblate Fathers) had begun to operate in northern Canada, and for a short time, there was conflict over who would cover this eastern part of Ontario.

The arduous task of covering such a wide territory necessitated that some missionaries were away from the home base for long periods of time. This left a few Brothers and, often enough, only one priest to manage the growing complex of buildings and activities comprising the early mission. That was a tension that would surface in later times as Jesuits tried to teach and administer the boys' residential school at Spanish while doing pastoral ministry in the local area as well. Later still, the situation persisted as contemporary Jesuits ran a ministries' formation centre for native people at Anderson Lake while also ministering to neighbouring parishes. Complicating matters were conflicts with government authorities, clergy of other denominations, whiskey traders, and white squatters. The constant strain took its toll. Travel was also difficult and treacherous, at times. In the summer months, one could travel by boat, but the winter required long treks on snowshoes while hauling heavy sleds. These were laden with supplies for the journey and a portable chapel for stops at remote camps, where there were no chapels or churches. Later, dog teams would make these arduous journeys more tolerable and a lot quicker.[40] Sick calls were frequently done on foot. After travelling many miles to minister to the sick and dying, the exhausted priest often discovered that the person was not sick or had left the premises. Yet, receiving the "last rites" of the Church was always important for native Catholics, and remains so.

Even in those early days, there were signs of a lay ministry that would blossom in the dioceses of Sault Ste. Marie and of Thunder

40 Paquin, *Modern Jesuit*, 62–63.

Bay after the Second Vatican Council. One example of this was to be found at the beginning of the Church in the newly established community of Michikinatonong, or West Bay, now known as M'Chigeeng. That community was located some 30 miles west of Wikwemikong. According to Paquin, M'Chigeeng "... was blessed with a good young chief named Louis Debassige, who looked upon his people as his children and fulfilled toward them the duties of a father. He gathered them on Sunday for prayer and instruction, and spent most of his time teaching the boys and girls."[41]

Other native men and women began to take up the work of teaching in those early years as assistants to Jennesseaux. Everyone worked at the day school in Wikwemikong village. The lay ministers' formal training was quite limited, as was the education they could impart to the children at this stage of Wikwemikong's development. In 1857, two girls from the community were sent to Montreal to become more proficient teachers, financed by the generosity of the Sisters of the Sacred Heart.[42] Occasionally, the community was able to hire qualified outside teachers, but due to government discrimination against the Catholic mission, their salaries were quite low, and thus they were not able to stay long. Economic developments during that period included a grist mill, the introduction of spinning, weaving, and knitting for women, as well as a root cellar for storing seed used for spring planting. All of this was done in conjunction with building up a model farm, which the missionaries hoped would spur their native neophytes to replicate these efforts on their own land, thus becoming self-sufficient. The farm also helped to sustain the Jesuit Community of two priests and four Brothers.

The discipline of a settled and farming way of life was often resisted or taken up half-heartedly as people hankered for the free life of a hunter-gatherer. Too often, unscrupulous traders took advantage of those nascent entrepreneurs, selling them inferior and shoddy goods far below the value of items such as the maple sugar, corn, potatoes, and fish that the native people produced. These traders also encouraged the natives to buy on credit, thus leaving them in

41 Ibid., 62.

42 Ibid., 91.

debt year after year. The missionaries tried to combat this situation by favouring honest traders and by selling produce to the people at fair prices. However, this only enraged the dishonest traders and raised suspicions among governmental authorities in Manitowaning. Occasionally, an honest trader would be found to treat the native people fairly, but they were the exception rather than the rule. Of course, the worst influence was alcohol. Traders would often entice people with this poison, which resulted in many deaths and much destruction. To make matters worse, authorities too often turned a blind eye to such criminal activity or doled out insignificant fines that deterred no one. The missionaries, for their part, tried to combat the evil with temperance societies and sometimes even excommunication. One has to wonder if years of alcohol abuse by traders and others had not already destroyed the native nations long before residential schools took their toll on the native population.[43]

Consolidation and Further Development of the Holy Cross "Reduction"

For most of the 1850s, Hanipaux was the Superior of the Holy Cross Mission. During his tenure, further improvements were made to the church, the Jesuit residence, and the school, with much attention also being paid to the farm, which continued to grow in size. The addition of a barn and stable were now essential to its proper functioning. Despite many setbacks and irritations, such as local dogs mauling and killing their sheep, and thieves stealing milk from their cows, the Jesuits persevered with the vision of creating a model farm. In such a way, they hoped to make the Jesuit Community self-sufficient and to inspire native farmers to emulate the "Blackrobes" by becoming self-reliant themselves. Parish life continued to develop, with great emphasis being placed on the important feast days of the liturgical year, especially Marian feasts. Interestingly, four sodalities operated during this period, one each for boys, girls, men, and women. These lay associations waxed and waned over the years, and eventually died out. Their successor in our time is the Christian Life Community, a lay

43 It is difficult to obtain exact figures for the actual percentage of native people attending school—residential or other—during this period. Reasonable estimates claim that about one in five native children attended residential schools.

movement of prayer and social action rooted in Ignatian spirituality and mission to others. Yet it remains to be seen whether this more recent development will appeal to and inspire native Catholics as the earlier sodalities once did.

During that early period, too, major liturgical feasts were celebrated with great solemnity and splendour. The feast of Corpus Christi, for instance, entailed three separate processions, which remained a popular attraction, as observed by the author when he visited Wikwemikong as a Jesuit novice in the early 1960s. After the Second Vatican Council, such practices were replaced by a vernacular liturgy, often with traditional native elements. Inculturation was aided by indigenous hymns and prayer books, some of which had been produced for the sodalities as early as 1855, when Jennesseaux had constructed his own printing press out of wooden blocks. By this stage, there were over 1,000 Catholics on Manitoulin Island, compared to 104 Christians of other denominations and 146 non-Christians. In the surrounding areas that were dependent on Wikwemikong for pastoral ministry, Catholics numbered 471, while there were ninety-eight Protestants and 370 non-Christian native people.[44] In the words of a missionary who chronicled this era,

> The moral and religious status of our Christians was quite satisfactory. Their faith, although simple, was sincere, and promised to endure in spite of temptations and bad example from their white neighbours—of which liquor traffic was the worst. One common blessing was to be theirs: a happy death marked with peace and the hope of eternal life.[45]

A Time of Troubles

During the 1860s, the humanistic hope of keeping the native peoples isolated from white encroachment—as previously advocated by Bond Head—was sorely tested. Already in the previous decade, non-native traders and settlers increasingly settled on Manitoulin Island. That led to much exploitation and corruption of the local native population. The colonial government of the day also contributed

44 Ibid., 95–96.

45 Ibid.

to the growing tension on Manitoulin Island. Beginning in 1859, the fisheries commissioner, William Gibbard, notified native residents that henceforth "they would have to buy, at auction in the open market, such fishing grounds that they wished to use."[46] They would now have to compete with white entrepreneurs, who could easily outbid the native fisherman. The measure, clearly in violation of the 1836 treaty, provoked great and justifiable anger among native residents of Manitoulin Island, setting the stage for violent confrontations to come. That policy also contravened the "fiduciary responsibility" of the Crown and later the Canadian government, which were expected to protect native rights and interests. Those actions later came back to haunt the federal government in the form of specific land and rights claims that were breached during the colonial period.

Hanipaux was present at a meeting held in Wikwemikong at the time to discuss this imminent threat to a vital source of employment, income, and nutrition. As he urged the native people to defend their traditional fishing rights, a petition was drawn up to be sent to the government. Their plan was sidelined, however, when they consulted the local superintendent, who advised them to trust the government, claiming the latter had their best interests at heart. That passive approach was endorsed by Jean-Baptiste Assiginack, a hero from the War of 1812 and an "arbiter" between native people and the colonial government.[47] A type of double agent, on the one hand he was a devout Catholic and Church leader who hosted and led services in his home. On the other hand, he was in the employ of the British government, and later signed the treaty of 1862 as a "grand chief". The historian Cecil King summed up Assiginack's life with a moving lament for a great man, who, as his life drew to a close, was ostracized by his own people:

> By signing the second Manitoulin treaty, Assiginack had desecrated the first treaty of Manitoulin and so doing had desecrated his people. Yet, Assiginack was a man whose life spanned almost a full century; a man who fought valiant

46 Ibid., 100.

47 DCB, vol. IX, 9–10; Cecil King, "J.-B. Assiginack: Arbiter of Two Worlds", *Ontario History* 86, no. 1 (March 1994), 47.

> battles for those he perceived as his friends; a man whose eloquence was noted above all others of his time. His story personifies the dilemma of those individuals from traditional societies who must confront the consuming force of a persistent and ruthless society overwhelming their own. Assiginack had to choose a path between the ire of his own people and the wrath of an imposed world that was ignorant and unsympathetic to his reality. ... In the coming of the fall (1866), Assiginack, holder of Tecumseh's wampum belt, was gone.[48]

On the fisheries and treaty issues, the Jesuits had sided with the majority of native inhabitants of Manitoulin Island, and thus were caught up in the conflicts of those years. After the McDougall treaty of 1862 was signed, the Jesuits, believing that a serious injustice had been done to the native people, attempted to have it overturned by Parliament.[49] In fact, the following year, Choné went to Quebec City, spending several weeks there to lobby the government on behalf of the native people, and testifying before a parliamentary commission.[50] Aided by the vicar general of the archdiocese of Quebec, Charles-Félix Cazeau, Choné strove mightily on behalf of Manitoulin Island's native population, but to no effect.[51]

In this case, as in others, political expediency trumped justice, as Brother Louis Carrez, s.j., related in a letter to the Jesuit Scholastics at Laval.[52] He cited Antoine-Aimé Dorion, the leader of the *Parti rouge* in Lower Canada, who on one occasion had interrupted Choné's plea for justice on behalf of the native people by exclaiming,

> Justice is not the point, Mr. Dorion responded, the question is very simple. If the lands of the island are good, your cause is lost; if they are bad, your cause is won. That is really the question! It was useless to continue. Choné left Quebec on the

48 Ibid., 48.

49 DCB, vol. XIII, 632–635. William McDougall was the superintendent general of Indian Affairs, and the colonial commissioner of Crown lands. The treaty is also referred to as the Manitoulin Treaty of 1862.

50 DJB, vol. 1, 59.

51 DCB, vol. XI, 167–173.

52 Louis Carrez, s.j., "Letter to the Scholastics of Laval, Collingwood, Sept. 12, 1863", in Lorenzo Cadieux, s.j., and Robert Toupin, s.j., eds., *Letters from Manitoulin Island 1853–1870*, trans. Shelley Pearen and William P. Lonc, S.J. (Toronto: Hammerburg Productions, 2007), 221–235.

fifteenth of October, spent three days in Montreal, and then returned to Manitoulin.[53]

In the end, the native community at Wikwemikong did not sign the treaty, thus retaining its section of Manitoulin Island, some 20 percent of the island's total area. The proviso that the Wikwemikong band had to accept any native person moving to their reserve remained in effect, a stipulation that had been central to the 1836 treaty. In the government's view, they had more land than they presently needed. The agreement was open-ended in the sense that at any time in the future, Wikwemikong could cede its land under the same terms and conditions that other bands had agreed to accept. This has never happened up to the present day, and still leaves many legal questions unanswered. For example, did Wikwemikong retain common ownership of the so-called fishing islands around Manitoulin Island, the North Channel, and Georgian Bay? Effectively, Wikwemikong's refusal to sign the new treaty maintained the status quo brought about by Bond Head's treaty of 1836.[54] Indeed, the native residents still thought of themselves as allies and not subjects of the British Crown, as had been the case before and during the War of 1812. The band even initiated early moves towards self-government, setting itself up for a shock when the next government decree was forcibly implemented.

The Fisheries Affair

Clearly, tensions were mounting over the matter of the fisheries. The situation was further aggravated by the presence of non-native residents on Lonely Island, one of the islands claimed by the Wikwemikong band for its exclusive use based on the 1836 treaty. One of those residents, Philémon Proulx, was the brother of Jean-Baptiste Proulx. Citing the terms of that treaty, the native community at Wikwemikong viewed the white fishermen as squatters, and thus not entitled to reside on that or any of the other surrounding islands. The fisheries commissioner, William Gibbard, saw things differently, as noted earlier, and even had the effrontery to demand fishing permits from native owners. In the meantime, the Wikwemikong band evicted

53 Ibid., 235.

54 Paquin, *Modern Jesuit*, 110.

non-native fishermen from Lonely Island, while a few other squatters on the reserve itself were removed. They protested to government officials at Manitowaning, thus beginning what has been described as a "period of open revolt against Canadian authorities … apparently countenanced by the missionaries." It was alleged that Kohler, the Jesuit Superior of the day, in a heated exchange with Gibbard, advocated an armed guerilla resistance to the injustice. Apparently citing the example of Osceola, the Seminole chief who had for a time waged a successful campaign against white settlers in Florida, he said he would join them had his health been better.[55]

As the drama unfolded, Gibbard reinstated on 27 June 1863 the legal right of Philémon Proulx and Charles de la Ronde to fish from part of Lonely Island and in the surrounding waters. While other parts of the island and vicinity were to be reserved for native fishermen, the Crown intended to back up this lease with force of arms, if necessary. To the native people of Manitoulin Island, this was yet another provocation; they gathered a force to reclaim their territory. On 24 July, Gibbard arrived at Wikwemikong by boat, joined by an interpreter and reinforced by twenty-two armed policemen. After asking to speak with native leaders in a home of their choice, they decided to meet instead at the rectory, with Choné present. When the latter declared they had referred the matter to the governor general and would await and respect his decision, Gibbard announced that he had come to arrest the instigators of the evictions from Lonely Island. Violence quickly ensued. When a man named Kinoshameg was about to be arrested, Choné resisted, and was himself arrested and handcuffed. What followed was described by Paquin as a riot.[56] Realizing matters had gotten out of hand, Gibbard finally released the prisoners with the proviso that they present themselves at a hearing in Quebec City.

After retreating to their steamboat, the *Ploughboy*, Gibbard's officials and the police force later headed for Sault Ste. Marie. En route, they stopped at Bruce Mines to arrest Chief Osawanimiki, the main

55 "*Daily Globe*, 27 July 1863, columns 4–6, 2", in Shelley Pearen and William P. Lonc. S.J., eds, *Letters from Wikwemikong 1845–1863* (Toronto: Hammerburg Productions, 2008), 185.

56 Paquin, *Modern Jesuit*, 112; Lecompte, 213–216.

leader in the eviction incident. Kohler, who was not arrested, was the chief's companion on this trip; he soon hired a visiting lawyer from Toronto to defend the chief at the subsequent trial held at Sault Ste. Marie. In defending the chief, David Blain argued that the court had no jurisdiction in the case, which he did not consider a criminal case. Since there were other charges pending against Chief Osawanimiki, he was released on bail put up by Kohler and Blain. The official investigator of the Wikwemikong incident later castigated both Gibbard and the Jesuits for their role in instigating and exacerbating the conflict.[57]

The final scene in this northern drama was yet to come. On 27 July, *Ploughboy* left Sault Ste. Marie with all the main protagonists on board, arriving at Killarney at four o'clock the next morning. When it was discovered there that Gibbard was missing, suspicion immediately fell upon Chief Osawanimiki and, to a lesser extent, upon Kohler. It was easily proven that both suspects were seen only on the lower deck, while Gibbard was last seen, and spoken to, on the upper deck at about a quarter past three in the morning—or so testified the first mate, who was piloting the boat on that shift. Other passengers corroborated that evidence.[58] Gibbard's body was eventually found with a laceration to the head. In the ensuing speculation as to the cause of death, three theories emerged. First, the press, especially the Toronto *Globe*, under its editor George Brown, assumed that he had been murdered by the chief and the priest. Some passengers thought the same, and even testified that Gibbard had been seen on the lower deck, which proved not to be the case. Others on board had noticed his depressed and distracted state of mind, and had presumed that he had committed suicide. That was the opinion of Kohler himself, and perhaps the most plausible one, given that Gibbard had been disgraced in the Manitoulin Island incident and had lost his legal case. The lawyer Blain, who had also been on board, offered a third possibility: "Some suppose that he may have turned giddy while gazing at the water and fallen overboard. There are several vague suspicions about his disappearance, none of which I think, are entitled to much weight."[59]

57 Paquin, op. cit., 113.

58 Ibid., 113–114.

59 Ibid., 114; Lecompte, 214–215.

At a subsequent hearing in Collingwood, Kohler and Chief Osawanimiki were exonerated by an all-Protestant jury. Their verdict of "murder by unknown persons", however, seemed tendentious.[60] In southern Ontario, Brown's *Globe* had poisoned the atmosphere, and "... the Catholic press preferred to see the hand of God not only in the fisheries officer's demise, but in the death two weeks earlier of the Indian Superintendent George Ironside—who had expired of heart failure at Manitowaning—as well as in the coincidental wreck of the *Ploughboy* on its southbound voyage."[61]

In a strange twist of fate, Kohler himself met a tragic end by drowning, when, on 14 October 1871, the *Cockburn,* the ship he was travelling on, sank in Georgian Bay during a violent storm.[62] What he said of himself would have made a fine epitaph: "God has done me the favor of having me persecuted for defending the poor against the rich and the weak against the strong."[63] Yet Kohler had not been the first drowning casualty in the northern Ontario mission. In 1854, Nicolas Frémiot, s.j., had drowned in the Mississagi River near present-day Blind River. As one commentator recounted, "His body was found drifting down stream four days later, covered with mud his scapular around his neck, glasses on his nose and a towel tied around his waist."[64]

A further ordeal of this period was the great Manitoulin Island fire of 1864. Beginning on the Wikwemikong reserve, the conflagration had enveloped the entire island by the end of that summer. Since many native people had lost their crops as a result, they had to be subsidized by the local government the following winter, which meant repaying this financial aid in the form of 450 cords of wood. One of the positive outcomes of the disaster was that native residents, in contrast with previous restrictions, were now free to cut wood when and where they wished, and to sell it on the open market.[65]

60 Paquin, op. cit.

61 Morrison, "Upper Great Lakes Record", 65; Lecompte, 215; DCB, vol. IX, 407–408.

62 DJB, vol. 1, 173; Lecompte, 229.

63 Morrison, op. cit.

64 Paquin, 104; DJB, vol. 1, 119.

65 Paquin, 114.

For the rest of the nineteenth century, all would not be easy as the mother-mission struggled on with limited resources and few priests. The Brothers kept the home fires burning by operating the farm and repairing the schools. Over time, relations with the government improved somewhat, but the plague of alcohol never ceased. The prospect of developing oil on the Wikwemikong reserve led to internal struggles over who should award the rights to explore. In the end, a compromise among all the parties allowed the enterprise to proceed. It all came to naught, as insufficient oil was found to justify a commercial operation.

Jesuit Intellectual Contributions

Amid their never-ending pastoral work and journeys throughout northern Ontario, the Jesuits also left a lasting intellectual legacy. They somehow found the time to keep diaries, write letters, compose local mission histories, and, in the case of Martin Férard, s.j., compile an Odawa-Ojibway dictionary of massive proportions during the 1880s. Comprising three volumes—some 1,374 pages—this major contribution to native linguistics remains largely (and surprisingly) unknown. In the spring of 1884, Férard was invited to attend a meeting of native language scholars at the Smithsonian Institute, Washington. While there, he presented the findings of his many years of studying the Ojibway language, the meaning and usage of its words, and specifically, the vast number of prefixes the Ojibway were accustomed to use in their speech.[66]

Férard's output of documents, letters, and other material on the Ojibway language was prodigious. Even after he was forced by declining health to retire in 1890 to the Novitiate at Sault-au-Récollet near Montreal, he continued to work on the Ojibway language right up to his death in January of the following year. Fortunately, in recent years many of his valuable manuscripts have been translated into English, edited and published under the direction of William P. Lonc, S.J., and Shelley Pearen. According to some scholars, if all of Férard's extant

66 Lecompte, 240–244; DJB, vol. 1, 108–109; Morrison, "Upper Great Lakes Record", 66. The texts still exist, and are kept in the Archive of the Jesuits in Canada, Montreal.

documents were published, it would be "even greater in volume than the seventeenth and eighteenth century Jesuit Relations."[67]

Joseph-Richard Richard, s.j., spent sixty-seven years on the missions of northern Ontario, the longest-serving Jesuit there at the time of his death at the age of 100 in 1954.[68] Although he had begun his missionary life in 1886 at Garden River, for almost six decades he worked on Manitoulin Island and all along the North Shore among the Ojibway people. His love for them and for their language and culture became legendary. In fact, in time he became proficient in their language, and encouraged them to use it in every possible way and on every possible occasion. To assist them and also to make sure that their language and culture would be preserved, he collected their oral expressions, stories, and songs. He even went so far as to argue that their language was an excellent means of communication because of its rich vocabulary and its sophisticated grammatical expressions. It was, he suggested, even superior to the classical Greek language, with which he was quite familiar.[69]

For almost fifty years, Richard corresponded with the bureau of ethnology at the Smithsonian Institute in Washington on the Ojibway's folklore, songs, and language. He also became a self-taught botanist and shared his knowledge with professional botanists. To that end he made himself familiar with over 500 different northern species of plants, wildflowers, and vegetables, and became an expert in their medicinal and healing properties. His prodigious memory, his love of Ojibway lore, his own remarkable ability to tell stories, and his exceptionally long years of service in the North set him apart as a remarkable and learned Jesuit among those who served the native people.[70]

Indigenization of the Jesuits

In 1865, the first Canadian-born Jesuit to work on the missions, Paul Nadeau, s.j., arrived at Fort William to take up the ministry in

67 Morrison, op. cit.

68 DJB, vol. 1, 303–305.

69 Ibid., 304.

70 When Richard died, he was the oldest Jesuit in the whole world, and the oldest priest in Canada.

Canada West.[71] Through the rest of the century, until his death on 6 May 1897, he exemplified the rigorous way of life that many of the Jesuits assigned to this work faced as they travelled the north country to minister to their far-flung people. He served in all three sectors of the northern missions: Manitoulin Island and environs, Fort William and vicinity, and the region around Sault Ste. Marie. By the time he arrived in north-western Ontario, that mission was well under way. Even prior to his arrival, it was thought by local missionaries that Canadian-born Jesuits would not willingly enter the native ministry. That was proven false by the arrival of Nadeau and later by the generations of Canadian Jesuits who have served afterwards in the North until the present day.

North of Lake Superior: The Mission of The Immaculate Conception

The north-western region of the Jesuits' native ministry began at Pigeon River in July 1848. After settling on the American side of the border, the Jesuits found that this earlier mission site had fallen into ruin. They also learned that local native people were in the midst of treaty negotiations with the American government. After rebuilding what they could amid trying circumstances, they realized this was not the place to start a mission. They soon moved to the shores of the Kam River near the Hudson Bay Company post at Fort William, Ontario.[72] There the land was better for farming, and many native people had already settled in the vicinity of the trading post, which provided a central departure point for the surrounding mission territory.[73] Beginning with a rudimentary house, chapel, and farm, they soon established day schools for both boys and girls. In 1870, the meagre Jesuit staff of this zone were bolstered by the arrival of the Daughters of the Immaculate Heart of Mary. An early form of a secular institute, these Religious women were called "Miss" instead of "Sister", since they did not wear a Religious habit, and could live in a community

71 Ibid., vol. 1, 256.

72 Jean-Pierre Choné, s.j., *Letters from the Ft. William Jesuit Mission, 1848–1862,* trans. Shelley Pearen and William P. Lonc, S.J. (Toronto: Hammerburg Productions, 2010), 46. "Kam" is the colloquial term for the Kaministiquia River.

73 Ibid.

or on their own. They began a convent school, which was really an orphanage, that provided an education for its residents. When the "Filles de Marie" were assigned to work elsewhere in 1884, the Sisters of St. Joseph of North Bay replaced them. The latter congregation went on to found and staff a hospital at Fort William and administer a residential school for native students from the surrounding area.

Early accounts of the mission described a difficult beachhead north of Lake Superior. Many of the native people were still nomadic and non-Christian. Those who settled near the Hudson Bay posts—for example, at Fort William and Nipigon, two of the earliest mission stations in the region—were often encouraged by the manager of the post to stay out hunting and trapping fur-bearing animals for long periods of time. Tension thus arose yet again between the reduction model of mission, as espoused by the Jesuit missionaries, and the itinerant-preacher approach that was necessary to foster contact with migrating bands. As Choné pointed out in a letter to the Jesuit Superior General in 1851, this was mitigated somewhat by the decline in traditional hunting during those years. As game became increasingly scarce, the native northerners were more likely to "settle down and cultivate the land."[74]

With missionaries and mission stations few and far between, progress was slow. The absence of resident priests made it difficult, if not impossible, to consolidate initial gains made by missionaries through early evangelization and baptism. Many native traditionalists clung tenaciously to their beliefs and practices, making it hard for neophytes to persevere without a permanent local clergy. To make matters worse, the bad example of many white traders and settlers—as in the Manitoulin Island region—brought the Christian faith into disrepute. Of course, missionaries were not above criticism, either, with some paternalistically treating the native people as "grown up children."[75] Others were overly strict and tried to run the churches on the reserves like monastic communities. There, too, reference was made to the reduction model as the way to proceed, as at the Immaculate Conception mission. Missionaries could see the

74 Ibid., 45.

75 Paquin, 246.

growing threats to a traditional way of life based on hunting, fishing, and gathering. In many cases, they expected that mission reductions would be a halfway station to eventual and inevitable integration with the growing non-native population.[76] The needs of Hudson Bay posts at this historical juncture, however, were exactly the opposite. For commercial reasons, they wanted native people to travel far into the back country to gather fur and fish to feed an ongoing demand in Europe and Canada.

For a time, it looked like the mission itself would be handed over to others, or abandoned altogether. To many, it seemed that Jesuit manpower was insufficient to handle the number of missions established further south, while Fort William was too difficult to reach.[77] In addition, at a time when few other priests were available for the North, those who were present had to minister to the growing number of non-natives in logging and mining camps as well as in towns and cities that began to dot the landscape. However, the Fort William mission soldiered on, reaching out further and further into the hinterland to numerous native communities and white settlements.

In more recent times, railways, highways, and air travel would aid these circuit riders of the North. In 1918, for example, the missions of the Albany River were entrusted to the Jesuits. Charles Bélanger, s.j., was the first missionary to visit the river's source at Lake Joseph.[78] Later, the far northern missions were bolstered by the presence of Joseph-Marie Couture, s.j., who was the first—and perhaps the only—Jesuit of the Canadian missions to use an airplane to reach his remote native parishes.[79] The Oblate Fathers had founded missions in this area and had resumed their ministry a few years later. This was part of a canonical mission to evangelize all of northern Canada, a mission they carry on to this day.

Today, the Immaculate Conception mission continues from its base on the Fort William reserve. Only one Jesuit remains active in

76 Du Ranquet, s.j., and Choné, s.j., *Letters from the Ft. William Jesuit Mission*, 73.

77 Ibid., 94.

78 DJB, vol. 1, 14–15.

79 Ibid., 72–73.

that region: Lawrence Kroker. In addition to parish ministry and liturgies on the reserve itself, the Jesuit team at Thunder Bay, which is based at St. Anne's Parish, founded and continues to be involved with the Kitchitwa Kateri Parish. This is a native parish within the city of Thunder Bay. They also administer a small retreat house. The one remaining Jesuit has been told recently that he will be the last Jesuit assigned to the region of Thunder Bay. Thus the Jesuits' presence in the native ministry will eventually be concentrated in the Algoma-Manitoulin region of the diocese of Sault Ste. Marie. This decision may be seen not only in the context of the shrinking numbers of priests and, especially, of Brothers in the Jesuit Order, but also as a sign of the times. Where Jesuits once served one immense diocese, there are now many dioceses, each with its own resident bishop and priests. The diocese of Thunder Bay also has two native priests among its presbyterate, another sign of the times. It is right and it is just that the dioceses of the North assume their rightful responsibility for all Catholics.

Sault Ste. Marie and Vicinity

At the juncture of Lake Superior and Lake Huron are the two Sault Ste. Maries: one in Michigan and one in Ontario. It was at Sault Ste. Marie, Ontario, that the third main hub of the Jesuit mission to northern Ontario was established. Initially planned by Chazelle, it developed with the arrival of two Jesuit priests in the region: Hanipaux and Kohler. Already fluent in Ojibway from his time at Wikwemikong, Hanipaux was based at St. Mary's Church in Sault Ste. Marie, Michigan. On the Canadian side, Kohler took up residence at Garden River, 10 miles east of Sault Ste. Marie, Ontario. After two years on the American side, Hanipaux was succeeded in 1848 by Jean-Baptiste Menet, s.j.[80] Five years later, this parish became the episcopal seat for the diocese of Sault Ste. Marie-Marquette under its first bishop, Frederic Baraga. At that time, Baraga had jurisdiction on the Canadian side as well. This saintly man, now a "servant of God", and someday surely a canonized saint, was not well received by the

80 DJB, vol. 1, 235; Lecompte 216–228.

resident pastor, Menet.[81] The bishop assumed ownership and direction of St. Mary's even though it was the Jesuits' property, and was therefore managed by an "exempt" Religious Order.[82] Resentment and conflict soon followed, with the Jesuits eventually leaving this mission for Sault Ste. Marie, Ontario, and Garden River.

As with the early years at Fort William, there was much pessimism about the future of the missionary enterprise. In writing to Clément Boulanger, s.j., his Superior in New York, Kohler was extremely blunt. He was also terribly depressed:

> All that I saw on my trip confirms me in the opinion that our missions have no future and that consequently I should have and we will all have, failed careers. I am now no more than an ignoramus who will not be any more use after leaving the missions than to cook for others.
>
> For a missionary to quit the missions is like a soldier leaving the army. He is good for nothing; he had been what he will be all his life. Despite that, however, I want, as much as it will be possible for me, to continue to walk along this road at the end of which I await utter uselessness. … My complete conviction is that we are cannon fodder. Once we are dead, there comes "The Deluge". No one will come to replace us in this task unless we take a different path.[83]

Writing later that same year, Menet was no less forthright and no less pessimistic:

> I swear to you, Very Reverend Father, that I am obliged to keep a tight grip on myself to refrain from saying to him what I would say to someone else. There is something so mean in such

81 This term indicates that Bishop Baraga has been accepted as a candidate for canonization. This is the first of four steps of the canonization process.

82 An "exempt order" means that the members were under the jurisdiction of its major superior, not the local bishop. In the case of the Jesuits, that would be the Provincial Superior. In reality, any Religious order operating within a diocese can do so only with the approval of the local bishop. This problem of the bishop usurping the Jesuits' building complexes occurred several times in the early days of the mission to Canada. For an example, see document # 6, Menet to Beckx, 11 June 1860, in *Letters from Sault Ste. Marie Jesuit Mission, 1850–1863*, trans. William P. Lonc, S.J., and Shelley Pearen (Toronto: Hammerburg Productions, 2010), 33–36.

83 Ibid., 12–13.

> conduct that only the respect that is due to his ecclesiastical status forces me to keep my mouth shut. I have kept Reverend Father Superior up to date and this letter will also be seen by him. After that, please make your decision and do with me what you will. But my opinion is that this place is not tenable.[84]

What accounted for such frustration? At the time, Menet considered that the bishop owed him money for expenses incurred, and that Baraga had assumed the house was his own, since "our house becomes an inn during the summer."[85] Given such concerns, the Jesuits eventually left the complex they had built up in Sault Ste Marie, Michigan. Later, in a letter to Pieter Jan Beckx, the Jesuit Superior General, Baraga seemed to indicate that tensions had eased somewhat. Even Kohler had visited Baraga to suggest that he petition Beckx and the "Propagation of the Faith" to have a permanent Jesuit residence re-established on the American side.[86] Without acknowledging their former ownership rights, the bishop made the Jesuits an offer that "I am willing to turn over the house where I live entirely to the Jesuit Fathers, and to move into another house; that is to say opposite the church, and to give them permanent title to the house and all the land that belongs to that house."[87]

Kohler ministered from Garden River until 1865, when he received a second assignment to Wikwemikong. For his part, Menet served as pastor in Sault Ste. Marie, Michigan, for fourteen years, until he was sent to Montreal to work at Collège Sainte-Marie. In 1864, he happily returned to Sault Ste. Marie for four more years of ministry to natives and newcomers.[88] The mission around Sault Ste. Marie continued to be served from the Jesuit residence at Garden River and, for a time, from St. Ignatius Parish in Steelton, later part of Sault Ste. Marie.[89] The last Jesuits to serve in the area were John D. Lynch and Clair L

84 Ibid., 17.

85 Ibid.

86 Ibid., 89.

87 Ibid., 90; Lecompte, 226–227.

88 DJB, vol. 1, 235.

89 Leonard J. Fischer, S.J., "Jesuit Mission History Northern Ontario: Among the Odawa and Upper Algonquins, 1641–1992" (unpublished document in author's possession), 9.

Fischer. The latter Jesuit came north after serving as president of Saint Mary's University, Halifax, and professor of communication arts at Loyola College (later Concordia University), Montreal. His older Jesuit brother, Leonard, had preceded him into the native ministry, remaining there well past the age of mandatory retirement; he later served in parish ministry in Nova Scotia and then in Guelph, Ontario. To any doubters, the Fischer brothers proved once again that the Jesuits in English Canada were willing to carry on the native ministry.

The Educational Dimension of the Native Ministry

From the beginning of the Jesuit mission, there was a concern for the education of youth, not only in matters of faith, but increasingly in trades and academic subjects. Day schools were started in many places and eventually staffed by a growing number of Religious women who joined the Jesuits on the northern Ontario mission. The Daughters of the Immaculate Heart of Mary and the Sisters of St. Joseph of North Bay were the main associates in this ministry. From the outset, it is important to remember the prominent role played by Jesuit Brothers. In addition to their academic contributions, their farm work was essential in keeping the schools at Wikwemikong, Fort William, and later at Spanish financially secure.

Over time, the educational dimension evolved through three distinct but related phases. First, there were the day schools on the home reserves of the students. That was followed by industrial residential schools located on the reserve. Finally, the industrial schools in their last years of existence included an academic high school curriculum. In the first phase, along with the catechism and hymn singing, students learned basic subjects like reading, writing, and arithmetic. In these early years, as noted previously, everything was taught in the native tongue. Later, as English came to dominate the surrounding culture, there was pressure to teach in that language. Pressure also came from governmental officials intent on promoting the assimilation of aboriginal peoples. Some parents also pushed for this policy, as they could see their children falling behind those on reserves where English was the language of instruction. By 1878, the second phase began at Wikwemikong when industrial boarding schools for both boys and girls were set up. These schools enabled the attendance of students who had to travel great distances from within the reserve. The boarding school also began to accommodate students from outside Wikwemikong. In 1895, for example, ten Iroquois students from Akwesasne, a Mohawk reserve near Cornwall, Ontario, were accepted at the request of the Department of Indian Affairs.[90]

All was not well, however, at the main schools in Wikwemikong. In 1885, fire destroyed both schools there under suspicious circumstances.[91] They were rebuilt. In 1911, the girls' school burned down again. It was suspected that a student had set the fire. Rebuilding was planned and started, but was interrupted by a strike, which occasioned a review on the part of the Jesuits and Sisters about the advisability of rebuilding on the reserve. At the time, the Jesuit Provincial Superior, Joseph Carrière, and the treasurer, Albert Bellemare, were highly critical of the results from the boys' school:

> It then held fewer than thirty students compared with the fifty at the girls' school. . . . The quality of teaching was inferior, and after a generation the school had graduated very few of the successful blacksmiths, carpenters, farmers and shoemakers it had hoped for. It was expensive and isolated, its legal status on the reserve unsure. Further, road and rail communication were now replacing travel by water, and new settlements, even of the Ojibway, were growing along the Canadian Pacific line and the transcontinental railway.[92]

Moreover, schools on reserves had difficulty keeping attendance at high levels. Parents often took their children with them to help with important seasonal activities such as the making of maple syrup, planting and harvesting crops, fishing, and hunting. While a governmental report of 1879 advocated the continued operation by missionary groups of the residential schools, it recommended that these be located off reserve, where parental influence would be minimal and full attendance could be enforced. Native students, unlike the rest

---

90 Ibid.

91 Paquin, 163.

92 DJB, vol. 1, 98.

of Canadian children, would have to stay in school until the age of eighteen.[93] Thus, for many reasons, including the growing assertiveness of the native population at Wikwemikong, a decision was made in 1911 to relocate off reserve to a farm property at the mouth of the Spanish River. Building went on through 1912 and 1913. The boys' school began to accept students in July 1913. The girls' school was not completed until March 1914, though female students had begun to arrive the previous year.[94]

As the federal government realized, conditions in most industrial residential schools across the country had deteriorated. Yet even the new facilities at Spanish were structurally inadequate, lacking proper ventilation and other features. Such problems hindered the control of a major disease that still takes a toll in northern native and Inuit communities: tuberculosis. The mortality from tuberculosis was shockingly high at this period in the residential schools of western Canada.[95] Later, after St. Peter Claver School for boys and St. Joseph's School for girls were relocated to Spanish, they experienced the devastation of the Spanish influenza epidemic of 1918–1919. According to the school diary for the period, nineteen registered students died at Spanish during the epidemic.[96] Before and after the epidemic, another twenty students registered at the school died. After 1938, and until the closing of the schools, there were no recorded student deaths at either of the schools. Tuberculosis also struck Spanish, claiming the lives of four students. In addition, two girls died in a drowning accident, while lightning struck and killed another youngster along with two teams of horses. Some students died of other identifiable causes, usually an infectious disease, while several entries give no cause of death.[97]

---

93 David Shanahan, *The Jesuit Residential School at Spanish: "More Than Mere Talent"* (Toronto: Canadian Institute of Jesuit Studies, 2004), 26–27; 29.

94 Ibid., 66.

95 Ibid., 55–57.

96 William P. Lonc, S.J., and Jacques Monet, s.j., eds., *The Residential Schools at Spanish Ontario: The Flu Epidemic of 1918–1919, A Translation of the School Journal October 13,* 31, 75. Figures for the death toll worldwide of the Spanish flu vary widely, from twenty-one million to more recent estimates of forty to fifty million. The higher estimate included some twenty million fatalities in India and other parts of Asia not considered in initial figures. In Canada, some 50,000 were believed to have died in the epidemic.

97 Ibid., 62, 63, 66, 74, for the page entries of these four students. I list the major causes of death

The eve of the Great War was not an auspicious time to start an educational enterprise in Canada's hinterland. Later, the Great Depression made scarce resources even more difficult to obtain, leading to six more years of sacrifice during the Second World War. All the while, the federal government kept the schools on a shoestring budget that never came close to covering costs. A new vision for the schools did not emerge until the post-war years, when the industrial skills model of education shifted towards an academic high school approach. This was reflected in a change of name in 1946 for the boys' school to Garnier College, the first native residential high school in Canada. Day schools at the elementary level were spreading fast across the native landscape, prompting the new Jesuit Superior at Spanish, Raymond Oliver, to focus on the high school level while phasing out lower grades or transferring them to the Filles de Marie. By meeting students' needs in a rapidly changing world, it was hoped the approach would garner support from the federal government, which held the purse strings, and would better harmonize with Jesuit educational institutions.[98]

Throughout the residential school era at Spanish, about half the manpower deployed by the Jesuits in the native ministry was assigned to work at St. Peter Claver Industrial School (later Garnier College). In 1925, for instance, fifteen of the twenty-nine Jesuits assigned to the native missions were living and working at the school. Though numbers can be deceiving, the Jesuit staff was a mixture of lifelong missionaries and short-term Jesuit Scholastics. Some were sent to convalesce from sickness and burnout after becoming burdened with extra ministry in the local parish or the neighbouring girls' school. Furthermore, many had to remain in the summer to provide activities for students, many of whom were orphans and could not go home for the holidays.[99]

---

because there is an effort at this time to accuse the churches and government of outright "genocide". My hypothesis is that the greatest number of students perished from two infectious diseases: tuberculosis and Spanish influenza.

98 Shanahan, 180–181. Cf. also DJB, vol. 1, 274–275.

99 Fischer, 11; Shanahan, op. cit., 177–178; 193.

Yet all was not doom and gloom in those last years of the school's existence. Under the direction of Hugh W. Barry, S.J., a new indoor hockey arena was built in 1950 at a cost of $35,000.00.[100] Students and staff were proud of their sports teams, which competed not just intramurally but against teams from other schools and towns in the area. The facility could also be used for many other activities, as David Shanahan noted: "The school now had, aside from a hockey arena for the winter, a meeting hall for concerts and plays, graduation ceremonies, and a place to show movies to the students and people from the village."[101] For students at the high school, the school day and culture changed in major ways. No longer required to work half-days on the farm or in the shops, they had more freedom to socialize. Occasionally, they visited the village or attended movies and dances with students from the girls' school. The boys even had their own pool room, where smoking was allowed![102]

Despite such social improvements, academic life was still greatly hindered by a shortage of properly trained staff. That situation plagued the school throughout its existence. Jesuits there often wrote to the Provincial Superior to point out this shortage and other serious problems. Many observers noted deterioration in standards. The inspector of schools, A. H. McKague, agreed with many Jesuits in attributing the decline to the shortage of trained teachers, and claimed "some subjects had been 'barely' covered because of illness and shortage of staff."[103] Moreover, it was likely the problem would not be solved. The federal government consistently underfunded native education, and, for their part, the Jesuits were already committed to running five other high schools from Halifax to Regina. In his well-researched history of the school, Shanahan summed up the situation:

> All the signs pointed to a massive failure of the people at Spanish to produce a high school of sound academic learning. Priests and Brothers were becoming disillusioned and exhausted by the continual drain on their spiritual, emotional,

100 DJB, vol. 1, 5–6.

101 Shanahan, 192.

102 Ibid., 194.

103 Ibid., 199.

> and physical resources. Questions began to be asked. What were the Jesuits doing at Spanish in the first place? What is it that the school was meant to do? Was it simply an orphanage/reform school run on behalf of the Indian Department, or was there potential for a traditional Jesuit centre of learning and development?[104]

Having shuffled the responsibility for native education off to the churches, the government could not succeed in an era of scarce resources and an assimilationist vision. Years later, both parties were called to account for charges of physical, emotional, and sexual abuse of students. Some have gone so far as to call it "cultural genocide" or "genocide" pure and simple, even likening it to the disease epidemics that had ravaged some of the schools. Some Jesuit priests and Brothers, Sisters, and lay staff have been accused of wrongs and abuses committed at the school. In the current age of redress and reconciliation, settlements have been reached with many, but not all, former students with claims. Those students retain the right to pursue justice on an individual or class action basis. In fact, all native students who had attended a residential school anywhere in Canada were eligible to be compensated for the years they attended those schools.

As with boarding schools elsewhere, much of the sexual abuse was perpetrated by older students on younger ones. Former students of Garnier College have confirmed this in private conversations over the years. In his chapter entitled "Cultures in Conflict", Shanahan stated,

> There is evidence of junior students [being abused] by seniors right up to the last days of the school. A Jesuit remembers hearing one morning of a senior caught in the bed of a junior boy the night before. Absolutely outraged, he called the offender out of class and faced him with the accusation. When the boy admitted his guilt, the Jesuit knocked him to the floor and gave him fifteen minutes to get out of the school before the police were called. To this day, the priest regrets his reaction, realizing how much the offender needed counseling. He also realizes that he lost the chance of learning the identities

104 Ibid.

of the offender's victims, who might also have gained from counseling and support for their ordeal.[105]

Since the closing of those schools fifty years ago, much has been learned about human psycho-sexual development.[106] According to some, same-sex boarding schools are not always conducive to healthy human development. Add to this milieu the familial and cultural deprivation of the students, many of whom were orphans or wards of the state and could never go home, and we have a recipe for dysfunction of all kinds. For these reasons alone, it was right that these schools were closed. A number of staff members—some of whom probably came through their own boarding school experiences—were, as reports of the time pointed out, dysfunctional. Long work hours and little sleep, the constant stress of looking after rambunctious children, and a Jansenist upbringing typical of the pre–Second Vatican Council era created conditions for serious pathology and abuse perpetrated by some staff. Some Jesuits in native parishes also were accused of sexual abuse. Since virtually all of the accused have died, they have never been to trial or been convicted in a court of law. In most cases, the testimony of victims has been accepted, resulting in apologies and compensation.

Despite this bad news (with "dire reports being sent to the Jesuit Provincial Superior year after year"), many who graduated from both schools at Spanish went on to lead productive lives. Shanahan's statistics for the period between 1951 and 1956 seem to support this conclusion. Of forty-one graduates from St. Joseph's School for Girls during this time, for instance, ten became teachers and another fourteen took up nursing.[107] At Garnier School, sixty-four students completed twelfth grade to enter an impressive array of occupations: "Alfred Cooper, was to become a doctor of medicine, another would become a university professor. Others got university degrees, became

105 Ibid., 195.

106 Examples include John E. Perito, *Contemporary Catholic Sexuality* (New York: Crossroad Publishing, 2003), and two works by John Money, *Love & Love Sickness: The Science of Sex, Gender Difference, and Pair Bonding* (Boston: Johns Hopkins University Press, 1980) and *Lovemaps* (New York: Irvington Publishers, 1986).

107 Shanahan, 199, 200.

electricians, carpenters, joined the Air Force and Civil Service. Overall, the graduates of Spanish generally did very well for themselves."[108]

Such success did not come soon enough to stave off a final decision to close the institutions. Garnier was the first to close, in 1958, followed by St. Joseph's four years later. At first, the Jesuits used their building as their residence, but it soon became too expensive to maintain. A last-ditch attempt to revive the school with governmental support took place in 1960, led by John E. McKey, who had been appointed the local Jesuit Superior the previous year.[109] That would have taken Garnier full circle to its original purpose, as outlined at its founding in Wikwemikong: "The proposal as it stands would be to have what academic studies are necessary for the particular jobs: Arithmetic, a smattering of Social Studies, English. The main purpose of the school would be to teach trades and the trades which are suggested are Motor Mechanics, Carpentry, Masonry, Bricklaying and Plastering."[110] However, the federal Department of Indian Affairs soon changed its mind about using the Spanish facility as a revived vocational school. The die had been cast. The school went up for sale in November 1960.

The Second Vatican Council Era

The vacuum created by the closing of the schools at Spanish was soon filled by a wholly unexpected event. In 1959, Pope John XXIII announced that he would convene a general council of the Church, which opened three years later—the first and only ecumenical council of the twentieth century. By that time, the circuit rider days in northern Ontario were drawing to a close. Yet even in that period of the council, there were key bases or parish hubs where resident priests ministered locally, while other Jesuits still travelled extensively across the North. In many cases, this practice has continued, as some resident pastors have several satellite churches to cover from a home base. The *societas perfecta* model of Church was outmoded and largely unworkable in an era of growing native self-determination and "revitalization." Anthony Wallace, an anthropologist, defined the process this way:

108 Ibid., 194.

109 DJB, vol. 2, 219–222.

110 Shanahan, op. cit., 255.

"revitalization is a deliberate, organized, conscious effort by members of a society to construct a more satisfying culture."[111]

Revitalization movements can take various forms, including the "nativistic" mode in which a culture tries to eliminate everything foreign from the original culture. This approach has proven totally unrealistic in the modern world. There is also the "revivalistic" mode, which attempts to retrieve and reintroduce cultural elements and practices that once existed or were thought to have existed in the culture. Unlike nativistic movements, this type is open to new and imported elements from other cultures. This is what we commonly see among those who are trying to revive and renew indigenous cultures. Whether it realized it or not, the Catholic Church itself was facing the need for an in-depth revitalization, a process in which the Second Vatican Council was a crucial first step. As the saying goes, "Without a vision the people perish" (Proverbs 29:18); the council developed such a vision, drawing from biblical, patristic, and contemporary sources, including gifts from contemporary cultures. As a result, the Church entered a period of revitalization in a "revivalistic" mode. Lately, however, it seems to be moving consciously into a "nativistic" period of retrenchment.

Amid this ferment, the Jesuit way of being present to the native Church of northern Ontario changed dramatically. Efforts were led by creative individuals such as Michael M. Murray, S.J., the builder and first director of the Anishinabe Spiritual Centre, founded at Espanola in 1979. As the process accelerated, the Jesuits in English Canada entered into a communal discernment process, meeting at Guelph under the direction of the late John J. C. English, S.J. On that occasion, the ministry to the native peoples was affirmed, while the Jesuit Community allotted significant funds to implement the vision of the Second Vatican Council.[112] The diocese of Sault Ste. Marie, in which the centre existed, had already adopted a similar direction at a local synod called by Bishop Alexander Carter and in which Daniel J. Hannin, S.J., a lifelong missionary and professor, played a coordinat-

111 Anthony Wallace, "Revitalization Movements", *American Anthropologist* 58 (1956), 265.

112 DJB, vol. 2, 90–94.

ing role.[113] He never tired of encouraging native people to take their future into their own hands. Having advocated for the reintroduction of the diaconate and the formation of women leaders in the Church's ministry, Hannin was instrumental in the early 1970s in setting up a programme to train native deacons. That project, in time, came to be among his signature contributions to the North, and eventually led to the setting up of the Anishinabe Spirituality Centre at Anderson Lake, Ontario. Its goal was to develop a strong, authentically native Catholic Church, and set the stage for similar developments elsewhere in the diocese. In time, programmes for formation in ministries for the English, French, and Native diocesan sectors were organized and funded by the diocese. Elsewhere, in the diocese of Thunder Bay Lawrence J. Kroker, S.J., who also had been associated with the earlier stages of the ministries' programme at the Anishinabe Spiritual Centre, initiated similar programmes in formation in Thunder Bay. Later, he would be instrumental in setting up an urban native parish, Kitchitwa Kateri, in the Fort William area of Thunder Bay.

Today, after more than a quarter century of offering ministries' programmes to the indigenous people of the North, Jesuits face new challenges, often with diminishing resources. From a high of thirty-eight Jesuits in the North in 1924, the number was reduced to only six Jesuits in 2012. As well, many of the first graduates from Anishinabe Spiritual Centre, both deacons and commissioned female ministers, have either died or retired. Nevertheless, the centre continues to receive candidates for ministry, the vast majority of whom are women. In addition to training seventeen men for the diaconate and nineteen women for the Diocesan Order of Women (now called the Diocesan Order of Service), the centre, in cooperation with Regis College, Toronto, has helped prepare two men, Milton McWatch and George Gardner, for the diocesan priesthood. McWatch now serves in the diocese of Thunder Bay, while Gardner ministers in the diocese of Sault Ste. Marie. Having come a long way from the reduction or *societas perfecta* model of the Church, such leaders have embraced a view of the Church that is consistent with the Second Vatican Council. In

113 Ibid., 120–122.

troubled times, their more person-centred models of the Church as the people of God and a community of disciples do not rule out the need for structures and institutions, but rather place them in their proper perspective.

Concluding Reflections

This brief history of native ministry by Jesuits in English Canada is, admittedly, selective. It would be difficult to include all those who served in this ministry, unnamed and unheralded, as priests, Brothers, Sisters, lay collaborators, and diocesan personnel since the Jesuits' return in 1842. A search of Jesuit records reveals that nearly 100 Jesuit priests served in the native ministry for a time or a lifetime. At least forty-three Jesuit Brothers also served in this ministry for some or all of their lives. The majority of those have been passed over or barely touched on in this account.

More could be said, as well, of the Alaskan mission, which was attached to the Province of Canada in 1907 before being transferred to the Province of California five years later. The modern-day urban native ministry likewise deserves a full study, as it has become an area of important involvement. For some time, in addition to Thunder Bay, which has been discussed briefly, Jesuits have ministered to native people in various major Canadian cities, such as Regina, Winnipeg, and Toronto. After a lengthy ministry in northern Ontario, for instance, Bernard A. Mayhew, S.J., moved to Toronto in 1973 at the request of the archbishop, Philip F. Pocock, to serve the city's growing native community. Working with another Jesuit, James J. Mara, and later assisted by two School Sisters of Notre Dame, he started a native parish that continues to this day. In Winnipeg, too, St. Ignatius Parish supported the Sisters of Zion in their efforts to educate native children in the city.

For decades, Regina has had a high proportion of native people living in its north and east side. Poverty, unemployment, and petty crime were widespread among them, but the city did little to alleviate their social situation. For the most part, too, the Catholic Church paid little attention to their plight. During the late 1970s and early 1980s, however, while teaching sociology at Campion College, Daniel

Hannin was especially helpful in organizing Wikiup, a social and religious centre for native people in the city's North Central district. He served there as the de facto pastor in an incipient native parish, while at the same time strongly supported the work of the Indian Federated College at the University of Regina, which later became the First Nations University of Canada.[114]

Upon his retirement in 1999, John D. Matheson, S.J., who assisted in the founding of the University of Regina's department of film studies during the 1960s, began an active ministry in the local prison, which held a large number of native people. Concerned especially with what became of them after their release from prison, he, along with others, established Friends on the Outside (FOTO). Supported by the archdiocese of Regina and benefactors, FOTO assists the families of prisoners, as well as aiding those released from prison by helping them to reintegrate into society and by advocating on their behalf. In that context, FOTO works closely with archdiocesan groups serving both urban and rural native people. In 2011, under the direction of Matthew W. Livingstone, S.J., Ruth Robillard, and Jenny Brown, FOTO produced a documentary entitled *Ashes and Tears*, which raised awareness of the plight of Métis who had been falsely promised land at Green Lake, Saskatchewan, in 1949 by the federal government.

Also in 2011, with the inspiration and financial assistance of lay groups in Regina, and with the strong encouragement of the local Jesuits and Campion College, Canada's first Nativity School, Mother Teresa Middle School, was begun. Part of a larger global network begun in 1971, the school is the first one to reach out to native people by adapting to the local context the Nativity model of educating young people from underprivileged backgrounds. In September 2012, Ivon Bellavance, a Jesuit Scholastic of the French Canadian Province, was appointed to the school's staff.

In Toronto, the social justice work so prominent in the early years of the mission was carried on partially through the Jesuits' Centre for Social Faith and Justice. Working ecumenically through Project North, later renamed the Aboriginal Rights Coalition, and

114 Ibid.

finally subsumed under Kairos, an ecumenical social justice group, the Jesuits in English Canada have worked on land claims and human rights issues. The publication of Michael J. Stogre's *That the World May Believe* in 1992 further raised awareness of Catholic social teaching on indigenous rights.

As well, several Jesuits in northern Ontario have been involved with local unresolved land claims. In that regard, the meticulous and painstaking work of William Maurice, S.J., in collecting and searching through church registers has been invaluable in reconstructing family trees and helping many reclaim their native status. Maurice and Hannin were also involved in the economic development of several northern native bands. The recent apologies by the Church's officials for abuse suffered in residential schools, as well as the canonization of Kateri Tekakwitha in October 2012 as the first aboriginal woman saint, mark a renewed attention to indigenous issues.

*

Ever since the time of the early Church, it has been said that pastoral ministry goes on until "the end of the age" (Matt. 28:20), while evangelization should be done within a reasonable amount of time. That seems to have been the approach of Saint Paul. After preaching the Gospel in a city or town, and after converting a large part of the population, he would appoint leaders from each community to carry on the work of ministering to it. As Jesus himself did during his public ministry, Saint Paul would then move on to other towns where people had not yet heard the Gospel message. Yet Saint Paul likely never envisaged a time when a new or second evangelization would be needed in vast areas of a once-Christianized world. This re-evangelization, or "New Evangelization", as described in recent years by Pope John Paul II and Pope Benedict XVI, has become our situation.

At the same time, some Jesuits who have served as pastors and missionaries in northern Ontario believe that it may be time for the Jesuits to move on. Given their declining numbers and their aging members, the English-speaking Canadian Jesuits may soon no longer be able to supply priests and Brothers for this sector of the northern Church. The dioceses of the North also face a similar diminishment in priestly numbers. Perhaps the number of diocesan priests will become sufficient in the near future, given the large migration of northerners to southern cities, along with a resultant and suitable restructuring and downsizing of diocesan institutions. Yet the fact remains that resident priests are becoming fewer and fewer, a situation already evident for some years in Quebec and in much of Europe and Latin America. In that context, therefore, the mission becomes primarily *ad intra*—that is, an effort to revive existing faith communities by calling forth gifts and ministries needed for a viable Church. At the same time, however, this may reflect more the missiology of Saint John than that of Saint Paul, with its aim of keeping the faith alive (John 6:29). Yet in the end, if local churches in Canada and elsewhere throughout the world are to have a future, they must begin to look beyond themselves to the "great harvest awaiting them" (John 4:35).

The key to this New Evangelization rests upon the revitalization of the Church's mission in the fullest way possible in today's society. This must encompass *kerygma* (proclamation/witness), *diaconia* (service/healing) and *koinonia* (community/communion/worship). The proclamation of the Gospel, without service to others and without a community of believers, lacks credibility; the Word of God must be shown to be living and active, transforming human hearts and societies. At the same time, having such service and community without the proclamation of the Word would be false to the great spiritual mission of the Gospel to make "disciples of all nations" (Matt. 28:19) and to teach them "to carry out all that I have commanded you" (Matt. 28:20). Within the Church, special charisms carry out this threefold ministry of witnessing to the Good News. Indeed, each Christian has been given special gifts for building up the *ekklesia* (1 Pet. 4:10; Rom. 12:6). Moreover, both the whole Church and each Christian is a missionary: "The Church on earth is by its nature missionary since, according to the plan of the Father, it has its origins in the mission of the Son and of the Holy Spirit."[115]

115 *Ad Gentes Divinitatus*, 7 December 1965, # 2, 814, in *Vatican Council II: The Conciliar and Post Conciliar Documents,* Austen Flannery, O.P., General Editor (Collegeville. MN: The Liturgical Press, 1979).

Today, in fact, every place is mission territory. In our time, the Gospel message must be preached to every tribe, tongue, people, and nation, to every class and strata of society, so that it may permeate every structure and institution. In this missionary effort, the laity plays a key role, for only it exists in sufficient numbers to take the Gospel where it needs to be proclaimed.[116] Through our witness of service and community, people will be moved to call us "to give an account of the Hope that is in us" (1 Pet. 3:15). This is evoked by the "good deeds of Christians" (1 Pet. 2:12) and by a good way of life. In this mission and ministry, Jesus has promised "to work with" us (Mark 16:20) and "be with [us] always until the end of the age" (Matt. 28:20b). In such a way, the Jesuits in English Canada, in their native ministry, have been committed to forming "a more independent, self-sufficient, energetic Church community actively handing on the faith in a culturally open and sensitive way to its young, and to help this Church relate to the wider community of the Church and bring to it the native's experience of God and human life."[117]

116 For a discussion of this topic, see Austen Flannery, O.P., "Vatican Council II", *Apostolicam Actuositatem,* 766–798.

117 The Jesuit Community of Manitoulin, unpublished draft of "Our Way Forward 2003–2013, Social Sector, Native Ministry, Manitoulin-North Shore", 2003.

II

The Witness of Jean de Brébeuf and His Companions Through the History of the Jesuits in Canada

MICHAEL L. KNOX, S.J.

On 29 June 1930, Pope Pius XI presided over the canonization of the Canadian Martyrs before thousands of pilgrims at St. Peter's Basilica, Rome. Among them were some 300 official French- and English-speaking delegates from Canada and the United States, with His Eminence Raymond-Marie Cardinal Rouleau, the archbishop of Quebec and primate of Canada, at their head. The delegation included five other bishops, the Honourable Honoré Mercier from the government of Quebec, university rectors, the Jesuit Provincials and their assistants, and a large number of priests and Religious, as well as many lay people, men and women, accompanied by their children.[1] Surrounded by the grandeur of Michelangelo's architectural masterpiece and thousands of candles that illuminated Bernini's grand *baldacchino*, and standing before the vicar of Christ,

1 Adrien Pouliot, s.j., *The Holy Martyrs of Canada*, translated by George F. Topp, S.J., library holdings, AJC, 3.

the pilgrims might have been excused for feeling a certain joyful satisfaction that Jean de Brébeuf (1593–1649) and his companions were now the first officially declared martyrs of North America and had finally joined the ranks of the venerable among the saints. "Now", Cardinal Rouleau might well have thought, "the faith of the Church in Canada, a faith that everyone knows to be gloriously rooted in the Church of Quebec, can truly be expressed in these heroic Frenchmen." Perhaps the Jesuit Provincial Superior of English Canada thought, "Finally we can refer to St. Joseph's Church in Midland as the Canadian Martyrs' Shrine." Together they must have thought, "At least we have our own genuine saints to help build up the faith on our continent."

A closer look at the history behind this momentous event, however, reveals that in reality, the devotion to the Canadian Martyrs did not abruptly begin in 1930 with their canonization, nor even in 1925 when they were beatified. As with most figures among the cult of the saints in the Catholic Church, devotion began during their lifetimes and, in the case of the Canadian Martyrs, has spanned over four centuries to the present day. Brébeuf and his companions were present at the beginning of Canada as edifying examples to many of its aboriginal peoples and its early European settlers. They have ever since been a part of the country's historical literature, its architecture, its national founding myth, and, most importantly, the Canadian Martyrs have been key figures for the faith of the Church in North America. If, therefore, a history of the Jesuits in English Canada is written, it would be less worthy without a reflection on the devotion to the Canadian Martyrs. Their lives to this day speak to Jesuits, to the larger Catholic Church, and even to secular culture about the members of the Society of Jesus in Canada and what they do.

The Earliest Days of Veneration: 1640 to 1800

An examination of the *Jesuit Relations* and other documents of the seventeenth century reveals that, even before their deaths, the Canadian Martyrs were extraordinary men whose efforts in the mission, even while they were still living, evoked the veneration of their contemporaries in New France. Before his death, Réne Goupil (1608–1642) is described as someone who was "lacking nothing in life to prepare for his martyrdom."[2] Jean de La Lande (d. 1646) is said to have had the virtues of a martyr while he worked among the aboriginal peoples in the mission.[3] The *Jesuit Relations* suggested that when the arrows reached his body, Antoine Daniel (1601–1648) died with a virtue that God had given him during his lifetime.[4] Noel Chabanel (1613–1649) is said to have been somehow predisposed for martyrdom, and when Charles Garnier (1606–1649) was buried, the Jesuits present stated that "It was truly a rich treasure to deposit in so desolate a spot, the body that lived as such a noble servant of God."[5]

In fact, the documentation on the lives of Isaac Jogues (1607–1646) and Brébeuf clearly emphasizes that they were already highly venerated among their contemporaries, both in New France and in Europe while they lived. After Jogues' return to France in 1644, despite his mutilated condition, he sought permission to celebrate Mass without his "canonical fingers". Pope Innocent X not only granted that dispensation, but went further to declare that "*Indignum esset Christi martyrem Christi non bibere sanguinem*" ("It would not be proper that a martyr for Christ should not be able to offer Christ's blood").[6] This communication was both an extraordinary expression of Jogues' renown in the universal Church and a public proclamation of the pope's belief in the missionary's sanctity.

From 1633 until his martyrdom in 1649, Brébeuf's life among the aboriginal peoples of Wendake (present-day southern Ontario) was filled with extraordinary accomplishments.[7] First as Superior of the mission, then as its acclaimed veteran missionary, Brébeuf wrote the first dictionary of the Huron language; he was the first to work

2 "Account of René Goupil (donné), by Father Isaac Jogues", *Jesuit Relations*, XXVIII, 125.

3 "Father Isaac Jogues Returns for the Third Time to the Country of the Iroquois, Where He is Put to Death", ibid., XXXI, 123.

4 "Of the Capture of the Villages of the Mission of St. Joseph, in the Summer of the year 1648", ibid., XXXIV, 93.

5 "Of the Death of Father Noel Chabanel", ibid., LV, 157; "Of the Capture and Devastation of the Mission of Saint Jean, by the Iroquois; and the Death of Father Charles Garnier, Who Was Missionary There", ibid., XXXV, 115.

6 "Lettre du père Jogues, captif chez les Iroquois, au gouverneur de Montmagny", BRH, XXXVI (1930),48–49, *Positio causae*.

7 The Wendake Nation was referred to by the French Governor and administration as Huron; this term continued both in academic and public use until the end of the twentieth century.

on translating parts of the Bible into local dialects, and he alone travelled, lived, slept, ate, and toiled alongside the Wendat people. Those efforts made Brébeuf, or *Echon* (as he was known among the Wendat), both a virtual "media star" in the early years of the printed page, and a magnet for anti-French sentiment among the many tribes of the region he served.

In the first documented act of veneration for the future Canadian Martyrs, his Religious Superior at Sainte-Marie among the Hurons, Paul Ragueneau, s.j. (1608–1680), ordered Brébeuf to write down in a journal his experiences during prayer. Excerpts of that journal were later published in 1652 as part of a larger series on the martyrs of New France.[8] The personal admiration that Ragueneau held for Brébeuf is also evident in his own correspondence to France. Among his reports on the religious, social, and economic progress of the mission among the Wendat, Ragueneau often offered admiring descriptions of Brébeuf's inner life of faith. In one letter, he suggested that the missionary's whole being was completely offered to Christ. He noted,

> He [Brebeuf] wanted nothing but Jesus Christ; he thought of and conversed only about Jesus Christ. His tongue spoke and his pen wrote only of Jesus Christ. All his activity was directed only to building up the body of Christ and if we had been able to perform a spiritual anatomy of his heart, in place of the desire for his own salvation, we would have seen a strong and passionate desire to belong completely and inseparably to Jesus.[9]

According to Ragueneau, Brébeuf's intense love for Christ was "Like a fire … enkindled in his heart" that cleansed every "interior impurity of fallen human nature", and permitted the grace of our Lord to rule over him.[10] Among his *confrères*, it was recorded several years

---

8 Paul Ragueneau, *Mémoires touchant / la Mort et les Vertus / des Peres Isaac Jogues / Anne de Noue / Antoine Daniel, Jean de Brébeuf / Gabriel Lallemant, Charles Garnier / Noël Chabanel & un Séculier René Goupil*, translated by William P. Lonc and George F. Topp (Hamilton, ON: Catlin, 2001), Introduction.

9 René Latourelle, *Jean de Brébeuf's Writings*, translated by William P. Lonc, S.J., and George F. Topp, S.J. (Toronto: William P. Lonc Inc., 2001), 336.

10 Ibid., 365.

before his death that no one ever saw him "angry or even showing any sign of resentment. . . . Some tried to catch him off guard in matters that they thought he must be very sensitive about, but his eyes were always kind, his words full of gentleness and his heart perfectly serene."[11]

Following the martyrdoms of Brébeuf and Lalemant at the village of St. Ignace II, the primary sources reveal the second major instance of veneration for the Jesuit martyrs in New France. After the news had come to Sainte-Marie among the Hurons that both men had been captured and put to death by the Iroquois, Ragueneau sent Christophe Regnault, the infirmarian at the mission hospital, to the decimated village to recover their bodies and bring them back to the mission through a heavy snowstorm. There he carefully examined Brébeuf's body. Regnault later wrote a moving account of his observations that clearly illustrates how, in his mind at least, the bodies were not only tragic manifestations of a mission on the verge of collapse, but already sacred relics, worthy of great care and veneration.

> I am about to describe to you truly what I saw of the Martyrdom and of the blessed deaths of Father Jean de Brébeuf and of Father Gabriel Lalemant. On the next morning, when we had assurance of the departure of the enemy, we went to the spot to seek for the remains of their bodies, to the place where their lives had been taken. We found them both but a little apart from each other. They were brought to our cabin, and laid uncovered upon the bark of trees—where I examined them at leisure for more than two hours, to see if what the savages had told us of their martyrdom and death were true. I examined first the Body of Father de Brébeuf, which was pitiful to see, as well as that of Father Lalemant. Father de Brébeuf had his legs, thighs, and arms stripped of flesh to the very bone; I saw and touched a large number of great blisters, which he had on several places on his body, from the boiling water which these barbarians had poured over him in mockery of Holy Baptism. I saw and touched the wound from a belt of bark, full of pitch and resin, which roasted his

11 "Some Remarks on the Life of Jean de Brébeuf", *Jesuit Relations*, XXXIV, 192.

> whole body. I saw and touched the marks of burns from the Collar of hatchets placed on his shoulders and stomach. I saw and touched his two lips, which they had cut off because he constantly spoke of God while they made him suffer. I saw and touched all parts of his body, which had received more than two hundred blows from a stick. I saw and touched the top of his scalped head; I saw and touched the opening, which these barbarians had made to tear out his heart. In fine, I saw and touched all the wounds of his body, as the [savages] had told and declared to us; we buried these precious Relics on Sunday, the 21st day of March, 1649, with much Consolation.[12]

Notice how both men emphasized their physical contact with Brebeuf's body in a manner that not only strengthens their eyewitness testimony, but seems almost prayerful, giving the reader a sense of the body's already sacred quality. They did not only observe the wounds on the martyr's corpse, but were moved to touch Brebeuf's legs, thighs, arms, head, and chest cavity, and finally referred to these as "relics." Ragueneau immediately went on to elevate the purposefulness of the martyr's life, suggesting that "His blood spoke much more loudly than his lips had done, and, his heart not being yet torn out, his tongue did not fail to render him service until the last sigh, for blessing God for these torments, and for animating the Christians more vigorously than he had ever done."[13]

Finally, in June of 1650, when the onslaught of Iroquois invaders had forced the Jesuits to retreat hastily from Sainte-Marie-among-the-Hurons, their two priorities were to see that as many Wendat Christians as possible, along with the bones of Brébeuf, Lalemant, and Garnier, accompanied them on their long journey to safety. Already possessing the bones of Garnier (removed from their grave in the Petun Nation during December 1649), Ragueneau turned his attention to the graves of Brébeuf and Lalemant. In the Jesuit Relation of 1649, he wrote that

12 "A veritable Account of the Martyrdom and Blessed death of Father Jean de Brébeuf and of Father Gabriel Lalemant, in New France, in the country of the Hurons, by the Iroquois, enemies of the Faith", ibid.

13 Ibid., 34.

> When we left the country of the Hurons, we raised both bodies out of the ground, and set them to boil in strong lye. All the bones were well scraped, and the care of drying them was given me. I put them every day into a little oven, which we had, made of clay, after having heated it slightly; and, when in a state to be packed, they were separately enveloped in silk stuff. Then they were put into two small chests, and we brought them to Québek, where they are held in great veneration.[14]

In both the Old World and the New World after 1649, veneration for these martyrs grew exponentially. When he was informed of their martyrdom, the archbishop of Rouen immediately ordered the Jesuits to gather together all significant and pertinent testimonies about them. The decision to first publish the *Jesuit Relations* was that of Paul Le Jeune, S.J. (1591–1664), the major Superior of the mission in New France between 1632 and 1639. Even after his return to Paris in 1649, he never failed in the task of overseeing the publication of a yearly *Jesuit Relation*.

Of all the *Jesuit Relations*, however, that of 1648–1649 became the most famous. Widely distributed and voraciously read throughout Catholic Europe, it was written by Ragueneau. In it, he told in dramatic detail the story of the invasion of Wendake by the Iroquois, and of the massacre of Wendat Christians along with the deaths of Brébeuf, Lalemant, and Antoine Daniel. Ragueneau also explained his difficult, even heart-breaking, decision to abandon Sainte-Marie in 1649.

Within a few months after its publication in early 1650, the 1648–1649 edition of the *Jesuit Relation* was sold out. Upon his return to Paris, Le Jeune published a second edition, which included a letter written on Christian Island by Pierre-Marie Chaumonot, s.j., (1611–1693). That same year, a third edition was distributed in Spanish Flanders, then two Latin translations at Innsbruck, Austria, and finally, in 1651, a Dutch translation of Le Jeune's work was distributed in Antwerp.

In fact, those *Jesuit Relations* became instant "bestsellers" in both France and Italy. As historian Allan Greer suggested, they combined

---

14 *Jesuit Relations*, 35.

two popular forms of writing at the time: the "travel narrative" and the "encyclopaedic catalogues".[15] The accounts of the Jesuits' martyrdoms spread not only across the Jesuit missions but also around the world, and went a long way in building up an extensive devotion to those popularly declared martyrs of New France. Certain notables among the colonists in Quebec City also wrote about the martyrs in their correspondence. For instance, in her memoirs, Mother Marie de L'Incarnation, the founder of the Ursuline Congregation in New France, dedicated several pages to her spiritual director, Jean de Brébeuf. In them, she suggested that he had the gift of "the spirit of the Sacred Word incarnate", a union with Christ that Saint Paul described in his letter to the Galatians when he wrote that "I am nailed to the cross of Christ; I live now, not I, but it is Christ who lives in me."[16] With this disposition, the nun wrote that his "soul makes more progress in one day than anyone else would make in a month."[17]

By the late seventeenth century, the Jesuits of New France would have the relics of only three of the eight martyrs, namely, Brébeuf, Lalemant, and Garnier. Until the capture of Quebec in 1759, those relics not forwarded to either France or Rome were housed at the Jesuit College in Quebec City, or were distributed among the Ursuline Sisters and the Augustinian Sisters of the Hôtel Dieu in Quebec City. The bodies of Jogues, Goupil, and de La Lande, martyred in the Iroquois territory in what is presently upstate New York, lie either at the bottom of the Mohawk River or elsewhere in the soil of Ossernenon, where the National Shrine of the North American Martyrs at Auriesville, New York, now stands. To this day, nothing has ever been found of Antoine Daniel, whose body was reduced to ashes in the flames that destroyed his church, or of Nöel Chabanel, whose remains were thrown into the Nottawasaga River.

The surviving relics, however, were almost immediately objects of great veneration. In the archive of the Jesuits in Canada, there are numerous accounts of miracles attributed to the martyrs between

---

15 Allan Greer, *The Jesuit Relations* (Boston: Bedford/St. Martin's, 2000), 16.

16 Albert Jamet, *Marie de L'Incarnation: écrits spirituels et historiques* (Paris, 1939), 255. Notes of Dom. Albert Jamet, O.S.B. on the life of Marie de L'Incarnation, the library holdings, AJC.

17 Ibid., 255.

1655 and 1700. In 1655, for example, J. Guion Dubrisson, a soldier in Quebec City, had asked that the relics of Brébeuf and Lalemant be placed over his two children, and, in doing so, he claimed that both were cured from "une colique estrange".[18] Another letter, written in 1674 by a Jesuit priest in Quebec City, Thierry Beschefer, s.j. (1630–1711), claimed that, after having prayed a novena to Brébeuf and applying the relics to his head, he was cured of a debilitating psychological condition.[19]

One of the most fascinating testimonies, however, comes from Madame Marie Regnouard, who wrote an eerie account of an exorcism that was performed on her servant, Barbe Hallay. In the letter, Madame Regnouard wrote:

> As on several occasions, when she was in the same state, I had applied the relics of different saints, that night I bethought me to apply the rib of the deceased Reverend Father Jean de Brébeuf which the Reverend Father Ragueneau had had the charity to give me on his return from the Hurons, which rib I placed on the side of the above mentioned girl… .
>
> At once the devil distorted in a variety of ways her arms and legs and her whole body, and tormented her more that night than I had ever seen before, and addressing me he repeated: "Take that away woman, take that away, for I am burning, I am burning!" I said to Him: "I conjure you in the name of the Living God, and by the Merits of the Most Holy Virgin Mary, Mother of my God, to declare to me whose relics they are you are in such anguish to have me remove from off this girl"… . [He replied,] "It is a relic of a saint who was martyred among the Huron, by the Iroquois." Then I again conjured him to tell me the name of the Saint whose relics they were. He answered in a rage, but with such volubility that I could not catch what he said.[20]

---

18 J. Guion Dubrisson, January 1655, AJC, Box C-319.

19 P. Therry Beschefer, December 1674, AJC, Box C-320.

20 "An Account of How Barbe Hallay, who was possessed, was delivered by the application of the Relics of Father de Brebeuf of Happy Memory", 15 October 1652, translated by Michael L. Knox, S.J., AJC, Box B-257.

This letter, along with those mentioned above, reveals several important details. First, that a portion of Brébeuf's bones were already distributed in Quebec City among certain Catholics—even lay Catholics—only three years after his death. Second, that the bones were already considered relics for veneration, and third, that they were even prayed with by those seeking cures.

Following the conquest of Quebec, relations between the new British governor and the Catholic hierarchy ensured that Jesuits were permitted to continue their ministry, but they were not allowed to take in any novices. Then, with Pope Clement XIV's suppression of the Society of Jesus in 1773, a slow process of attrition finally left Jean-Joseph Casot, s.j. (1728–1800), as the sole remaining Jesuit in Canada. Shortly before his death on 16 March 1800, he entrusted the remaining skull of Brébeuf and the femurs of Lalemant and Garnier to the Augustinian Sisters of the Hôtel-Dieu.

The Beatification of the Canadian Martyrs: 1842 to 1930

In 1840, only twenty-six years after the official restoration of the Society of Jesus, Bishop Ignace Bourget (1840–1876) of Montreal wrote to the then Superior General, Jan Roothaan, s.j. (1785–1853), urging that the Jesuits return to Canada. In his letter of 2 July 1841, *Appel aux Jésuites*, Bourget appealed to the spiritual heritage of Brébeuf.[21] Two years after the Jesuits' arrival on 31 May 1842, the mission's Superior, Pierre Chazelle, s.j. (1789–1845), interrupted his expedition to Manitoulin Island in order to celebrate Mass on the site of Sainte-Marie among the Hurons. Greatly moved by that experience, he wrote to Roothaan, strongly urging that an archaeological project should begin on the site as soon as possible:

> Nevertheless, the ruins of Sainte-Marie have not completely disappeared. Look through these bushes, Father, and through this thickly clustered growth, you see these mounds; they are piles of stone, bastion debris I think. But where could our house have been? Probably here to the west. I know that

21 The *Appel aux Jésuites* is quoted in full in Gérard Jolicoeur, *Les Jésuites dans la vie manitobaine, 1885–1922* (Saint-Boniface: Centre d'études Franco-Canadiennes de l'Ouest, 1985), 218–219.

> the river reached its walls, and besides, I recognize the spot described to me by an old chap who used to travel among the [Indians]. Nearly fifty years ago, he saw the remnants of the missionary dwelling and near the groundwork he noticed a stairway leading down to the river where, he tells me, they used to carry water. Here then, I think, was the house our Fathers loved to call: "*Notre maison de Sainte-Marie.*" The church could not have been far away for over here are more ruins. . . . But where then is the cemetery? Where should we look for it? Where shall we find the hallowed soil that received the torn and burnt limbs of those martyrs of Jesus Christ? Now an idea strikes me Reverend Father—and a very natural one too! Why not make excavations? It would not be a big undertaking in a place like this, and for the purpose I have in mind.[22]

Meanwhile, Félix Martin, s.j. (1801–1886), took up the task of assembling Ragueneau's documents, as well as copies of the dispersed thirty-eight volumes of the *Jesuit Relations*, among which was the famous 1648–1649 document.[23] In 1848, he wrote the first modern article on the Canadian Martyrs, entitled "La destruction des Hurons", published in *L'Album littéraire de la Revue canadienne.*[24] In 1852, he prepared the first translation of the Relation of Joseph Bressani, s.j. (1612–1672), written by the missionary in 1644.[25] Then on 7 August 1855, Martin, with a grant of $250.00 from the government of the province of Canada, did fieldwork in Huronia.[26] He left Montreal for the northern section of Simcoe County, and after two weeks, returned with maps, drawings, and notes. Using this research, in 1856 he submitted a report of his expedition, which he entitled *Voyages et Recherches, 1855.*[27]

---

22 R. J. Sloan, "Historical Documentation", in *Sainte Marie Project Manual* (1970), AJC, Box D, 1.

23 Guy Laflèche, *Les Saints Martyrs Canadiens* (Québec: Singulier, 1980), vol. 1, 270.

24 Ibid., 270.

25 *Relation abrégée de quelques missions des pères de la Compagnie de Jésus dans la Nouvelle-France par le R. P. Bressany de la même compagnie*, ed. Félix Martin (Montréal, 1852).

26 Sloan, 4.

27 Collection, Félix Martin, Library and Archives Canada, Ref. MG18-H27; R6387-0-4-F.

Years later, the former president of the University of Western Ontario, Sherwood Fox, described the importance of Martin's early work:

> … the historian and archaeologist of Huronia Father Martin was, as it were, the first Surveyor-General; his conspectus of the territory was the chart, which enabled all those who came after him to find their way about in the bewildering network of ancient settlements that covers a large part of Simcoe County. To him must be accorded the tribute of having gone ahead even of the pathfinders.[28]

In 1858, again with financial help from the Canadian government, Martin collected in three large volumes the first complete set of the original seventeenth-century *Jesuit Relations*, which were later published by the government, and have since been known as the "Quebec Edition".[29] In 1859, Charles-François Baillargeon, archbishop of Quebec (1855–1870), asked Martin to prepare the first survey of documents on the Canadian Martyrs as a background for the possible submission of a postulatum for their cause. Six years later, in 1865, he published the biography of Jogues, and then, in 1873, the biography of Jean de Brébeuf.[30]

In 1884, while staying in Trois-Rivières, Edward J. Devine, S.J. (1860–1927), found what would become his life's passion. He uncovered in an abandoned corner the old records of the parish kept during the 1640s by the Jesuit missionary Jacques Buteux, s.j. (1599–1652).[31] For most of the next forty years, Devine would devote every spare moment to archival research. Among other discoveries that he made was that of 1892, when he found the 1644 parchment granting Pope Urban VIII's plenary indulgence to the Wendat who would visit the

---

28 Sherwood Fox, *St. Ignace: Canadian Altar of Martyrdom* (Toronto: McClelland & Stewart, 1949), Introduction.

29 Laflèche, 271.

30 Félix Martin, *Le P. Isaac Jogues de la Compagnie de Jésus: premier apôtre des Iroquois* (Paris: Édourde Baltenweck, éditeur, 1873); Félix Martin, *Le P. Jean De Brebeuf; Sa Vie, Ses Travaux, Son Martyre* (Paris, 1877).

31 DJB, vol. 1, 157.

chapel of St. Joseph at Sainte-Marie.[32] Devine's publications began soon afterwards. The first edition of his *Jesuit Martyrs of Canada* was published in 1916.

Between 1896 and 1901, a protégé of Martin's, and archivist of Collège Ste-Marie, Arthur Edward Jones, S.J. (1838–1918), assisted American historian Reuben Gold Thwaites (1853–1913) in publishing his monumental critical edition of the *Jesuit Relations* in a seventy-three-volume set.[33] Within those Latin, French, and Italian documents was included their first professional English translation. In 1902, Jones visited the Huronia region around Sainte-Marie, where he mapped various sites that were already dug up, and worked hard to identify them with the various mission sites described in the *Jesuit Relations*. It was during that expedition that Jones reported to have discovered the old Wendat village of St. Ignace II where Brébeuf and Lalemant were put to death. It was some 10 kilometres from the site of Sainte-Marie.[34] In 1909, the literary fruit of Jones' extraordinary work, entitled *Old Huronia*, was published as the Sixth Report of the Ontario Bureau of Archives. In it, he not only included appropriate sections of the *Jesuit Relations*, but also Martin's watercolour sketches and various seventeenth-century maps of the region.

All of that interest in the history of the early Jesuit martyrs played a huge role in the growing devotion among Catholics in both Canada and the United States. In 1884, the American bishops at the Third Plenary Council at Baltimore formally proposed the introduction of the causes for Isaac Jogues and René Goupil along with the young Mohawk Christian, Kateri Tekakouitha (1656–1680).[35] Rome responded to their proposal in 1885 with a letter allowing the Catholic Church in the United States to begin officially its research. Almost immediately after Rome's approval, a pilgrimage was organized to Auriesville in the summer of 1855, where some three thousand Catholics travelled to the newly built chapel dedicated to Our Lady of the Martyrs. Attendance

---

32 Ibid.

33 Ibid., 158

34 Ibid.

35 Laflèche, *Les Saints Martyrs Canadiens*, 273.

at what was eventually to be called the National Shrine of the North American Martyrs continued to grow. Then, in 1886, the American bishops put forward to Rome a *postulatum*, largely based on Martin's biography of Jogues, hoping that that document would further spur on the cause of the martyrs.[36]

Meanwhile, in 1886, the provincial council of bishops in Quebec put forward their own *postulatum* in support of the American initiative, but they also added Antoine Daniel, Brébeuf, Lalemant, and Garnier to the list. Once again, that proposition was greatly inspired by Martin's work on the life of Brébeuf.[37] That same year, a memorial church to the martyrs was dedicated in Penetanguishene, Ontario (now known as St. Anne's Church), approximately 10 kilometres from the ruins of Sainte-Marie, with the idea that Brébeuf and Lalemant had died somewhere close to its location. In 1890, Elzéar-Alexandre Cardinal Taschereau of Québec approved the first official prayer in Canada for the glorification of the Canadian Martyrs.[38]

The first canonical process for the beatification of the Canadian Martyrs was initiated in 1904 under the stewardship of Louis-Nazaire Bégin. At that time, two other Jesuit missionaries, Jean de La Lande and Nöel Chabanel, were also added to the list, but Kateri Tekakouitha's name was absent.[39] Soon afterwards in 1909, the bishops of the Plenary Council of Quebec wrote to Pope Pius X asking the tribunal in Rome to give immediate attention to the report sent them on the martyrs of Canada. With that, a clear momentum was building within the Catholic hierarchy.

Based on the discoveries of Jones, in 1906 Denis T. O'Connor, archbishop of Toronto (1899–1908), asked the Society of Jesus to found the parish of St. John the Evangelist, Waubaushene, Ontario. The hope was that the church would become a pilgrimage destina-

36 Ibid.

37 Ibid., 277

38 Pouliot, 3.

39 The name of Kateri Tekakouitha was removed since, according to Catholic tradition, a martyr can be immediately beatified, whereas, for one who has not been martyred, such as Kateri, the Church requires two miracles before their proclamation as blessed.

tion close to the proposed site of St. Ignace II.[40] Jean-Baptiste Nolin, s.j. (1849–1914), was assigned to the task; in 1907, he constructed a pilgrimage chapel on the newly christened "Martyrs' Hill." That same year, on the feast of the Assumption, the first pilgrimage to Martyrs' Hill took place. Twenty-five thousand pilgrims gathered to pray at the site.[41] Over the years, the numbers grew. The chapel remained in use until 1925, when the present Martyrs' Shrine church was built on the hillside across from the ruins of Sainte-Marie.

Paul Bruchési, archbishop of Montreal (1855–1939), while focusing his efforts specifically on Brébeuf, Lalemant, Jogues, Daniel, Garnier, Chabanel, Goupil, and de La Lande, sent out a *Mandement* on 8 February 1909, proclaiming that

> The dream of a native Church on our shores was not entirely realized, but "the blood of the martyrs is a seed of the faith"; a new people has emerged, and Christian virtues flourish on the shores of the St. Lawrence and the Great Lakes. If the Church today is indeed so prosperous, she should perhaps count among one of its graces the admirable generosity of her first apostles, their blood given for Christ, and the divine protections they provide.[42]

The archbishop went on to insist that "[i]n virtue of this apostolic instruction, all the faithful in this diocese, without any exception, are obliged, under pain of censure, and with grave consequences to surrender, either directly to the Archdiocese, or through their priest, all the writings or documents they might have from these servants of God."[43] In 1912, the report on the martyrs presented to the Congregation of Sacred Rites was approved, and the formal cause for Brébeuf, Jogues, Lalemant, Daniel, Garnier, Chabanel, Goupil, and de La Lande was formally introduced.

---

40 DJB, vol. 1, 261.

41 Laflèche, 286.

42 Paul Bruchési, archbishop of Montreal, *Mandement*, dated 8 February 1909, in "The Canadian Martyrs' Shrine", AJC, Box D, 1.

43 Ibid.

During the period between 1919 and 1923, an intense investigation began of all the acquired records from France, Canada, and Rome. These were carefully scrutinized, and every effort was made to secure both the sanctity of the martyrs' lives and the motives for their deaths. During those years, too, Devine dutifully recorded a surge of popular devotion among Canadians in the regular editions of *The Messenger*.[44] Indeed, he would once again play an important role in the beatification of the Canadian Martyrs. In 1907, he had cards with prayers to the martyrs placed in every edition of his magazine, and invited anyone to write in who had experienced their intercession.

Theopile Hudon, s.j., now the first official vice-postulator for the cause in Canada, was officially responsible for evaluating the alleged "favours", or miracles, attributed to any of the missionaries put forward in the cause, and for sending the most genuine of those to Rome.[45] The final *positio* for the beatification of the Canadian martyrs was then gathered by Hudon and Devine, along with their American counterpart, John J. Wynne, S.J., and officially sent to Rome in 1919. In 1922, a formal apostolic commission was established to review the *positio* put forward to Rome, where Devine testified as a witness for over eighteen hours, never faltering in his detailed knowledge and appreciation of the lives and works of the early Jesuits.[46] Thirty years of painstaking research had gone into making those hours decisive in the forwarding of the cause. He wanted the beatification to take place on or near the 300th anniversary of the arrival of Brébeuf in Canada on 19 June 1625.

Another driving force behind the beatification was John M. Filion, s.j. (1878–1962), who was appointed Provincial Superior of Canada on 1 July 1918. He had admired the Canadian Martyrs ever since his childhood in Ottawa. As their cause progressed, especially after 1919, he became fervent in his promotion. It was no surprise, then, that their beatification stood as one of the principal issues in his mind when he became Provincial Superior.[47] There is no doubt that Filion's attend-

---

44 DJB, vol. 1, 83.

45 Pouliot, 1.

46 DJB, vol. 1, 83.

47 Ibid., 112.

ance at the Twenty-Seventh General Congregation of the Society of Jesus in the autumn of 1923 (fewer than two years before the martyrs' subsequent beatification) was largely taken up by efforts to promote their cause. In fact, it was his decision to promote the "Jesuit Martyrs of New France" as the "Canadian Martyrs" that was the decisive factor in winning over Pope Pius XI, who had canonized several French saints the previous year.[48]

After the official investigation was completed, their cause was brought back to the Congregation of Sacred Rites, and, in November 1924, they were declared Servants of God. To prepare for the beatification, all of the bones that had been preserved in Canada, either at the Hôtel-Dieu or at the Ursuline Convent, were officially identified, and some important fragments were sent to Rome.[49] Soon afterwards, those two Religious communities decided to share the remaining bones equally with the Society of Jesus in Canada. The Ursuline Sisters who had the ribs of Brébeuf and Lalemant, as well as an anklebone of Charles Garnier, divided them into two equal sections. The Hospitalers, who had the femurs and two vertebrae of Lalemant and what was left of the fibula of Garnier, gave the Jesuits one femur, one vertebrae and another section of the fibula.[50] As for the skull of Brébeuf, it was sawed in two, vertically down the middle of the face, by a surgeon from McGill University, Montreal, and one half was given to the Jesuits.[51]

Meanwhile, the Jesuits of France also donated their relics of Garnier to the Canadian Jesuits, along with a beautiful reliquary. During the three days of prayer celebrated at Quebec City in honour of the newly beatified martyrs, and amid some 40,000 participants, all the relics were ceremonially transferred to the Society of Jesus on 12 November 1925 in a solemn procession to the Jesuits' Sodality Chapel.[52] On that day, courts were adjourned, government offices were closed, and everyone in Quebec City was encouraged to attend

48 DJB, vol. 1, 112.

49 Pouliot, 23.

50 Ibid., 24.

51 Pouliot, 23.

52 Ibid., 24.

the event. On 21 June 1925, the 300th anniversary of the arrival of Brébeuf to New France, Pope Pius XI beatified the Canadian Martyrs in St. Peter's Basilica, Rome.

Construction and Canonization: 1925–1930

As early as 25 November of the same year, the Congregation of Rites ordered the cause of the martyrs to be taken up once more. It observed that

> … the devotion, reverence and confidence of the faithful towards these martyrs have grown to such an extent that, on their invocation and by their intercession, some remarkable cures, it is claimed, have been obtained from God. Because of these, we consider it fitting and very useful to institute apostolic procedures in view of advancing their cause for canonisation.[53]

That same year, too, it was decided that the old shrine at Martyrs' Hill should be dismantled. It was too far from the railway line, and the water supply for the pilgrims was inadequate. As well, its historical authenticity was being questioned.[54] Filion acquired the property across from the ruins of Sainte-Marie, and promised to have a church built there for the first anniversary of the martyrs' beatification. Taking on the project personally, he secured a bank loan for $20,000.00 and drew up the plans for the new church. He remained on site as the foreman. He hired some fifty labourers who normally worked on the Great Lakes boats during the summer months, begged over 75,000 board feet of wood from various local lumber companies, and acquired discarded fixtures from both a Paulist Church and the Catholic Cathedral in London, Ontario, to adorn the building's interior.[55] By 1 December, the roof of the church was in place, and by May, Filion had hired stonemasons to align the limestone facing around the building's exterior. Finally, on 26 June 1926, the shrine to the Canadian Martyrs, placed under the patronage of Saint Joseph, was officially

53 Correspondence, in "The Canadian Martyrs' Shrine", AJC, Box D, 1.

54 In 1918, on his deathbed, Jones told Filion that he had his doubts whether the shrine built in Waubaushene was truly on the site of Brébeuf's and Lalemant's martyrdom.

55 Jacques Monet, s.j., "Millennial Jesuit Anniversaries", in the *Jesuit Bulletin* (2000), 8.

opened by William Henry Cardinal O'Connell of Boston (1859–1944), while Charles McCrea, minister of Forestry and Mines, government of Ontario, unveiled bronze statues of Brébeuf and Lalemant that were prominently displayed at the front entrance to the church. The following day, a delegation of Canadian bishops led by Neil McNeil, archbishop of Toronto (1851–1934), offered the first mass in the newly opened church before some 13,000 pilgrims.[56]

While Filion was hard at work building the shrine to the Canadian Martyrs, John J. Wynne, S.J., the vice-postulator in the United States for their canonization and founder of *America* magazine (1909) published *The Jesuit Martyrs of North America*.[57] This book became important since it highlighted the miraculous nature and the very large number of cures obtained through the intercession of the Canadian Martyrs—a fact that was said to have inspired great devotion throughout North America. Though the proven holiness and martyrdoms of the French missionaries were the only requirement for their beatification, the Catholic Church required two legitimately recorded miracles for them to be canonized. Among the numerous cures referred to the Congregation of Rites and submitted to the examination of experts, two were chosen for the purpose of canonization. Both were cases of tubercular peritonitis that had been completely cured. One was that of the Acadian Religious Marie Robichaud of the Religious Hospitalers of St. Joseph on 9 July 1926; she was cured on the last day of a novena to the martyrs that the Sisters in her convent had been praying. The other case was a French Canadian Religious, Alexdrine Ruel, a Presentation Sister, on 30 December 1927.[58] Both Sisters had invoked the help of the Blessed Canadian Martyrs. Ruel had had relics of the martyrs applied to her body on three different occasions. The miraculous nature of those two cures was officially recognized by the Congregation of Rites on 11 May 1930; Pope Pius XI signed the decree authorizing the

---

56 It was dedicated to honour St. Joseph, the patron saint of Canada since 1624 and of the Jesuit Mission to the Wendat between 1634 and 1650.

57 John J. Wynne, S.J., *The Jesuits Martyrs of North America* (New York: University Knowledge Foundation, 1925).

58 Pouliot, 3.

beginning of the canonization on 18 May 1930.[59] The day of solemn proclamation was set for 29 June 1930, which was the solemnity of the apostles Saints Peter and Paul. Meanwhile, in Canada, as the eight martyrs became the first saints of North America, over 7,000 pilgrims were attending an outdoor Mass at the shrine, with Archbishop Neil McNeil of Toronto as presider.

Pilgrimage and Devotion 1930 to 1984

For over a century since its opening, the Canadian Martyrs' Shrine has remained a priority commitment of Canadian Jesuit ministry. Thousands upon thousands of pilgrims have indeed come to the shrine, as pilgrims elsewhere throughout the ages and in all the great religions have visited sacred sites. They come to Martyrs' Shrine because it is thought to be a holy place. Saints have lived there, miracles have occurred, and the shrine brings a great sense of peace to its visitors.

In 1927, Joseph A. Keating, S.J. (1893–1952), was appointed the first director of the new Canadian Martyrs' Shrine. During his time there, he oversaw the completion of both Fort Sainte-Marie Inn and the stone towers of the church.[60] He also supervised the design of the grounds with trees, shrubs, and pathways. Most especially, he managed the installation of the outdoor Way of the Cross on what would be named "Calvary Hill". Its almost life-size bronze figures were fashioned by French sculptors in Vaucouleurs Studio, Paris, and make up the fourteen stations winding along the hillside. They were made possible by a gift of $6,000.00 by Mary McMartin Campbell of Montreal.[61] On 11 September 1927, Archbishop McNeil presided at their solemn blessing with a Mass at the twelfth station, set on the highest point of the grounds.

For over a third of its history, the Canadian Martyrs' Shrine was under the direction of Thomas J. Lally, S.J. (1898–1953).[62] He was

59 Laflèche, 299.

60 Monet, 11.

61 Ibid., 11.

62 DJB, vol. 1, 179.

appointed as director in 1928, and would remain there until 1953. During that period, and especially during the 1930s, there was such an increase of pilgrims that the inn had to be enlarged to accommodate the crowds. Diocesan pilgrimages became annual events. Pilgrims would travel to the shrine by car, bus, train, and boat: French-Canadian and English-speaking Catholics at first, then aboriginal peoples: Wendat, Ojibway, Mohawks; then Americans from the Midwest; afterwards, and in ever-growing numbers since the first Ukrainian pilgrimage in 1946, new Canadians from different cultural communities and different religious traditions, including Mexicans and Germans; Czechs, Poles, and Italians; Jamaicans, Slovenes, Greeks, and Tamils; Mennonites, Lutherans, the Bethel Bible Church; Quakers and Presbyterians; and Third Order Franciscans.

Lally worked hard to keep this growing population informed, and in 1930, founded the *Martyrs' Shrine Message*, which was published four times each year. He wrote many of the articles himself, and, within a few years, was mailing them out to some 12,000 subscribers.[63] Within the first thirteen years of its publication, 527 cures were dutifully reported in its pages.[64] In 1932, he supervised the transport and proper installation of a beautiful reliquary, given to the Shrine by the Society of Jesus of Paris.

Clearly, too, Lally considered it of the greatest importance to support all forms of devotion to the Canadian Martyrs. He genuinely assisted bestselling author F. W. Davey McDowell in his writing of *The Champlain Road* and the Canadian poet E. J. Pratt in writing his epic poem *Brébeuf and His Brethren*.[65] Lally also encouraged the work of amateur archaeologists Alphonse Arpin and Thomas Connon in verifying the discovery of St. Ignace II, which was located off present-day Rosemount Road, the accepted site where Brébeuf and Lalemant

---

63 Ibid., 179.

64 After the opening of the Canadian Martyrs' Shrine, it quickly became a custom for pilgrims to attest to the director, in person, or by mail or telephone, experiences they had of being healed by God through the intercessory prayers of the Canadian Martyrs. With the permission of the pilgrims, Lally began to publish these miracles in each edition of the *Martyrs' Shrine Message*, under the title "Cures". Bound volumes of this magazine can be found at the Archive of the Jesuits in Canada, Montreal, and at the Archives of the Canadian Martyrs' Shrine.

65 DJB, vol. 1, 179.

were martyred. Soon afterwards, in 1937, excavations of the site began on behalf of the National Museum of Canada by W. J. Wintemberg.

As director, Lally approached both the Jesuit Provincial Superiors and various local Jesuit Superiors yearly for adequate summer staff. Judging from his correspondence, he never flinched from making forceful presentations in order to get what he wanted. In 1937, he confidently wrote to the then Provincial Superior, Henry J. Keane, S.J. (1876–1956), "My prayers for help have been unceasing, and I know that the martyrs will not permit us less than what we need!"[66]

The 1940s at the shrine began with the proclamation of Pope Pius XII on 16 October 1940, naming the Canadian Martyrs secondary patron saints of Canada, the primary being Saint Joseph. That year, too, Lally succeeded in persuading benefactors and friends to help him in acquiring the sites of Sainte-Marie and St. Ignace II. As a result, that same year, the Jesuit Fathers of Upper Canada finally purchased the site of Sainte-Marie across from the Martyrs' Shrine. To authenticate those sites, Lally initiated contact with the Royal Ontario Museum and later with the University of Western Ontario.[67] Between 1941 and 1943, the Royal Ontario Museum and the University of Toronto carried out excavations under the field direction of archaeologist Kenneth E. Kidd (1906–1994). He excavated the area outlined by the stone remains. The results of his work were published in *The Excavation of Ste. Marie I*.[68]

During the Second World War years, pilgrims continued to visit the Canadian Martyrs' Shrine in vast numbers. Many of them would journey there to pray for their family members who were fighting overseas, and to seek the intercession of the martyrs on their behalf. On 9 September 1945, a Mass of Thanksgiving was celebrated at the shrine for the military; it was attended by over 1,000 soldiers from Camp Borden near Barrie, Ontario.[69] In 1947, Lally initiated a project to reconstruct the bastions at Sainte-Marie, and over the years

66 Thomas J. Lally, S.J., letter to Joseph P. Monaghan, S.J., 12 March 1937, AJC, Box 173.

67 DJB, vol. 1, 180.

68 Kenneth E. Kidd, *The Excavation of Ste. Marie I* (Toronto: University of Toronto Press, 1950).

69 Steve Catlin, *A Pictorial History of the Canadian Martyrs' Shrine* (2005), Canadian Martyrs' Shrine Archive, Tay Township.

he conscripted the help of several Jesuit novices who were there on pilgrimage.

Two years later, the University of Western Ontario, under the direction of Wilfrid Jury, curator of its Museum of Indian Archaeology, once again undertook extensive archaeological excavations at the site. His discoveries completely changed the accepted beliefs of the extent of this central Jesuit residence. It was found to be much larger, surrounded by a double palisade and designed for both living and defence purposes.[70] In 1948, he discovered the North Court of the compound with its artificial waterway system, and the following year, the artificial locked waterway, the first to be discovered in North America. As well, in 1950, he unearthed the south court of the mission and a cemetery, in which had been buried both French and several aboriginal Christians. His efforts over those years, with the support of both Lally and the wider Society of Jesus, led to finding of animal and fowl bones, seeds, nails, hinges, keys, locks, rosary beads, knives, forks, scissors, surgeon's materials, leather goods, wooden artefacts and metals. All these discoveries helped to transform our understanding of the earliest days in Canadian history.[71]

That support from the Society of Jesus was, in the end, not only of the moral kind, but also physical and intellectual. In June 1949, Denis A. Hegarty, S.J. (1907–1996), was assigned to the Canadian Martyrs' Shrine to help the American author Francis-Xavier Talbot, S.J., complete his biography on the life of Saint Charles Garnier. While there, Hegarty became friends with Jury, and after Hegarty had taken course work in archaeology at the University of Western Ontario, Lally gave him permission to join the archaeologists in their excavation of Sainte-Marie.

In 1954, long after Jury had finished his work at Sainte-Marie, Hegarty fulfilled the long-standing hope that Chazelle had expressed to his Superiors in 1842: he found the graves of Brébeuf and Lalemant at Sainte-Marie.[72] That discovery was of national significance, and was

70 R. J. Sloan, "Archaeological Excavations", in *Sainte Marie Project Manual* (1970), AJC, Box D, 1.

71 Ibid., 2.

72 DJB, vol. 2, 130.

later to be a major factor in the Jesuit Order's decision to encourage the reconstruction of the historic site. Until 1967, Hegarty remained a member of the staff at the shrine. His devotion to the martyrs, mixed with his extraordinary gift of storytelling, indeed inspired generations of visitors.

Earlier, in 1949, Lally had invited the American author and director Daniel J. Lord, S.J., to stage a giant pageant in commemoration of the tercentenary of the deaths of the Canadian Martyrs. He entitled it *Salute to Canada*.[73] With a cast of some 500 participants, including actors, musicians, dancers, makeup artists, stage crew, and production staff, the show entertained over 25,000 pilgrims that July.[74] That same year, on 26 June, pilgrims from Quebec brought a relic of the skull of Brébeuf to the shrine.

Over the years, Lally welcomed hundreds and hundreds of people to the shrine. Among those was Louis St. Laurent, the prime minister of Canada (1948–1957) and his wife, Jeanne; they visited the shrine on 29 August 1952 and later toured the beautiful Midland area.[75] Lally, the longest-serving director of the shrine, the man who was often heard to say, "There is nothing I would not do for the martyrs", finished his last season in early October 1953. He died a few days later.[76]

John F. McCaffrey, S.J. (1906–1972), was assigned as the new director of the Canadian Martyrs' Shrine in 1954. He took great personal interest in continuing the archaeological work at Sainte-Marie, and his friendly relationships with both William Cranston, then chairman of the Economic Council of Ontario, and John Robarts, then premier of Ontario (1961–1971), greatly aided the establishing of a formal agreement between the Jesuit Fathers of Upper Canada and the government of Ontario to restore the Jesuit mission of Sainte-Marie among the Hurons.[77] To that end, on 19 March 1964, Robarts announced the formation of the Huronia Historical Development Council for the purpose of reconstructing the site. That council was

73 DJB, vol. 1, 179.

74 Monet, 11.

75 Catlan, op. cit.

76 DJB, vol. 1, 180.

77 Ibid., 215.

comprised of a five-man committee representing the government of Ontario, the University of Western Ontario, and the Society of Jesus. The university accepted responsibility for the reconstruction work and for the necessary research to ensure the site's authenticity. Work commenced on 15 June 1964, with Jury once again responsible for the project.[78] Not only did various Canadian scholars comb through sources at numerous public archives, but also, with the support of the Canadian Jesuit John L. Swain (1907–1987), Vicar General of the Society of Jesus, they were able to examine documents in Jesuit institutions across both North America and Europe.[79] After much research and consultation with the then Provincial Superior, Angus J. Macdougall, S.J. (1918–1993), as well as with McCaffrey, construction began on Jury's plans for the site. It was officially opened in 1968.

During the year leading up to the opening of Sainte-Marie-among-the-Hurons, Canada's centennial year, devotions to the martyrs played an important role in the way many young Jesuits decided to celebrate their "centennial project." On 13 August 1967, twenty-five Jesuit Scholastics and priests from the Provinces of French Canada and of Upper Canada—along with some American Jesuits—set out from Sainte-Marie among the Hurons to follow the historic 550-mile route of the early Jesuit missionaries to Montreal.[80] Travelling in canoes, some adorned with the name "Brébeuf", dressed in rugged wear, and often camping along the way, these men were enthusiastically welcomed at the Christian Pavilion at Montreal's Expo 67 on 4 September. That same year, Pedro Arrupe, s.j., the first Superior General of the Society of Jesus (1965–1983) to visit North America made a pilgrimage to Huronia.[81] There, with the Provincial Superiors of both Canadian Jesuit provinces, he was given a tour of the shrine by McCaffrey, and later was presented at St. Ignace II with a vivid description by Hegarty of the martyrdoms of Brébeuf and Lalemant.

Throughout the 1970s, the directorship of the Canadian Martyrs' Shrine was held first by Macdougall (1918–1983), who served in the

78 R. J. Sloan, "Reconstruction" in *Sainte Marie Project Manual* (1970), AJC, Box D, 1.

79 Ibid.

80 Monet, 16.

81 Ibid., 17

role from 1969 to 1974; J. Winston Rye, S.J., who succeeded him between 1974 and 1979; and then Edwin Merchant, S.J., between 1979 and 1981.

During Macdougall's tenure, the shrine continued to flourish, with annual numbers of pilgrims reaching over 200,000.[82] Soon after his appointment, he realized that certain aspects of the "pilgrimage culture" at the Shrine were changing. More and more pilgrims were arriving by cars or by coach, the costs to maintain the grounds were growing, and certain buildings around the church were starting to pass out of use.[83] One of his first decisions in 1970 was to have the Fort Sainte-Marie Inn, which had become a firetrap, demolished.

Macdougall also made the difficult choice of setting the first gate fee of $1.00 per car to pay for the upkeep of the grounds. Furthermore, aware of growing tensions in the province of Quebec, he negotiated with the government of Ontario to have bilingual signs placed on several highways to indicate directions to the shrine. Macdougall also helped to promote devotion to the Canadian Martyrs through writing and preaching retreats outside of the shrine's season. Gifted with knowledge of both Latin and French, he immersed himself in the early history of the Canadian Mission. As a result, he wrote several pamphlets about the martyrs, and produced the small book entitled *The Martyrs of New France*, which to this day remains an excellent reflection on the lives of Jesuits in seventeenth-century Huronia.[84]

His successor, Rye, continued to welcome pilgrims from 1974 to 1979. Filled with youthful energy and passion for the Canadian Martyrs, Rye was the youngest director ever to be appointed. In 1975, he worked tirelessly with different aboriginal groups in Ontario to erect "The Native Prayer Garden". He dedicated it on 29 August 1976.[85] That same year, on 8 July, Rye greeted an important guest to the cause of the Canadian Martyrs: Sister Marie Robichaud, who had been cured through the intercession of the martyrs in 1926. She was

82 Catlin, op. cit.

83 DJB, vol. 2, 174.

84 Catlin, op. cit.

85 Ibid.

on her first pilgrimage to the shrine.[86] Later that month, on 26 July, he also led a large number of dignitaries and pilgrims in celebrating the fiftieth anniversary of the Canadian Martyrs' Shrine at a Mass of Thanksgiving. The following year, on 26 June 1977, he unveiled a statue of Kateri Tekakouitha, which was beautifully placed along the path leading to the Native Prayer Garden. Three years later, during Merchant's time as director, this statue became the site of a celebratory Mass in honour of Kateri's beatification by John Paul II on 22 June 1980.[87] That same season, Merchant drew national attention to the shrine when he welcomed Edward Schreyer, governor general of Canada (1979–1984), and his wife, Lily Schreyer, on 19 June.[88]

The seventh director of the shrine, James J. Farrell, S.J., assumed the office in 1981. During his tenure, he oversaw an unprecedented period of growth and renewal. The number of large pilgrimage groups from the Polish, Italian, German, Slovak, Slovenian, Croatian, and Belarusian ethno-cultural communities continued to grow every year. Farrell worked hard to adapt the presentation of the lives and deaths of the martyrs to these cultural groups. His gentle, kind-hearted nature and outlook always made pilgrims of every background feel very welcome.

To accommodate the rapidly growing numbers of visitors, Farrell had the base of the church excavated to accommodate a new set of rooms.[89] This centre, named after the shrine's founder and primary architect, John Milway Filion, S.J., serves to this day as a museum, theatre, lecture hall, and secondary chapel for any overflow of pilgrims attending Mass. Farrell also brought the cafeteria on the property up to modern standards, kept all of the roadways and parking lots on the grounds well paved, and hired additional staff to ensure that each pilgrim would be greeted by beautifully kept grounds.[90] All of those initiatives reflected a growing national interest and devotion to the

86 Pouliot, 4.

87 Catlin, op. cit.

88 Ibid.

89 DJB, vol. 2, 104.

90 Monet, 15.

martyrs among Catholic Canadians and many others. By then, the annual number of pilgrims had grown to over 250,000.

At the centre of Farrell's labours, however, was the anticipated visit of Pope John Paul II to the Martyrs' Shrine in 1984. This would be the visit that would remain in Canada's Catholic consciousness as the best and strongest memory of the pope's tour of Canada that year. Assigned by the Catholic hierarchy to coordinate the visit, Farrell worked tirelessly for well over a year, attending meetings with bishops, parishes, government officials, the military, municipal figures, both federal and provincial law enforcement, technicians, caterers, volunteers, fundraisers, and vendors. He sometimes had to work late into the evening, only to get up the following day at an early hour to begin again.[91] All of this was done while he continued his normal duties as director of the shrine.

In collaboration with advisors from the Holy See, Farrell masterfully centred the event on a special liturgy of purification involving various aboriginal elders and newly ordained aboriginal permanent deacons.[92] After visiting Sainte-Marie among the Hurons, the Pope went up to the church to pray before the relics of the Canadian Martyrs, and then to preside over a special healing service with the sick.[93] Then, at an enormous altar especially designed by liturgist Toby McGivern, O.M.I., to evoke the architecture of Sainte-Marie-among-the-Hurons, John Paul II stood as the first Pope to visit Huronia. At this "Papal Altar" he began the solemn liturgy of thanksgiving before the entire country, with much of the population watching on television or listening on radio, by saying "Chay" (the traditional Huron word of welcome).[94] "My dear brothers and sisters in Christ", he continued. "I greet you all … at this holy place, the Martyrs' Shrine, which stands as

91 DJB, vol. 2, 105.

92 *The People's Pope* (Canada: Trillium Publishing, 1984), 85.

93 For the visit of John Paul II, the Jesuits of French Canada lent their portion of the skull of Brebeuf for the pope's veneration. Subsequently, in 1992, during a ceremony marking the 150th anniversary of the Jesuits' return to Canada, at the Canadian Martyrs' Shrine, the then Provincial Superior of French Canada, Bernard Carrière, s.j., offered the portion of the skull and its reliquary on indefinite loan for the veneration of all the faithful.

94 Ibid., 76.

a symbol of the unity of faith in a diversity of cultures… . St. Jean de Brebeuf dreamed of a Church fully Catholic and fully Huron as well!"[95]

During this prayer service, different aboriginal leaders burned sweetgrass and presented Pope John Paul II with an eagle feather, the symbol of knowledge and direction. Then he blessed six permanent deacons of different aboriginal tribes who would return to minister among their people. Now that they were prepared to take on that ministry anew, the Pope told them plainly, "Not only is Christianity relevant to the [Indian] peoples, but Christ in the members of His body is Himself Indian."[96]

*

Around the world, for over 375 years, the lives of Jean de Brébeuf and his companions have inspired, in many different forms, the devotion of lay people, bishops, priests, and Religious women and men including members of the Society of Jesus. Their stories dwell at the heart of Canada's founding myth, inspiring in the midst of adversity countless thousands throughout Canada's history to resolve—through architectural ingenuity and artistic endeavour, through historical debate and scholarly research, through faith and pilgrimage and prayer, through healing of body and soul—to resolve divisions between peoples and divisions between people and Jesus Christ.

Even while still alive, their way of living inspired their fellow missionaries of the Society of Jesus, and indeed their writings inspired popes, prelates, Religious, and laity across Europe. Immediately after the deaths of Brébeuf and Lalemant, their bodies were venerated, and cures were sought through their intercession. As the last Jesuit in Canada, Jean-Joseph Casot, prepared to die in 1800, one of his primary concerns was the care of their relics; after his death, bishops who sought to restore the Jesuit presence evoked the memory of the martyrs.

When the first missionaries of the Jesuit Order returned to Canada in 1842, a principal and immediate journey of the Superior of that first

95 Ibid.

96 *Celebrate Jesuit* (Toronto: Jesuits in English Canada, 2012), 11.

mission was to the ruins of Sainte-Marie. Soon afterwards, learned men among the Jesuits such as Chazelle, Martin, Devine, Jones, and Talbot made it their goal to mine the deep wells of literature describing those Jesuit martyrs' lives and works. Later, too, Canadian icons of literature, such as Pratt and McDowell, put the martyrs' lives to paper, while archaeologists such as Jones, Arpin, Cannon, Wintemberg, Kidd, and Jury painstakingly searched the missionaries' Canadian landscape, one layer of earth at a time.

Of uppermost importance, too, has been the devotion to the Canadian Martyrs most beautifully seen in the faith of those who have believed in them and their power to heal spiritually and physically. Throughout the centuries, many have sought the martyrs' intervention to heal their own souls and bodies, or those of someone for whom they cared deeply. Countless thousands of pilgrims, too, from various cultures and religious backgrounds, have travelled to the Canadian Martyrs' Shrine over its long history to seek similar healing. For some, the testament to their faith is poignantly expressed in the crutches, braces, canes, and walkers that they have left in the church's sanctuary. Yet to most others who have been touched by the lives of Jean de Brébeuf and his companions, whether or not within the context of the Christian faith, their testament to that fact has remained within the subsequent quality of their lives.

III

Communities of Sacrament and Prayer Committed to Justice: Jesuit Parishes in English Canada since 1842

J. WINSTON RYE, S.J.

On 31 May 1842, the Jesuits returned to Canada after the suppression of the Society of Jesus was rescinded by the papal brief *Sollicitudo Omnium Ecclesiarum* of 7 August 1814. Although the brief of suppression, *Dominus ac Redemptor* of 21 July 1773, had not been promulgated in Canada,

> … the Jesuits in Canada were doomed to extinction. Under the terms of the Capitulation of Montreal, they had not been permitted to receive new members. The result was that, at the time of the Suppression, their members were only thirteen in number. These were allowed to remain at their posts until their deaths. A careful watch was kept on them and their personal property was seized by the Crown as soon as they died.[1]

1 E. J. La Jeunesse, C.S.B., *Outline of the History of Assumption Parish* (n.p., 1967), 20.

The Jesuits' arrival in Montreal in the nineteenth century was 200 years to the month of the first Mass offered on the island by Barthélemy Vimont, s.j., in 1642.

The majority of the parishes founded or undertaken by the Jesuits were in Canada West, or present-day Ontario, beginning with Sandwich in 1843 and continuing into the new millennium with new parishes, as in Guelph in 2000 and Thunder Bay in 2005. During this same period, however, small forays were made into western Canada: Brandon in 1888, Winnipeg in 1908, Vancouver in 1924, and Winnipeg again in 1955. The east coast of Canada fared less well, with only two Jesuit parishes: in Halifax in 1952 and, ten years later, in St. John's. The parishes that follow and whose history is recounted here are those listed in the Mission, Vice Province, or Province Jesuit annual catalogues over the various years. Their insertion in the catalogues indicated a responsibility taken on by the Major Superior to supply Jesuit manpower for the work of the parish and an accountability for the running of the parish. It is in this sense that they are here referred to as "Jesuit parishes".

It is difficult to find a pattern in the history of the Canadian Jesuit parishes, except in the early years, when the Jesuits followed along the Great Lakes from Windsor to present-day Thunder Bay. Among the founding pastors, these are the only ones who established more than one parish: Pierre Point, s.j., at Assumption, near Sandwich, and St. Mary's near Sault Ste. Marie, Michigan; Jean-Baptiste Nolin, s.j., at Sainte-Anne-des-Pins in Sudbury and St. John's in Waubaushene; finally, Clarence P. Hinphy, S.J., at St. John Brebeuf in Winnipeg and Our Lady of Lourdes in Toronto. Thus this chapter will follow the chronological establishment of the parishes. The one exception to this rule is in the area of Thunder Bay, in northern Ontario, which will come out of order so that the historical continuity of that region's story will be kept intact.

The Nativity of Our Lady Parish, La Prairie, Canada East

The first ministry the Jesuits undertook was the direction of the parish of the Nativity of Our Lady in La Prairie, Canada East, just south of Montreal. It became their headquarters for the first twelve years of their return to Canada. The parish had been under the direction of Michael Power, who encouraged the Jesuits to take it over since he had just been named first bishop of Toronto. Originally, upon their arrival, it had been suggested by the bishop of Montreal that the Jesuits open a college at Chambly. Pierre Chazelle, s.j., however, declined, causing tension between the two men. In this stressful and delicate situation, bishop-elect Power suggested the parish alternative, and the possibility of opening a college there, to which both the bishop of Montreal and the Jesuits agreed.

It was not by chance that the Jesuits returned to Canada at this time. One of the first Jesuits in the group of six priests and three brothers was Chazelle, the first Superior of the restored Society of Jesus in Canada.[2] Montreal was not unknown to Chazelle. He had conducted the diocesan clergy ten-day retreat in August of 1839, and at that time met for the first time the future bishop of Montreal, Ignace Bourget. Bourget became the bishop of Montreal on April 23, 1840; he was an auxiliary at the time of Chazelle's visit. It was Bourget who later would petition the Jesuit Superior General, Jan Roothaan, s.j. (1829–1853), for the return of the Jesuits, which was recorded in the document *Appel aux Jesuites* of 2 July 1841.

Once settled in La Prairie, the Jesuits were called upon to give parish missions, offer priests' retreats in both the diocese of Quebec and the new diocese of Toronto, as well as promote the work of the Temperance Society. It was from this base that they expanded their work to include ministering to the native population, as well as opening the first Canadian Jesuit Novitiate on 31 July 1843, with Paul Luiset, s.j., as the Novice Master. In 1854, the Jesuits left the parish at La Prairie, but not without regret and with the great appreciation of the people of the parish. Rémi-Joseph Tellier, s.j., was said to have exclaimed, "C'est vraiment un peuple d'élus!"[3]

---

2 The first nine Jesuits came from three Jesuit Provinces in Europe: from the Province of Lyon, Pierre Chazelle and Brother Emmanuel Brenans; from the Province of Paris, Félix Martin, Paul Luiset, Dominique du Ranquet, Joseph Hanipaux, and Brother Joseph Jennesseaux; and from the Province of Turin, Rémi-Joseph Tellier and Brother Pierre Tupin; Lecompte, 36.

3 Ibid., 78.

Assumption Parish, Sandwich, Canada West

On 31 July 1843, at the invitation of Bishop Michael Power, the Jesuits accepted Assumption Parish at Sandwich, near present-day Windsor, which was associated mainly with the aboriginal or First Nations peoples, one of the priorities mentioned in Bishop Bourget's *Appel aux Jésuites*. The first Jesuit pastor was Pierre Point, who was accompanied by Jean-Pierre Choné, s.j.; both had been sent from France specifically for this assignment:

> By a happy coincidence, they said their first Masses at the new abode the next day on the feast of St. Ignatius, the founder of the Society. The arrival of these new evangelical labourers changed the face of things. They had at their head a man possessed of rare talent for organization, an ardent zeal for souls and the heart of an apostle. Simultaneously and successively he was assisted by Father Nicolas Point (his brother), Choné, Chazelle, Jaffré, Menet, DuRanquet, Férard, Grimot, Maginguy and Conilleau.[4]

This particular parish had been under Jesuit administration from 1701 to 1781, and during the intervening years had been serviced by priests from Canada East.[5] The mandate given by Bishop Power was the pastoral care of the inhabitants of Essex, Kent, and Lambton counties in south-western Ontario. The population of the area was made up of people of French origin, some recent Irish immigrants as well as the native people. The first order of business was the completion of the church. This parish would remain under the direction of the Jesuits until 1859, when it was handed over to the then newly formed diocese of London, Ontario, amid controversy with the new bishop,

---

4 La Jeunesse, *Assumption Parish,* 38.

5 "Father [Pierre] Potier, a Jesuit, was at Assumption at the time of the Brief suppressing the Society issued by Pope Clement XIV in 1773, and remained there until his death eight years later. This was because the Brief went into effect only when the bishop of the diocese promulgated it. Bishop Briand did not promulgate it because Governor Carleton wanted the Jesuits to continue their labors. There is no evidence that Potier was ever officially notified. If not, he likely learned of the Suppression from Father Pierre Gibault who visited him during the winter of 1775–76 while on his way to Quebec from the Illinois mission of Prairie du Rocher. From that place on March 29, 1775, Father Meurin, S.J., had written a letter to Bishop Briand asking to be adopted as a priest in his diocese as a consequence of the Suppression". Ibid., 19–20.

Pierre-Adolphe Pinsonnault, over the establishment and running of a college.[6]

In the beginning, the Jesuits accepted the care of parishes or missions linked to the aboriginal or First Nations peoples, mainly in Canada West (Ontario). Their Superior was situated at Sandwich from 31 July 1844 onwards, when this administrative division was agreed to by Roothaan on the recommendation of Chazelle. The First Nation Missions are taken up in another chapter of this work and will not be dealt with here. This chapter will deal with those parishes that primarily ministered to the Canadian population of European origin. The Jesuits moved north along the Great Lakes, where they founded parishes along the way.

St. Mary's Parish, Sault Ste. Marie, Michigan

The next stopping-off point was Sault Ste. Marie, which was situated in both present-day Michigan and Ontario, directly across St. Mary's River from each other.[7] In 1846, St. Mary's Parish, today known as Holy Name of Mary Parish, in Sault Ste. Marie, Michigan, was begun with the arrival of Pierre Point, s.j., who was sent to study the conditions for the establishment of a residence.[8] In 1853, Upper

6 "In 1856 the diocese of Toronto was divided. Out of its westernmost section was formed the diocese of London, with the Most Reverend Pierre-Adolphe Pinsonneault at its head. On his first visit to Sandwich he was much pleased with the reception accorded him by the people, and he declared that he would have preferred being Bishop of Sandwich to being Bishop of London. In 1859 he realized his wish, transferred his See to Sandwich, and Assumption church became the Cathedral of the diocese". Ibid., 40. Three articles by Francis J. Nelligan, S.J., present a good overall view of Sandwich and the college. These were published in *The Messenger* in July, September, and December 1955. Typed copies are kept in the AJC, Box C-401.

7 The place name was given by Jacques Marquette, s.j., who had a vision of the Blessed Virgin Mary there in 1668. He named the place Sault Sainte-Marie and founded a mission there. From 1680 to 1840, there is a gap in the history of the place due to troubles with the Iroquois and the founding of Detroit, causing "the centre of the western missions to be transferred eastward". The information and quotation are taken from an unpublished manuscript entitled "Sault Ste. Marie–Historical Background", AJC, Box C-405.

8 He left on 25 July after performing thirty-four baptisms. Jean-Baptiste Pedelupe, s.j.,was sent to preach a retreat and open a residence in preparation for the arrival of the first Superior. He performed his first baptism on 16 September 1846, and said the first High Mass on 20 September, the feast of Our Lady of Seven Dolours, patron of the mission. The first curé, Jean-Baptiste Menet, s.j., arrived on 3 November 1846. They all came from Sandwich. Brother La Coste, s.j., opened a school in the sacristy. The population of the Sault was around 400. A laywoman, Mrs. Sarah Cadotte, opened a school for girls until a Religious community could be found to assist. Finally, in the fall of 1853, the Ursulines from Faouette, Brittany, France, sent Mother Mary

Michigan became a vicariate apostolic and Sault Ste. Marie the episcopal seat. The first bishop was Federic Baraga, who was consecrated on All Saints' Day in Cincinnati, but did not arrive at Sault Ste. Marie until the summer of 1854. Immediately after his consecration, he went to Europe to raise funds and recruit priests for his diocese. Baraga arrived on 21 August 1854, and took up residence with Jean-Baptiste Menet, s.j. The church became the cathedral, and Menet was given the spiritual responsibility of the parish. In 1860, the Ursulines moved to Chatham, Ontario; Baraga blamed Menet for their move, so Menet also moved away that same year. Since Baraga could not get priests for the Sault, eventually he asked the Jesuits to return; it was Menet and Brother Adrien LaCoste, s.j., who returned in 1864.[9] The problem of recruiting priests for the diocese continued, so to solve the situation, a convention was signed on 24 January 1881 between Bishop James Vertin of Michigan and Pieter Jan Beckx, S.J., Superior General of the Jesuits, giving the responsibility for the care of souls in Sault Ste. Marie and environs to the Jesuits.[10] The last permanently assigned Canadian Jesuit in the area was Edouard O'Gara, S.J., who arrived on 10 May 1910. He stayed until 1914.

Sacred Heart Parish/Precious Blood Parish, Sault Ste. Marie, Canada West

On the Canadian side, a parish was also established at Sault Ste. Marie: Sacred Heart Parish, now known as Precious Blood Parish. A church also had to be constructed there, but by 1854, the church was still not completed. A log church was used until 1876, when a new stone church was ready after two years of construction.[11] In 1859, the following information was sent by Menet to the Superior:

> At the Sault, but on the Canadian side, a piece of land on which the church is situated (if one dare call 4 bare walls a church) with two rooms, a stable, a barn, a cemetery and about 5 acres of land of which I bought a part. They were presented and

Xavier, née Yvonne de Hihan, who opened a school for girls with a class of twenty. See Antoine Rezek, "History of Sault Ste-Marie and Marquette Diocese", in AJC, Box C-405.

9 Ibid.

10 Ibid.

11 Ibid.

> paid for to the government as Catholic Church property and put down in my name (in trust). I have the official deed. If we cease being in charge of the mission, we will naturally have to transfer this deed to the Bishop of Hamilton, at least in part.[12]

By 1869, the Jesuit Superior of Garden River, Auguste Kohler, was given charge of the Sault and environs, while Jean-Baptiste Menet was Superior on the American side. On 2 August 1874, a major change took place when the vicariate of Northern Canada was created by Pope Pius IX. Jean-François Jamot was appointed vicar apostolic. When he took up residence at Sault Ste. Marie, there were about 8,500 Catholics living in the vicariate.[13] The original church became the cathedral seat, which was established as Precious Blood Cathedral in 1875. The Jesuits remained in the area until 1937.[14]

Sault Ste. Marie was an important site both during the fur-trading period and that of the building of the railways. In the former period, the Northwest Fur Company in 1787 built a canal on the Canadian side of the river to be used by the English Canadian and French Canadian traders to get canoes and bateaux around the rapids. It was the entrance to Lake Superior, and was named Sault du Gaston, in honour of Prince Gaston d'Orléans, the younger brother of Louis XIII, but the name did not stick, since it was more generally known and accepted as Sault Ste. Marie. One hundred years later, in 1887, the Canadian Pacific Railway used Sault Ste. Marie to connect with the United Railway System in the United States.

Immaculate Conception Parish, Fort William, Canada West

Two years after the establishment of the Jesuits at Sault Ste. Marie, the parish of Immaculate Conception in Fort William, Ontario, was begun in 1848. It was founded by Pierre Choné, s.j., and Nicolas Fremiot, s.j., on the left bank of the Mission River at the junction of the

12 Ibid.

13 Booklet entitled *1904 Diocese of Sault Ste-Marie 1979: United in Faith: We Celebrate*, AJC, Box C-405.

14 The diocese of Sault Ste Marie was set up in 1904 with David Joseph Scollard as first bishop; he served until 1934.

Kaministiquia River.[15] This was to serve the Catholics of Fort William as well as to become "the base and headquarters for Jesuit missionary activity extending over an immense area from Grand Portage and Grand Marais on the north-western shore of Lake Superior in the United States to White River, 320 kilometres east of Fort William."[16]

The Jesuit Superior also served as pastor of Immaculate Conception Parish, which consisted of approximately 250 First Nations parishioners. On any given Sunday, however, the modest church was crowded with "more white people than Indians".[17] This was true even though there was no bridge across the Kaministiquia River, which separated the mission from the rapidly expanding town of Fort William. It is said that all the parishes in the present diocese of Thunder Bay were founded or begun by Jesuits. The book *Hope and Charity: Diocese of Thunder Bay, An Illustrated History*, by Roy Piovesana, is a good source to understand the work of the Jesuits in this area of the country:

> The Most Rev. Richard A. O'Connor noted in his journal how "deeply grateful" he was for the "great zeal and unwearied energy of the Jesuit Fathers" who laboured in the western portion of his diocese. In addition to the Fort William Reserve, they had been engaged as pastors at St. Andrew's in Port Arthur since 1874 and later at St. Patrick's in Fort William when it became a parish in 1893.[18]

The Fort William Mission was important to the history of Thunder Bay and to the establishment by the Jesuits in the mid nineteenth century of a firm presence of Roman Catholicism in north-western Ontario:

> To be sure, the predominance of Roman Catholicism along the Lake Superior's north shore during the first two decades of the twentieth century must also be attributed to the large number of Roman Catholic European immigrants who settled

---

15 For more on this, see the article by William Maurice, S.J., in *The Northwestern Catholic* (1998), also found in AJC, Box C-407.

16 Roy H. Piovesana, *Hope and Charity: An Illustrated History of the Roman Catholic Diocese of Thunder Bay* (Thunder Bay, ON: Diocese of Thunder Bay, 2002), 6.

17 Ibid., 16.

18 Ibid..

there. But the Jesuit evangelization of the Indian People and CPR workers from Chapleau to Fort William during the late nineteenth century established fertile ground from which a thriving Roman Catholic community could grow. From the Fort William Mission the Jesuits and the Sisters of St. Joseph filled an important void in a frontier society with the creation of the social institutions such as a school, church, and orphanage.[19]

Although the Church of the Nativity and St. Agnes claim to be founded by the Jesuit missionary Richard Baxter in the mid 1880s, the two parishes that the Jesuits were more generally associated with were St. Andrew's in Port Arthur and St. Patrick's in Fort William.

St. Andrew's Parish, Port Arthur, Ontario

St. Andrew's Parish was founded in 1875 at the corner of Algoma and Red River Road, and was named to recognize a financial contribution of $100.00 for its construction by Scottish Catholic labourers. The first pastor was Richard Baxter, S.J.:

> In 1881 a new church was built to replace the original which had been destroyed by fire. Within a year fire again struck and not only destroyed the vestry where it had originated but also the altar and some of the pews and windows. By Christmas of 1882, the fire damage had been repaired and the church refurnished.[20]

Twenty-five years later, another new church became a necessity, not because of fire, but rather because the city was growing rapidly. The process to build a church was not an easy one, and many complications and delays were initiated by Bishop David Joseph Scollard.[21]

Not only did the church minister to the local population, but it also served as the home base for the Jesuits who were chaplains to workers of the Canadian Pacific Railway along the north shore of Lake Superior. There is an amusing story about Edward J. Devine, S.J.,

19 Ibid., 23.

20 Ibid., 35.

21 The struggle, from 1907 to 1924, is wonderfully outlined in Piovesana, *Hope and Charity,* 36–40.

who replaced Baxter when the latter retired at the age of seventy-two. "Devine rode in the caboose with the railway crews, and during these long hours, his creative mind led to the invention of an electrical device that would allow the engine crew to communicate with the caboose and once patented in 1895 it became known among the CPR railway workers as 'the Devine Signal.'"[22] The Jesuits continued to work in St. Andrew's Parish until 1997, when the decrease in manpower led their superiors to pull back on parish commitments.

St. Patrick's Parish, Fort William, Ontario

St. Patrick's in Fort William was founded at a later date, mainly because the Immaculate Conception Mission seemed to be covering the needs of the area. In 1892, however, the first Mass at St. Patrick's in Fort William was celebrated on 21 August:

> … [i]n the yet unfinished 40' by 80' frame church, with a sacristy built on the side, the first mass was celebrated … before a large congregation by Father Remi Chartier, s.j., (1839–1906) Superior of the Jesuits in the Thunder Bay District and pastor at St. Andrew's in Port Arthur. There was a saying among St. Patrick parishioners at the time concerning their first church: "The French built it, and the Irish named it."[23]

Officially, the Jesuits undertook the administration of the parish in 1900, but it was first listed in the Jesuit catalogue for 1901 with Ludgar Arpin as pastor. He continued as such until 1906. The population of the parish doubled by 1902, and church renovations were needed. These were blessed in 1904 by Bishop Richard O'Connor, assisted by three Jesuits: Olivier Neault of St. Andrew's, Prosper Lamarche of the Fort William Mission, and Arpin.[24] Both St. Patrick's Parish and Arpin were key to the growth of the Church in the area. As Piovesana put it:

> St. Patrick's Parish, under the leadership of their pastor Father Arpin, provided the catalyst for the development of Roman Catholic institutions in Fort William at the beginning of the

22 Ibid., 44.

23 Ibid., 28.

24 Ibid., 34.

> twentieth century. The Fort William Separate School Board, St. Stanislaus School, St. Patrick's Cemetery, and the Sisters of St. Joseph Convent on Myles Street all found their origins with this parish. Little would have been accomplished, however, without the vision and risk-taking of Father Arpin. St. Patrick's became the parish around which the first and second generation Polish, Slovak, and Italian immigrants rallied. Father Arpin was a source of encouragement to each cultural group to practice their faith within the context of an Anglo-Saxon and French-Canadian dominated parish.[25]

Arpin was replaced by Albini Primeau, s.j. (1906–1911), and assigned to Collège de Saint-Boniface, where he was procurator. He was then moved to Collège de l'Immaculée-Conception in Montreal, where he died on 1 July 1908 at the age of sixty-seven after forty-five years in the Jesuit Order. A series of Jesuit pastors followed: Aloysius Heroux (1911–1912), John MacDonald (1912–1919), Julien Paquin (1919–1920), Daniel J. Donovan (1920–1922), and, finally, Aloysius Cotter (1922–1924). The parish came under the direction of priests from the diocese in 1924. The first diocesan pastor was Peter Joseph Monahan. Four years later, before becoming the third bishop of Calgary, he founded the first private Catholic high school in northwestern Ontario. He named it in honour of Arpin: St. Patrick Arpin Memorial High School.[26]

Church of Our Lady Immaculate, Guelph, Canada West

Beginning in 1827, a large number of German-speaking immigrants settled in Waterloo County, south of Guelph. In 1847, Michael Power, bishop of Toronto since 1842, asked that German-speaking Jesuits be sent to minister in that area of the diocese. The bishop's request was made through the Jesuit Superior in New York, and some Swiss Jesuits as well as others from the Austro-Hungarian Empire were recruited to serve among these immigrants, mainly at Wilmot (St. Agatha) and New Germany (Maryhill).[27] John E. Holzer, s.j., arrived

---

25 Ibid.

26 Ibid., 35.

27 John W. Keleher, "The Reverend Father John E. Holzer, s.j.", *Historic Guelph: The Royal City* [The Guelph Historical Society] 26 (1986–1987), 51, 53; also in AJC, C-406.

in 1848 with three other Jesuits: William Kettler, Rupert Ebner, and Brother Francis Marckhgott. Within three years, they were caring for about 6,000 souls, prompting the new bishop of Toronto, Armand de Charbonnel, to have them expand their ministry to include Guelph and areas northward towards Lake Huron and Georgian Bay. As a result, in 1852, Holzer moved to Guelph with three Jesuit colleagues: Gaspar Matoga, Joseph Fruzzini, and Brother Charles Hoch.

The city's founder, John Galt, had granted land to local Catholics, who were mainly Irish, in an area that became known as "Catholic Hill". On the hill stood an unfinished church, replacing St. Patrick's (1835–1844), which had burned down, and also a very unsuitable residence. The first task was to complete the church, now called St. Bartholomew's. Holzer, however, did not stop there. He oversaw the building of a convent school for the Loretto Sisters and St. Ignatius College for boys, which later became the parish rectory. He also helped the Sisters of St. Joseph found a hospital, an orphanage, and a home for the aged. The accompanying priests took up the enormous task of travelling and seeking out Catholic families in the many new settlements and outlying farms. They said Mass, administered the sacraments, taught catechism, and encouraged the people to assist other Catholic families and, where possible, to build mission churches. Holzer also took his turn in these hazardous, long trips on horseback. It was not unusual for the Jesuits to be harassed and threatened bodily, given the strong anti-Catholic sentiment harboured by many settlers of the area.

John Galt, although not a Catholic, wrote to a friend in England in 1827 that he was "Desirous of seeing the effect of a rising ground, at the end of the street where a popish church, about twice the size of St. Peter's at Rome, is one day to be built… ."[28] Holzer also had grand plans for that hilltop. Of course, this was only after the bishop of the diocese of Hamilton, which had been created in 1856 with John Farrell as its first bishop, agreed to have the Jesuits take over St. Bartholomew's Parish. The conditions for taking over the parish

28 Cited in *Fraser's Magazine* (1830) and found in an anonymous manuscript entitled *A Brief Survey of the History of the Parish of Our Lady, Guelph, Ont.* (1939), 2. AJC Box C-406.

were set down in a letter dated 21 May 1860.[29] In 1863, Bishop Farrell laid the cornerstone for a new church, which was to occupy most of the hilltop, but construction halted when a debt of $20,000.00 accumulated. Holzer's pastorate ended in 1864 when he had a stroke; he was moved to Georgetown University near Washington, D. C. Holzer's dream lay dormant until it was taken up in 1874 when Pierre Hamel, s.j., set out plans for the Church of Our Lady Immaculate. Two years later, Bishop Peter Francis Crinnon of Hamilton turned the sod for the new church, and in 1877, Bishop George Michael Conroy, apostolic delegate to Canada, laid the cornerstone. Within ten years, the work had progressed enough that St. Bartholomew's could be demolished; in October 1888, the Church of Our Lady Immaculate was dedicated by Bishop Thomas Joseph Dowling of Peterborough, the *cathedra* of Hamilton being vacant at the time.

At the beginning of the twentieth century, the Church of Our Lady Immaculate was no longer a mission centre, but was becoming more and more a city parish for Guelph. The many mission churches begun by the Jesuits throughout the countryside were themselves becoming parishes. A separate historical chapter would be needed to cover the development of each of these parishes. Even Guelph was growing enough to require a second parish, Sacred Heart, which was built in 1924, situated in an area served by John C. Sinnett, S.J., and William Dunn, S.J. As the area was developing and growing, the Jesuits also desired to relinquish the Church of Our Lady Immaculate to the diocese because of "the need to use the manpower elsewhere".[30] This was done in 1931 by an agreement between the Provincial Superior, William H. Hingston, S.J., and John T. McNally, the fifth bishop of Hamilton. The last Jesuit to serve as pastor was George Bradley, who had been appointed in 1930 mainly because of his natural ability to be tactful in such a sensitive situation where the Jesuits were relinquishing the direction of the parish after so many years.[31] His term was exactly one year to the day, beginning 6 September 1930 and ending on 6 September 1931.

---

29 Bishop John Farrell, letter to Rémi-Joseph Tellier, s.j., 21 May 1860, AJC, Box C-406.

30 *Brief Survey of History of Parish of Our Lady*, AJC, Box C-406.

31 DJB, vol. 1, 26.

Not everyone, however, was pleased that the Jesuits were leaving the Church of Our Lady Immaculate; the archives contain a letter from Mother Mary Constantia, a Loretto Sister, expressing disappointment.[32] A wonderfully crafted letter on the departure of the Jesuits was prepared by Hingston and read at the Masses as well as issued to the press. In part it read,

> A choice had to be made. The Jesuits would be unfaithful to their vocation, untrue to their traditions, and unworthy of their brethren, those noble priests of Guelph, whose memories we cherish in common with you, were they to prefer the comparative comfort and even the consolations of well-organized parochial ministry in your midst, to the more urgent need of souls elsewhere, or were they to allow their feelings of attachment to you to over-rule their judgment. They must do as did the early Jesuits who left home and country to labor in Guelph, as these men would do now were they in our midst today. They must place the need of souls above all human considerations.[33]

St. Joseph's Parish, Chatham, Canada West

The work of pastoral care continued in Canada West, the Jesuits sending a priest occasionally to Chatham to minister to the Irish settlers in the area. The Superior in New York, Jean-Baptiste Hus, was reluctant at first to have the Jesuits take on responsibility for the Chatham parish. Hus conceded, however, and in 1857, Jean Jaffré, s.j., was appointed pastor of St. Joseph's Parish, where he would remain until 28 August 1860. The Superior's concession came only after the new bishop of London, Pierre-Adolphe Pinsoneault, had failed to convince the Oblate Fathers to take on the parish to preach missions in the diocese. In Pinsoneault's letter, he described the parish as half French Canadian and half Irish, 1,500 to 2,000 communicants in

32 Mother M. Constantia, I.B.V.M., letter to William H. Hingston, S.J., 27 September 1931, AJC, Box C-406.

33 Article entitled "New Rector is Appointed for Guelph Parish", *Guelph Mercury*, 9 September 1931, ibid.

all.[34] Jaffré's term was short, as he was strong-headed and did not get along with either the parishioners or the members of the Jesuit community.[35] He did convince the Ursuline Nuns to come to Chatham, which caused problems mentioned above, to open a school in 1860.

Jaffré was followed by Martin Férard, s.j., for two years, then Charles Conilleau, s.j., from 1862 to 1870. It seems that Rémi-Joseph Tellier, the Superior of the New York–Canada Mission, had withdrawn Férard, and appointed Conilleau without consulting the local bishop, which did not help to raise the Jesuits there in the opinion of Bishop Pinsoneault.[36] The situation improved after a number of letters were written and consultations took place. In a letter to Conilleau, Bishop Pinsoneault gave him canonical approbation "very gladly", saying that he wanted to have the best of relations with the Jesuits. He also declared his sorrow that Férard had been ill, even inviting him to convalesce in the bishop's house.[37] The last Jesuit pastor was Alphonse Baudin, who served from 1870 to 1874, after which the Jesuits withdrew from the parish.

Ste-Anne-des-Pins, Sudbury, Ontario

In 1883, the parish of Ste-Anne-des-Pins in Sudbury was founded by Jean-Baptiste Nolin, s.j., with Louis Côté, s.j., and François Xavier Santerre, s.j. It remained in the hands of the French-Canadian Jesuits at the time of the division of the Province of Canada in 1924. Two other churches founded in this early period were also continued by the French Canadian Province after 1924: l'Église du Gésù, Montreal (opened in 1865), and l'Église de l'Immaculée-Conception, Montreal (founded in 1889 and consecrated in 1898 by Archbishop Bruchési). The latter church was turned over to the archdiocese of Montreal in 1999, while the Gésù continues to be administered by the French-Canadian Jesuits today.

---

34 Bishop Pierre-Adolphe Pinsoneault, letter to John Walsh, 2 February 1867, as outlined in notes by Francis J. Nelligan, S.J., AJC, Box C-401.

35 DJB, vol. 1, 153.

36 Bishop Pierre-Adolphe Pinsoneault, letter to François de Sales Cazeau, 23 June 1862, as outlined in notes by Francis J. Nelligan, S.J., AJC, Box C-401.

37 Bishop Pierre-Adolphe Pinsoneault, letter to Charles Conilleau, s.j., 29 July 1862, as outlined in notes by Francis Nelligan, S.J., ibid.

St. Augustine of Canterbury, Brandon, Manitoba

In Brandon, Manitoba, St. Augustine of Canterbury Parish was canonically erected on 6 December 1883, and the first pastor was Joseph Robillard, a diocesan priest.[38] It seems that Bishop Alexandre-Antonin Taché and Robillard did not see eye-to-eye on a number of items, and in 1888 Robillard was replaced by the Jesuits. John Alister Somerled MacDonald, S.J., arrived at the end of May; during the two-month hiatus between Robillard leaving in March and MacDonald arriving in May, Lewis H. Drummond, S.J., performed the Sunday Masses. Drummond took advantage of his time in Brandon to deliver public lectures. He continued with these lectures, and gave one in the roller-skating rink on 21 July 1889 entitled "The Life and Work of the Jesuit Order". On another occasion, he tried to lecture at Plum Creek (Souris) on the Jesuit Estates Question, but was prevented by the local Protestants. The local newspaper, *The Mail*, commented: "It was a pretty courageous undertaking for Fr. Drummond to attempt a lecture in the Orange Hall at Plum Creek."[39] Other Jesuits were assigned to assist in the parish: Edward Proulx in 1888 and Daniel J. Donovan in 1889.[40] Brother George Brown, S.J., who had arrived in 1888, was replaced by Brother Thomas Stakum, S.J., in 1890. Besides his work in Brandon, Donovan preached in Portage la Prairie once a fortnight. The Jesuits remained in the parish for three years and three months, leaving in August 1891, when the parish reverted to the diocese. The Reverend Onésime E. Bourdeau arrived the following month.

St. John's Parish, Waubaushene, Ontario

The Jesuits always had a longing to be back in the land of the Canadian Martyrs. In 1905, Arthur E. Jones, S.J., identified the possible site of St. Ignace II (where Jean de Brébeuf and Gabriel Lalemant had been put to death) on the Campbell farm, Tay Township, VII Concession, the east half of lot 4, in Simcoe County. Shortly thereafter, the Jesuits asked the archbishop of Toronto if they could take

38 Article by Patrick J. O'Sullivan, "By Steps, Not Leaps: St. Augustine of Canterbury Parish, Brandon, Manitoba, 1881–1981", in AJC, Box D-501.

39 Ibid.

40 DJB, vol. 1, 88–89; 327–328.

over the Waubaushene Mission, which was about 5 miles from the identified site.[41] Accordingly, St. John the Evangelist Parish was begun in 1906; the first pastor was Jean-Baptiste Nolin, who was moved from Sudbury and whose first task was to build a church.[42] Prior to the Jesuits being installed in the new parish, Mass was held occasionally in Waubaushene by the pastor of St. Anne's Parish in Penetanguishene from 1873 to 1883, and then from 1883 to 1906 by the pastor in Midland.

Nolin was to die of smoke inhalation on 16 November 1914 when his church burned down, also taking the life of a carpenter. Five days prior to the fire, the carpenter had moved into a room above the kitchen in the residence and had been working on placing double windows on the church. Around midnight on the thirteenth, a passer-by noticed a glow coming from the cellar window. He immediately woke up the Jesuits, who had to vacate the house so quickly that Brother Alfred Langevin made his way onto the roof, from where he jumped to the ground. The carpenter was not so fortunate, and perished in the fire. Nolin, whose room was on the ground floor, had escaped, but then realized he had left a 5-gallon can of methyl alcohol in his room. He went back to get it before it exploded. He did not reappear. Langevin went in and found him unconscious on the floor, overcome by smoke. With some difficulty, he got Nolin out, and Joseph Drolet, s.j., administered extreme unction. The residence and hall were destroyed, as were the chapel and church. Nolin was taken to Midland, where he died: "the opinion of the doctor and of most of his friends was that he died of a heart attack, caused by the destruction, in a few hours, of all his undertakings at Waubaushene."[43]

The present church was built in 1915–1916 by the workmen of the Georgian Bay Lumber Company under the direction of Stanislaus Bouvrette, s.j., who was to be its pastor for twenty-two years. When the parish was founded in 1906, a small church had been built at what was then thought to be the site of Brébeuf's and Lalemant's deaths.

41 Manuscript by L. Desjardins on Jean-Baptiste Nolin, s.j., AJC, Box C-421.

42 Description of boundaries by Bishop Dennis O'Connor, 12 November 1906, ibid.

43 Manuscript by L. DesJardins on Jean-Baptiste Nolin, s.j., ibid.

That church served as a summer shrine until the present Martyrs' Shrine Church was built in 1926 near Midland. From 1933 to 1943, apart from the first year when Bouvrette ministered there, the care of native people on Christian Island was the responsibility of the Jesuits at Cape Croker. In 1943, Thomas J. Mullally, S.J., the Provincial Superior, added St. Francis Xavier Mission among the Beausoleil First Nation on Christian Island to the care of the pastor at Waubaushene.[44] In 1999, a new church was built by Carl J. Matthews, S.J., on Christian Island and blessed by Aloysius Cardinal Ambrozic on 17 June. It is situated across from the ruins of Ste-Marie II, where Christian Hurons and Jesuits spent one year (1649–1650) before their long voyage at the end of the Huronia mission, eventually reaching L'Ancienne-Lorette near Quebec City. For a number of years, a Presentation Brother, Henry Spencer, and students from Brebeuf College School, Toronto, a former Jesuit school, have taught catechism on the Island as part of the school's outreach programme. The boundaries of St. John the Evangelist Parish were expanded to take in the surrounding area towards Cold Water, but in 2010, the parish was handed over to the archdiocese of Toronto due to lack of Jesuit manpower. Today, the mission on Christian Island continues to be served by Jesuits from the Martyrs' Shrine.

St. Ignatius Parish, Winnipeg, Manitoba

The early 1900s saw the Jesuits expand parish ministry into western Canada. The growth of Winnipeg with the influx of Irish and Eastern Europeans fuelled the demand for more parishes in the St. Boniface archdiocese.[45] While national churches were begun for Eastern Europeans, there was some hesitation on the part of Archbishop Adélard Langevin, O.M.I., to found more English-speaking parishes for the Irish and others. The archbishop was confronted with a three-fold petition in December 1906, asking firstly for new English-speaking parishes staffed by English-speaking or Irish clergy who could better understand their ways; secondly, urging the establishment of an English-speaking Catholic college; and

---

44 Thomas J. Mullally, S.J., letter to James Howitt, 17 June 1943, ibid.

45 Anonymous booklet, *St. Ignatius: A Growing Community* [a souvenir of the 75th anniversary of St. Ignatius Church], AJC, Box D-501.

finally, requesting an English-speaking bishop, suffragan to the archbishop of St. Boniface and located in Winnipeg. Although Langevin seemed to be open to the first request, he was slow to respond to the last. Regarding the establishment of an English Catholic college, the archbishop referred them to the then bilingual St. Boniface College, where they could obtain an English-language classical education. Finally, the idea of an English-speaking bishop was totally out of the question, and he reminded the petitioners that it was outside of their competence to request and decide such a matter.

A second petition was sent to Archbishop Langevin in April 1907. It asked only for a new English-speaking parish for the Fort Rouge area. He was open to this, and officially began negotiations with the Jesuit Provincial Superior, Édouard Lecompte, in Montreal. An agreement was reached, and at a meeting on 8 December 1907, the archbishop informed the Catholics of Fort Rouge of the terms, stating that if they were ready to accept these, the parish could go ahead. Due to an economic slump at the time and the small number of potential parishioners, it was thought that a Jesuit priest from St. Boniface College could begin a small-scale ministry to the group. Lewis H. Drummond, S.J., was assigned to this work. The first Mass of the parish was celebrated in a small rented store at 109 Osborne Street on 16 February 1908. By April, it became apparent that the space was too small, and that another accommodation must be found. A site, consisting of two lots, was selected at the corner of McMillan and Nassau streets, and a former wooden Baptist church building that had been purchased was moved to the site. On 10 May 1908, this new church was blessed by the Rector of St. Boniface College, Jacques Dugas, s.j. In December 1908, a house was purchased at 476 McMillan Avenue for Drummond to use as a rectory, which spared him from having to walk each Sunday from St. Boniface College to Fort Rouge and back the same day. By the time the purchase was completed, Drummond had been replaced by John C. Coffee, S.J., who moved into the rectory. In February 1909, the archbishop canonically erected the parish, making it formally a part of the archdiocese.

As early as the summer of 1909, the parishioners realized that the wooden church would not be adequate for long; they took an option on a block of property bounded by Stafford, Corydon, Jessie, and present-day Harrow streets. Two years later, in 1911, they decided to build only the basement of a new church, and to use this area for worship until they could afford to complete the full structure. The basement was completed in early 1912. A school was an integral part of the parish plan, and in January 1912, St. Ignatius School opened with nineteen students in a small building next to the basement church. Two Sisters of the Holy Names of Jesus and Mary staffed the school; they came each day by horse and buggy from St. Mary's Academy. By September 1912, the school population had grown to eighty-eight students. In 1917, an addition was built to the original school. A rectory for the Jesuit Community had also been built on the Stafford Street site.

Amidst this flurry of activity, the new archdiocese of Winnipeg was created on 4 December 1915 from part of the archdiocese of St. Boniface, and the new archbishop, Alfred Arthur Sinnott, was officially installed on 24 December 1916, one year and twenty days after the announcement of the formation of the archdiocese. In 1928, it was decided that the time had come to complete the church and build upon the basement structure. Also included in the plans was an addition to the school. Over the summer and fall of 1928, construction took place, and the new gothic church was ready to be used on 10 February 1929 by Edward O'Gara, S.J., who had become pastor in 1914; he was to stay until 1934. Archbishop Sinnott was in Rome at the time, begging for funds; he instructed O'Gara to use the church, and said that he would dedicate it when he returned. The dedication was on Sunday, 6 October 1928, on the feast of Our Lady of the Rosary.

With the advent of the Great Depression, the parishioners were forced to become creative in finding events and ways to finance their new church and school. It was a long process that continued until 1945; there were many financial ups and downs over those years, with more downs than ups. It was under the leadership of A. Earland Reddin, S.J., appointed pastor in 1939, that the turnaround in the finances, helped by the upturn in the economy after the war, was finally achieved. A unique situation occurred in 1944, when Bishop Gerald Murray of Saskatoon was appointed coadjutor archbishop of Winnipeg. Murray moved in with the Jesuits, as Archbishop Sinnott was not ready either to retire or to give Murray office space at the chancery.[46] Murray was comfortable with the Jesuits, since he had been educated by them at Loyola College in Montreal. He was never to take over the see, however, because he died in 1951, a year before Sinnott retired.

Out of the original boundaries of St. Ignatius Parish, two new parishes were begun: Our Lady of Victory in 1946, and Saint John Brebeuf in late 1955. Brebeuf was under the direction of the Jesuits, and will be dealt with more fully later in this chapter. Our Lady of Victory was the official memorial church of the archdiocese; its first pastor, James MacIsaac, had been a chaplain during the war.[47] In 1956, the present layout of the site at St. Ignatius was devised and the overall plan started to be put into place, with the new school and convent built in 1959 and the administration centre and rectory in 1964. The Jesuits worked hard over the years to build and set the ground for an active and dedicated parish. In his annual letter to Rome, the Provincial Superior, William F. Ryan, S.J., wrote to the Delegate of the Society of Jesus, Paolo Dezza, that "This is, I believe, our best parish with considerable outreach to native peoples, to youth, divorced people, etc."[48]

St. Ignatius Parish, which remains a Jesuit parish, continues to be an active centre encompassing many parishioners in a wide variety of ministries that were built up over the years and that will carry it forward into the future. In the hundredth-anniversary booklet entitled *The St. Ignatius Centennial Book: Who We Were, Who We Are, 1908–2008,* the following ministries were listed: St. Ignatius Elementary School, Sunday School, RCIA (Rite of Christian Initiation of Adults), Marriage Preparation, and Infant Baptism Preparation.[49] Under the umbrella of the Spiritual Exercises of St. Ignatius, the following were included: Annotation 19, Annotation 18, "Finding God

---

46 A. Erland Reddin, S.J., letter to Thomas J. Mullally, S.J., 7 June 1944, ibid.

47 Norman J. Chartrand, *History of the Archdiocese of Winnipeg* (Winnipeg: Éditions du Signe, 2004), 104.

48 William F. Ryan, S.J., letter to Paolo Dezza, s.j., 7 December 1981, AJC, Box D-501.

49 For a description of each ministry, see Christine Butterill and Richard Lebrun, eds., *The St. Ignatius Centennial Book: Who We Were, Who We Are, 1908–2008* (Winnipeg: St. Ignatius Parish, 2008), 42–74.

in the Dark" film series, Christian Life Communities, and Ignatian Lay Volunteer programme. The list continued with the Stewardship Team, Youth Ministry, Parish Choirs, Knights of Columbus Council 5808, Healing Prayer Team Ministry, Intercessory Prayer Group, Bereavement Ministry, St. Ignatius Parish News, Catholics Coming Home, Ladies Marathon Bridge, Prayer Shawl Ministry, Toastmasters, Community Health and Well-Being Programme, and a Social Justice Group, which included the Refugee Claimants and Refugee Rights Advocacy, Development and Peace Group, the El Sitio Committee, Prison Ministry, Environmental Committee, and Christmas Lite and Housing Advocacy Committee. This long list tells the real story of involvement, commitment, and reaching beyond the parish boundaries. The Superior General, Pedro Arrupe, s.j., challenged alumni/ae of Jesuit institutions to be "men and women for others", an ideal truly lived out in this parish.

St. Ignatius Parish, Montreal, Quebec

Another parish by the name of St. Ignatius was begun in Montreal, and is linked to the move of Loyola College from Drummond Street to the Sherbrooke Street West site in the Notre-Dame-de-Grace area of the city. The history of the college can be found in volume 1 of this series, which deals with Jesuit schools. The move took place in 1916. On 5 August of that year, a Mass was celebrated to mark the opening of the college's new campus, which some have also considered to be the first Mass of the parish. The college chapel was located at that time in the east-wing basement of the high school building, with the sacristy located at the rear of the chapel. Right from the opening of the college, the people of the neighbourhood, which was within the boundaries of the parish of Notre-Dame-de-Grace, located at the corner of Décarie and Notre-Dame-de-Grace Avenue, began to attend Mass in the college chapel. Extra Masses were added to accommodate their attendance, even though Archbishop Paul Bruchési had insisted that the chapel be used "en principe ne servir qu'aux élèves tant que la paroisse ne sera pas érigée."[50] To formally open the chapel to the public would require the permission of the archbishop and the agree-

---

50 Paul Bruchési, letter to Édouard Lecompte, s.j., 28 November 1910, AJC, Box D-515.

ment of the curé of the local parish. This stipulation can be found in Article 9 of the agreement between the archbishop of Montreal and the Dominican Fathers in a document dated 1 April 1910.[51]

In 1917, a group of English-speaking Catholics from the area around Loyola College held the statutory meeting in preparation to petition the archbishop to erect an English-language parish, which was granted the same year. It seems the regular steps were taken, and the consent of the Provincial of the Dominicans was given. Normally the civil law required the erection of the parish under the "Fabrique Act", which meant a petition to the commissioners in Quebec City; it seems this was not done. From this period until 1932, regular parish activities were organized and run out of the college chapel. The exact civil status of the parish was not clear, but the best designation would be that it was a mission, operated for the convenience of the people. Mission churches were usually attached to a particular parish or designated as such, but there is no indication that it was so designed in this case. The only clear status was its ecclesiastical existence as set up by the archbishop, "but only for the spiritual duties of the English-speaking Catholics under the patronage of Saint Ignatius of Loyola."[52] The Jesuits assumed the financial responsibility of the parish, and financial books were kept even though no wardens were elected. A proper chapel and the amount of ministry undertaken by the Jesuits were always a concern, which was exemplified in the visitation report of the Provincial Superior, John M. Filion, in 1927:

> Too much ministerial work was accepted in and around the city. Ministry across the border [to the USA] should be refused. Ours, especially the teachers, need free time on Sunday to do justice to their work. The needs of our parish must have priority over those others. … All ours are recommended in their Masses and prayers to appeal to God's Holy Providence to provide Loyola College with a suitable chapel in the near future.[53]

51 A copy of this document was in the office of St. Ignatius Parish at one time.

52 Document dated 16 June 1917 signed by the archbishop and James S. McCrory, Chancellor, ibid.

53 The visitation report can be found in AJC, Box C-417.

In 1930, the question arose as to whether the Jesuits should continue to administer the parish. In a letter dated 10 December 1930, E. Leo Burns, S.J., outlined to Hingston, the Provincial Superior, the reasons for and against keeping the parish. Burns favoured the keeping of the parish.[54] With the planned building of a proper college chapel for Loyola that was made possible by the F. C. Smith renunciation, Joseph Primeau, s.j., the pastor, met in 1931 with Archbishop Georges Gauthier to get permission for the new chapel and to clarify the status of the parish. In a letter dated 14 September 1931, Primeau put into writing what he had discussed with the archbishop. He had asked for permission to set up the parish and for the pastors to be Jesuits. He also confirmed with the archbishop the original purposes of the parish, with some special Masses for the French-speaking people of the immediate area.[55] The fruit of this meeting and follow-up letter was that the parish would be left in the hands of the Jesuits of Loyola College; that the Jesuits were to supply a church and services as part of the contract; and that the blessing of the Superior General in Rome be obtained for this project. The date of 15 August 1933 was set for the official acceptance by the Jesuits of the parish after the agreement had been approved and signed by the Sacred Congregation of Religious on 14 July 1933 and by the Superior General of the Society of Jesus, Wlodimir Ledóchowski, on behalf of the Jesuits.[56]

The exclusive character of the parish, namely, for the English-speaking people of the area, was to be maintained. The Jesuits, however, were asked to look after the French-speaking Catholics of Notre-Dame-de-Grace Parish who lived in the vicinity of St. Ignatius Parish, which meant a special Mass on Sundays and Holy Days with a sermon in French, French-speaking confessors, and visits to the sick in the area. Baptisms, marriages, and funerals for the French-speaking people of the area were to be supplied by their canonical parish, namely, Notre-Dame-de-Grace Parish. It was not until 1950 that Sainte-Catherine-de-Sienne, the local French parish church, was

54 E. Leo Burns, S.J., letter to William H. Hingston, S.J., 10 December 1930, AJC, Box D-515.

55 Albini-J. Primeau, s.j., letter to Archbishop Georges Gauthier, s.j., 14 September 1931, AJC, Box D-515.

56 Document found in AJC, Box D-515.

opened. The construction of the new chapel was begun in July 1932 and completed and officially opened on Palm Sunday, 23 April 1933.[57] Many of the furnishings were donated; these are listed in the Loyola College Review for 1934:

> The beauty of the College chapel was further enhanced by several commemorative gifts, and it is our pleasant duty to express our sincere gratitude to Mrs. J. K. Foran, who donated the rose window of the south transept, a symbolical treatment of the different titles of our Blessed Lady. The window was installed in memory of the late Dr. J. K. Foran, K.C., Litt.D., LL.B. The large west window depicting the Jesuit Martyrs of North America, is the gift of the Irish-Canadian Rangers, in memory of their fallen comrades. It was solemnly dedicated by Reverend Father Rector on Armistice Day, on the occasion of the laying-up of the colours of the regiment in the College chapel. These windows are the work of Mr. C. W. Kelsey of Montreal. A precious addition to the collection of sacred vessels is the gift of the Timmins family, in memory of the late M. J. Timmins—a handsomely wrought silver monstrance of original design, whose lines are in strict keeping with the other adornments of our chapel.[58]

At the blessing of the new chapel, Archbishop Gauthier told the people that this was their church, even though it was mainly built by funds donated through Loyola College. Agreements were worked out between the parish and the college for rental of the facilities, for salary, and for room and board for the parish priest. The parish was permitted to use the hall beneath the chapel, as well as other facilities of the college. Extra ministerial assistance was to come from the Jesuits teaching at the college. It seemed that each time plans were begun for the building of a separate parish church, the pastor was reassigned. Was this a coincidence or not? It happened in 1944 when John H. Keenan, S.J., began the process; he was moved that year to Winnipeg. This occurred again in 1951, when Arthur C. Wilson, S.J., was planning

---

57 See article by Horatio P. Phelan, S.J., in *Loyola College Review*, 1946.

58 *Loyola College Review*, 1934.

to buy the land where the present Sainte-Catherine-de-Sienne church stands; the land was to be bought by his brother and two others who were willing to hold it until the parish was ready to begin construction. Wilson was moved that same year to Saint Mary's University in Halifax. Ten years later, in 1961, John J. Masterson, S.J., announced a campaign for funds for a new church, but then was moved to Winnipeg. Masterson's announcement caused the clarification of the status of the parish, and, in 1962, wardens were elected under the new Quebec "Fabrique Act", assuming the responsibilities of the parish. Two years later, under the pastorship of Joseph F. McDonald, S.J., the college sold to the parish a corner of its property, fronting on West Broadway. Church construction began in early 1965 and finished a year later. In 1969, the Provincial Superior, Edward Sheridan, in his visitation report of 10–21 February, described the parish:

> It is a well organized and well run parish. The pastoral service is excellent, and the houses are visited on a regular basis. Mass attendance and the use of sacraments, remain good. A number of younger people and some young married couples often assist at the College Sunday Mass (really a student Mass), and this is a mild source of friction between the parish priests and the College chaplains. The College liturgy is, of course, more lively and attractive for young people. … Our priests are respected and admired. On the other hand, our parishes do not display any particular strong leadership in new forms of parochial ministry or parish reform. Perhaps, in this regard, we tend to be over conservative. Moreover, a lot depends on the personnel engaged in our parishes; good people, yes, but usually not creative or imaginative.[59]

The Jesuits continued to administer the parish until 1982, when it was transferred to the archdiocese. In a letter to the wardens of the parish, the reason given for leaving the parish was the lack of manpower and a reassessment of the Jesuit commitment across Canada.[60] This letter was prompted by a letter from the wardens expressing their dis-

59 Visitation report in AJC, Box C-417.

60 William F. Ryan, S.J., letter to wardens, 26 March 1982, AJC, Box D-515.

appointment and surprise.[61] Disappointment because the Jesuits were leaving at a crucial and uncertain time for the English-speaking people of Quebec, and surprise that the wardens were not informed beforehand, and only found out during the homily preached by Kenneth C. Casey, S.J., at the Sunday liturgy. Casey had had a long history with Loyola High School, having been its Principal for twenty-five years, and spending three more years in high school ministry in Toronto before going into parish ministry in 1979 at St. Ignatius Parish. The Jesuit document entitled *Our Way of Proceeding in the '80s*, published on 31 May 1981, which had been approved by the Jesuit Superior General, Pedro Arrupe, stated about St. Ignatius Parish, "Given that we already have a strong and multi-form pastoral presence in this archdiocese, we will consult with the archbishop concerning the feasibility of a creative disengagement from the administration of St. Ignatius in exchange for putting some senior Jesuits at his disposal for pastoral work in the archdiocese."[62]

Over the years, the parish had a number of schools within its jurisdiction. The first was housed in property belonging to Loyola College at 3500 Belmore Avenue and the house next door. There were playgrounds for the children on either side of these two houses. The school was popularly known as "The University", and it continued until 1932. In that year, St. Ignatius School on the corner of Terrebonne and West Broadway streets was built, and was large enough for the number of students until the 1950s, when an Annex was added on West Broadway near Fielding Avenue. In the early 1960s, St. Francis Borgia School was opened to accommodate the growing number of children in the parish. Today, there is only one school in the boundaries of the parish, and that is St. Ignatius School on Coronation Avenue.

Immaculate Conception Parish, Vancouver, B.C.

The move into western Canada continued with a new parish on the west coast. Immaculate Conception Parish in Vancouver, which officially opened on 2 March 1924, was under consideration as early as 1922, when the Provincial Superior, John Milway Filion, visited the

61 Wardens, letter to William F. Ryan, S.J., 14 March 1982, ibid.

62 *Our Way of Proceeding in the '80s*, 41, AJC, Box B-311.

area on 27 May. This latter event was recorded in the house journal of the Convent of the Sacred Heart by the Sisters. It stated that Filion made a survey of the 250 acres of the B. C. University Lands and the ten acres of this land granted to the Jesuits by the government, "provided they build a College."[63]

On 4 October 1922, John D. Knox, S.J., was assigned to be chaplain to the Sisters of the Sacred Heart in Vancouver, a post he had held between 1918 and 1920 as a secular priest before he entered the Jesuits in 1920. Knox had been a chaplain in the armed forces during the Great War, had risen to the rank of major, was made an officer in the Order of the British Empire in recognition of his service, and eventually rose to the rank of lieutenant-colonel. He had converted to Catholicism in 1910, having been ordained an Anglican priest in 1909. Some consider Knox to be the "unnamed first pastor" of Immaculate Conception Parish, which had been canonically established in 1922 but only opened in 1924. He sang the first High Mass for the parish in the convent chapel. In November, Knox received a letter from Archbishop Timothy Casey of Vancouver, stating, "Will you please inform your Father Provincial that I invite you to establish a parish, and when possible a Classical College, in this archdiocese. The territory in which I permit you to establish the parish and future College, is that of Point Grey, Vancouver, BC."[64] The boundaries of the new parish were also defined. The territory had originally been in the parish administered by the Redemptorist Fathers, Our Lady of Perpetual Help.[65]

On 13 December 1923, Filion wrote to the General Superior, Wlodimir Ledóchowski, s.j., who responded on 31 December 1923 with permission to accept the parish. Walter McManus, S.J., arrived in Vancouver on 12 August 1924 as pastor of the new parish. Five days later, Knox left for eastern Canada, where he worked for the next thirty years. Not everyone was pleased that the Jesuits were now officially working in the archdiocese. It seems the Irish Christian Brothers had

---

63 Anonymous report, "Immaculate Conception Parish, Vancouver, B.C.", c. 1972, AJC, Box D-519.

64 The original letter is in AJC, Box D-519.

65 The parish boundaries were further defined in the letter of 1 March 1924, ibid.

entered into an agreement with the archbishop in June of 1922 to open a classical college. Thus, in a letter, the archdiocesan administrator, William P. O'Boyle, O.M.I., revoked the invitation to the Jesuits to open a classical college.[66] On the other hand, negotiations went well with the Sisters of the Sacred Heart, which led to their agreement to teach in the parish school. The Sisters ran their own academy in their convent, and since they were not allowed to walk on public streets or sidewalks due to the fact that they were semi-cloistered, an adjustment had to be made for the site of the church and the school. The latter was the reason that the church was not built on Dunbar Avenue, which was more accessible to cars and to those using city buses, but rather eventually on West 28th Street, about three blocks from Dunbar.

In December 1924, it became clear that the parish could no longer use the Sacred Heart chapel indefinitely as a parish church. In March 1925, Filion asked Ledóchowski for permission to build a small temporary chapel. As he wrote, "It is merely a little wooden structure, shingles on the roof and the sides and wood sheeting inside. No architect would want to sign his name as the author of such a temporary and flimsy construction."[67] In actuality, the church ended up being a bit more than "temporary and flimsy". The reason Filion had written to the General Superior was to obtain permission to use the money from the Jesuit Order to build the church. As a result, a builder was engaged and a church and a basement school were completed; these were blessed on 12 December 1926 by Archbishop Casey. Filion assisted. Previously, in August of that year, John H. Keenan, S.J., took over as pastor, replacing William Dunn, S.J. (September 1925 to August 1926), who in turn had replaced Walter McManus (August 1924 to September 1925). Keenan remained as pastor for fifteen years, during a period of rapid growth for the Point Grey area and the parish.

Three months before the blessing, the basement school was opened on 7 September 1926, with forty-one children enrolled in the first class. Even though the school was in session in the basement, work on the church section was under way and continued until 1928, when

66 Ibid.

67 John M. Filion, s.j., letter to the Assistant (Rome), 4 March 1925, AJC, Toronto, in file folder entitled "Letters to and from Father General 1924–1925".

the choir loft was added. The beginning years were a period of firsts: the first crowning of Mary, the first First Communion class, the first Corpus Christi procession, the first bazaar, the founding of the Altar Society, the St. John Berchman's Sodality, the Sodality of Madeline Sophie, the Holy Name Society, the St. Vincent de Paul Society, and so forth, all of which demonstrated how active and organized the parish was. For the first field day on 22 June 1928, William H. Hingston, S.J., the new Jesuit Provincial Superior, was present. He had donated the prize, and also had paid for the new Christmas crib. In 1932, construction began west of the church on a separate two-room addition to the school for grades seven and eight. It was ready for use that fall, when eighty-nine pupils were registered in the school. This was not the end of construction. In 1932, Scout Hall was added, and in 1940, the Catholic Youth Organization (CYO) Hall. The Sisters of the Sacred Heart taught in the school until 1948, when the administration was taken over by a lay person, Mrs. Walton; in 1954 the Sisters of St. Ann took over the teaching duties and moved into the new school, which was officially opened and blessed during the school year on 27 January 1954.[68] In 1980, the Sisters left the school; since then, it has been under lay direction. To this day, the Jesuits have maintained contact with the school through the awarding of four bursaries to top students who are destined to attend a Catholic high school.

In 1941, after 15 years, Keenan was replaced as pastor by Raphael E. Kennedy, S.J., who was transferred from Montreal. It was Kennedy who extended the nave of the church and eliminated the debt. He also bought a new rectory and persuaded the Men's Association to launch an action to purchase three lots on 27th Avenue for additional playgrounds. J. Adalbert (Bert) Leahy, S.J., arrived in February 1946; he was to give the next thirty-eight years of service to the parish and the archdiocese, especially as chaplain for thirty-five years of the British Columbia Catholic Hospital Conference and, beginning in 1957, as administrator of St. Michael the Archangel church on the Indian Reserve at Musqueam. In August 1963, St. Michael's burned

68 *The 75th Anniversary Commemorative Album* states that the school was blessed by Bishop Martin Michael Johnson. Johnson was the bishop of Nelson in 1954, while the archbishop of Vancouver was William Mark Duke (1931–1964).

down. The archbishop gave permission in February 1964 to build a new church that could also be used on occasion for non-Catholic funerals and other special activities. This was an ecumenical first for the reserve and for the archdiocese. Kennedy was replaced in 1951 by Thomas J. Mullally, S.J., who held the pastorship until 1959, and who in turn was replaced by Clarence P. Hinphy, S.J., who was to remain for ten years. Almost as soon as he arrived, Hinphy was elected to the Senate of Priests in the archdiocese. He made a number of changes in the church facilities. For example, the drapes were taken down and a new altar was built. It was during this time, too, that the liturgical changes following the Second Vatican Council came into effect. Beginning in 1965, Mass was celebrated facing the people, and in 1967, the Eucharistic prayer in English was proclaimed for the first time.

In 1969, John (Jack) F. McCaffrey, S.J., began as the new pastor, arriving from the Martyrs' Shrine, Midland, Ontario, where he had been the director for fifteen years. Carefully preparing for the education of the parishioners in the new liturgical rules, McCaffrey planned to renovate the sanctuary of the church. On 24 August 1972, however, after attending a diocesan meeting, as he was walking in the grounds of the Sacred Heart convent, he suffered a fatal heart attack. Archbishop James Francis Carney celebrated the funeral Mass; McCaffrey's remains were translated to Toronto for a memorial Mass before the burial at the Jesuit cemetery in Guelph. The planned renovations proceeded after McCaffrey was replaced by Harvey D. Seasons, S.J., who in turn was replaced by J. Brendan Cloran, S.J., in 1974, and who remained until 1980. The Jesuits stayed on for only four more years afterwards, as three pastors succeeded each other: Patrick J. Boyle (1980–1981), W. Ross Feeley (1981–1982), and the return of Clarence P. Hinphy (1982–1984). Hinphy had to leave slightly before the official end of the Jesuits' tenure at the parish in order to be admitted into Princess Margaret Hospital in Toronto for treatment for cancer. He died on 12 July 1984 in Pickering, Ontario.

Once it was clear that Archbishop Carney would not allow the Jesuits to develop an Ignatian Spiritual Centre involving the training of lay people as spiritual directors, William F. Ryan, the Jesuit Provincial Superior, decided that given the Province's priorities outlined in *Our*

Way of Proceeding in the '80s,[69] the Jesuits could no longer continue at Immaculate Conception Parish.[70] So on 31 July 1984, on the Feast of St. Ignatius Loyola, in the sixtieth year of the parish, Leahy, the longest-serving Jesuit in the parish, handed over the parish to the Reverend Stephen Jensen, now a monsignor, of the archdiocese of Vancouver. In the week prior to this event, Edward J. Dowling, S.J., acting pastor, and Leahy celebrated a farewell Mass on 22 July, which was also the formal archdiocesan farewell to the Jesuits.

Canadian Martyrs Parish, Halifax, Nova Scotia

It was some thirty years before another parish had been accepted by the Jesuits in English Canada. This was Canadian Martyrs parish in Halifax. In 1940, the Jesuits had undertaken the direction of Saint Mary's College on Windsor Street in Halifax amid some disagreements between Archbishop John McNally and the Christian Brothers, who had administered the college. In 1951, the college and high school were moved from Windsor Street to 35 Robie Street, and the college was granted university status. In the following year, the Jesuits at the university were asked to take on Canadian Martyrs Parish, the university's chapel, as its home. This was confirmed in a letter from Rome and quoted by George E. Nunan, S.J., the Provincial Superior in English Canada, in a letter to J.Frederick Lynch, S.J., the Rector:

> The following letter was received this morning from Father Bolland in the name of Father General: "Absente P. Generali placet respondere ad RVae litteras die 26a martii datas et approbare ut Halifacense Collegium curam assumat paroeciae eidem Collegio adnectendae, sicut P. Generalis iam conditionate approbaverat. Cuius paroeciae P. Eduardus Brown videtur

---

69 The Jesuit document, approved by the Superior General, Pedro Arrupe, s.j., *Our Way of Proceeding in the '80s,* 31 May 1981, stated: "Should the archbishop agree to our proposal to open a small spirituality centre in Vancouver, our parish will continue for the time being as a good small parish serviced by one full-time Jesuit. Should the archbishop not want us to locate a small spirituality centre in the archdiocese, we will offer this service to the bishop of Calgary and begin to explore the feasibility of withdrawing from the administration of this parish". 41, AJC, Box B-311.

70 William F. Ryan, S.J., letter to Clarence P. Hinphy, S.J., J. Adalbert Leahy, S.J., and parishioners, 4 May 1983; Archbishop James F. Carney, letter to parishioners of Immaculate Conception Parish, 4 July 1983, AJC, Box D-519.

> bonus parochus future." This is for your information. I shall send official notice of the appointment to His Grace.[71]

Once the permissions were granted, the parish boundaries had to be set and a temporary alternative to the university chapel found since the construction of said chapel was only beginning. These items were discussed in the letter from the pastor-designate, Edward M. Brown, S.J., to the Provincial Superior on 27 June 1952:

> His Grace, the Archbishop, gave me the boundaries of the parish. According to the document the new parish will have 630 families or more. One hundred and thirty of these are from St. Thomas Aquinas Parish and five hundred or more are from St. Mary's Basilica Parish … the Vicar-General told me that he would ask us to take charge of the Old Folks Home and possibly the T. B. Hospital. The Basilica would keep the large V.G. Hospital, Childrens' Hospital and Grace Maternity… Monsignor Burns is of the opinion that we should start Sunday Masses in the auditorium of the new St. Francis School as soon as it is available. The auditorium may possibly be ready in a month's time. His Grace, the Archbishop, stated very emphatically on several recent occasions that he wanted our own chapel to be closed in as quickly as possible… . Even if work started on our own chapel in July I doubt that it would be useable, even in an unfinished state, before October. That is why the Vicar-General thinks that it would be wise to use St. Francis school auditorium as a temporary Sunday chapel.[72]

It took a while for the construction to be completed, but it was finally done. The new church was formally opened and the first Mass was celebrated on Saturday, 28 November 1953. The university chapel was to be used for the next eighteen years when the parish was moved from Saint Mary's University to temporary quarters on Inglis Street in 1970 and then in the following year into the new parish church at 5900 Inglis Street. Although this move was contemplated before 1967, there was some contention over the site of the new parish church,

---

71 George E. Nunan, S.J., letter to J. Frederick Lynch, S.J., 7 April 1952, AJC, Box F-625A.

72 Edward M. Brown, S.J., letter to George E. Nunan, S.J., 27 June 1952, ibid.

which delayed the project.[73] With the move of the parish into new quarters, an agreement was drawn up between the archdiocese and the Jesuits. It was signed on 30 November 1970 by Edward F. Sheridan, the Jesuit Provincial Superior, and on 23 November 1970 by Archbishop James M. Hayes and Chancellor John W. Burkley.[74] The following was reported in the Jesuit Province *Newsletter* of November–December 1971 and is also found in "The Jesuits of Halifax: the 1970s", compiled by William Lonc, S.J.:

> On December 11, Archbishop J[ames] M. Hayes, officially opened and blessed the new parish church bringing an end to the 16-month wait for this facility during which the parishioners used the parish hall for the Sunday liturgy. … Frs Johnson and Pianfetti moved into the rectory after Christmas and the move marked the beginning of a new Jesuit community in Halifax.[75]

The Jesuits remained at Saint Mary's University for only three more years before they returned the administration to the archdiocese of Halifax in 1974. Although some Jesuits continued to teach at the university, the Order was no longer responsible for the administration. The Jesuit Community remained in Halifax. As a result, Canadian Martyrs Parish became more and more the focus of their work. In 2005, however, the Jesuits informed the archdiocese that they could no longer staff the parish, and it, too, was returned to diocesan administration.

St. Elizabeth of Hungary Parish, Toronto, Ontario

Although the Hungarian parish has its roots as far back as 1928 with the assignment of a Hungarian Seminarian, László Forgách, and a Franciscan friar, Lelemen Burka, to minister to the needs of the small but growing Hungarian population of Toronto, it was only in

---

73 For more information on the controversy, see Robert L. MacDougall, S.J., letter to Angus J. Macdougall, S.J., 21 January 1969, ibid.

74 Copy of agreement in AJC, Box F-625A.

75 *Province Newsletter* (November–December 1971); William P. Lonc, S.J., "The Jesuits of Halifax: the 1970s", ibid.

1948 that the Jesuits became involved.[76] In the beginning, members of the Hungarian community had Mass available to them in a variety of locations. It was only in 1944 that they settled into a permanent site when they bought an unused Anglican church, St. Philip's, built in 1885 and located at the corner of Spadina and Dundas streets in Toronto. This church was consecrated by Archbishop James Charles McGuigan on 19 March 1944 and dedicated to Saint Elizabeth of Hungary. The traditional mortgage-burning ceremony was held three years later on 14 December 1947 in the presence of the archbishop. Just prior to this period of setting up the parish, no Hungarian-speaking priest was available, so the Reverend Leo Austin of the archdiocese was assigned as pastor in 1939. Although he did not speak Hungarian, he took on the challenge. He became responsible for the parish until a Hungarian Jesuit was appointed pastor in 1949. Cardinal McGuigan enquired about where he could find Hungarian-speaking priests for the parish, and was informed that there were some Hungarian Jesuits in Boston, in the New England Jesuit Province. The Cardinal then wrote to the New England Provincial Superior, John J. McEleney, requesting that one of the Hungarian Jesuits be sent to Toronto to assess the situation. István Békési was sent. He celebrated Mass at St. Elizabeth's on 21 November 1948. Several months later, on 1 July 1949, he was appointed pastor. Although Austin was reassigned to work in an English-speaking parish, he kept close ties with the Hungarian parish until his death.

This particular period was one in which the parish was expanding because of immigration. It grew so fast that a second priest was assigned in 1952, and a third a year later. In 1955, the parish bought property in Streetsville (Mississauga) and renamed that property Mindszenty Park; the parish used it for a variety of activities. In the meantime, the church windows were replaced with stained glass, and a fundraising campaign was begun for a new organ.

In 1956, after the Soviets brutally put down the Hungarian Revolution, thousands of refugees fled the country; many arrived in Toronto as well as in other cities across Canada. The parish was

76 Anonymous booklet, "Saint Elizabeth of Hungary R.C. Parish" (2009). This was published by the parish, and printed in Hungarian and English.

accordingly taken up with helping settle these refugees by providing shelter, food, and English classes. Even when the federal and provincial governments stepped in to help, the parishioners continued to assist their fellow Hungarians. This influx of Hungarians prompted the appointment of a fourth priest to help with the parish's pastoral and social ministries. In 1958, the St. Elizabeth of Hungary Credit Union was formed to assist the newcomers. By 2006, when it was dissolved, the credit union had provided loans to over a thousand Hungarian Canadians for the purchasing of homes and cars as well as funding to support small businesses. Another result of this great influx of Hungarians was an increase in the number of children who needed instruction in language, history, and geography. In 1961, to expand the school facilities, the parish purchased a site at 263 Spadina Avenue. The following year, the parish bought a 130-acre farm in Orono, which was named Loyola Park. This area was a favourite spot for the youth as well as for the whole parish community, and was the site for the Hungarian Scout Jamborees in 1975, 1980, and 1990. The year 1978 marked the 50th anniversary of the founding of the parish. A gala dinner was held to commemorate the event, and a new pipe organ, a Casavant two-manual organ with 1120 pipes designed by Dr. Ferenc Gergely and György Zadubán, was inaugurated.

Slowly but surely, the parishioners began to migrate from the city core to the suburbs, and it was becoming more and more difficult to find parking near the church. In 1983, people began to ask for the parish to be relocated in the suburbs, where most of the parishioners were living. After permission was granted by the archdiocese, a new site was selected, and on 7 June 1984, a purchase agreement was signed for the land at 430-432 Sheppard Avenue East. The following year, plans for a new church, parish office, hall, and youth wing were completed, and in the spring of 1985, the sod-turning ceremony was held. By 28 July, the move from Spadina and Dundas was completed. The first Mass was celebrated on 4 August, and the consecration of the church took place on 5 October. The move revitalized parish life, with many events organized by parish groups and the school becoming a stronger focus for the parish. The number of students increased, prompting the addition of a third floor in 1993 on the school section of the complex, adding the needed classrooms for more students.

The World Youth Day congress held in Toronto in 2002 involved many members of the parish in housing, feeding, and caring for 180 pilgrims from Hungary and Transylvania. The following year marked the seventy-fifth anniversary of the founding of the original parish, and numerous events were held over a six-week period to celebrate the jubilee. The move to the new church, the integration of Hungarians into Canadian culture, and the aging of the parishioners and the Jesuits are today challenging the parish to embrace young people who have Hungarian roots and sentiments, yet do not speak the language. To accomplish this aim, the noon Mass on Sundays is now focused towards those who are less familiar with the Hungarian language. Also, a new advisory council was established to facilitate better communications between parishioners and the clergy. The foundations laid in 1928 are being built upon with new eyes looking towards a new future within the Hungarian community in Toronto.

St. John Brebeuf Parish, Winnipeg

St. Ignatius Parish ministered to the Catholic population of the area of River Heights in Winnipeg in the 1940s and 1950s, as the area and the Town of Tuxedo expanded rapidly. The archdiocese, led by Archbishop Philip F. Pocock, decided that a new parish was needed in the area, so half a city block, bounded by Lanark, Fleet, Renfrew, and Corydon, was purchased by the archdiocese.[77] In 1955, Clarence P. Hinphy, S.J., was named the first pastor of the new parish, and a patron was chosen: St. John Brebeuf, the leading figure among the Canadian Jesuit Martyrs. In the spring and fall of 1955, Hinphy began visiting the parishioners within the boundaries, which had been carved out of St. Ignatius Parish, and which consisted of the Assiniboine River to the north, McGillivray Boulevard to the south, the west side of Cambridge on the east, and the boundary of Tuxedo and Charleswood on the west. Since there was no building on the land, arrangements were made with the Canadian Army to hold Masses at St. George

---

77 Joseph C. Johnson, S.J., "History of St. John Brebeuf Parish" and "Thirty Seven Years of Jesuit Service: 1955–1992", both in AJC, Box D-501.

Army Chapel on Kenaston Boulevard at Fleet Street beginning on Sunday, 4 December 1955. Seventy-five parishioners attended the first Mass. In the beginning, three Masses were celebrated on Sunday: at nine, ten, and noon. By January 1956, however, attendance had increased enough to warrant the addition of a High Mass at 11 a.m. and another at 12:15 p.m. The parishioners were asked to organize two basic groups: a board of advisors, which met on 10 January 1956, and the Ladies Auxiliary, which met for the first time on 23 March that same year.

The work of building church and school began by interviewing various architectural firms so that one could be chosen to draw up plans. In the beginning, it was thought that the plans would include an eight-room school, a gymnasium, and a church building; this was soon changed to a school, a parish administration area, and a gymnasium. The architectural firm of Libling, Michner and Associates was chosen. In the meantime, the men of the parish met to discuss the financing needed for the project. On 30 May, a fundraising drive was decided upon, with a goal of $75,000.00. This campaign was to begin in early September 1956 and to run for a month. Hugh Carmichael was named campaign chairman. On 9 September at the 12:15 Mass, the solemn opening of the campaign was held, with Archbishop Pocock preaching and Captain Laureat L. Lord, O.M.I., army chaplain of St. George Chapel, presiding. A special blessing was given to the parishioners as a whole, and individual blessings to each of the men who were to go out to solicit the funds. By 11 September, $20,000.00 had been pledged; by 1 October, the campaign had exceeded the goal, with $75,241.00 pledged and still more people to be contacted.

The plans were adjusted again before the campaign began, when Archbishop Pocock, Hinphy, members of the church board, and Mel Michner held a meeting on 30 August. They decided that the project would now include an auditorium/chapel combination, an administration area, and an eight-room elementary school. The cost was not to exceed $242,000.00, including architect fees and furnishings. In November, after the success of the initial campaign, a men's parish society, eventually called "The Men of Brebeuf", was organized. At its first meeting on 9 December, J. L. "Dooley" Freeman was elected president. Goodwill was evident in the parish, and by May 1957, the pledges for the fundraising campaign totalled $125,000.00, just over half of the determined cost of construction. Even though a great deal of energy was going into the fundraising campaign, the parish was also functioning very well. The first class of forty children, combined with those from St. George Chapel, received their First Holy Communion on 26 May 1957; two days later, confirmation was administered by Archbishop Pocock to fifty children and adults.

The contract for the construction was awarded to Bocksteel Construction on 12 June 1957 for the sum of $223,000.00, under the proscribed limit set the previous August. The plans were slightly adjusted again: they now included an auditorium, which would also serve as a chapel and meeting area, and a basement with rooms for teachers, nurse, pastor, mechanical equipment, and washrooms. On the main floor would be four permanent classrooms and four temporary classrooms, the latter eventually becoming the parish administration area. The foundations were poured to accommodate three storeys: the second storey for more classrooms and the third for a convent. Construction began almost immediately, and by the middle of August, the concrete had been poured for the basement and the first floor.

With construction well under way, the Sisters of the Holy Names of Jesus and Mary agreed to undertake the administration of the school. They assigned two sisters, Sister Maureen Patricia as Principal and Sister Guy Marie, to the teaching staff. The lay staff were hired by the end of August. The school opened at a temporary location and moved to the new construction on 25 November 1957, with a total of 123 students. The solemn blessing of the school took place on 9 February 1958 by Archbishop Pocock. Many people attended, including Manitoba Premier Douglas L. Campbell. The first parish Mass was celebrated on 11 February by Hinphy in the new chapel/auditorium, and the following Sunday, regular Masses at nine and ten were begun. On 1 June, the first First Holy Communion group was received in the new chapel, and the first wedding took place in the chapel on 19 July. A few days later, on 22 July, news was released that Hinphy, who had guided the beginnings of the parish, was to be transferred to Regiopolis College in Kingston, Ontario, and that Roderick A. MacGilvray, S.J., from St. Ignatius Parish was to be his successor. Although many parishioners found it difficult to see Hinphy leave, the majority knew and respected MacGilvray. The change-over took place on the Feast of Saint Ignatius, 31 July 1958.

The first problem that MacGilvray faced was the cost of running the school, which was an added expense to the parish. A new financial scheme was instituted to help alleviate the problem. It consisted of a pledge of 4 percent of a parishioner's income, less $500.00 for each dependent (not counting husband and wife). At the Sunday Masses on 9 November 1958, MacGilvray gave a fine and convincing sermon on the giving programme. This was coupled with the men of the parish going door to door to speak personally to the parishioners who were late with their pledges. Thus, an excellent response was achieved. In 1959, the house at 570 Renfrew Street was purchased for a rectory. Up to this time, the Jesuit pastors had been travelling from either St. Ignatius Parish or St. Paul's College at Ellice and Vaughan, where they had been living. The college had moved from downtown to the campus of the University of Manitoba in 1958, which meant a long commute once the residence was completed on the University of Manitoba campus.

As time went on, many new parishioners moved into the area, and the school became overcrowded. Three years later, a decision could no longer be put off; in May 1961, a contract worth $87,000.00 was awarded to Bocksteel Construction to build an addition, which was completed by December of that year.

The next step in the programme of construction, a church, was also beginning to demand immediate attention, since Masses were often congested. Moreover, funerals and weddings could not be held in the chapel/auditorium on weekdays, for the space was needed for the school. So in 1963, a study was undertaken to look at what was needed in the construction of a church. Although a cruciform design was first proposed, after consideration of the new liturgical movement, a circular church was proposed that would not cost more than $350,000.00. At the same time, it was decided that a preliminary fundraising campaign with a goal of $150,000.00 be undertaken before construction began. Hugh Carmichael, the senior parish trustee, was elected as chairman of the campaign. On Sunday, 29 February 1964, the "Church Building Campaign" was begun with a special Mass at noon dedicated to its success. The campaign was to take place over three weeks. By the end, they had raised $135,000.00; by mid 1964, they had exceeded the goal by $15,000.00. Tenders were called in May 1964, and Sawatsky Construction was awarded the contract. The total cost of the church with furnishings was to be $365,000.00. The archdiocese guaranteed a loan for $200,000.00 from the Toronto Dominion Bank to make up the amount. On 19 June, the sod was turned, and construction began immediately. The eventual cost was reduced to $325,000.00 by making economies during the construction period.

Due to the stress of construction, MacGilvray suffered a mild heart attack in early September 1964. He was sent to Misericordia Hospital. His Jesuit Superiors decided that the burden was too great for him, so he was moved to St. Paul's College to work as spiritual director beginning on 1 November. J. Raymond Oliver, S.J., was appointed as MacGilvray's replacement. Just before the farewell Mass on 29 October, MacGilvray collapsed; he died a short time later in the rectory. His funeral was held at St. Ignatius Parish, with over fifty priests concelebrating. On a cold January day in 1965, Archbishop George Bernard Cardinal Flahiff, in a three-hour meeting, assisted the new pastor, trustees, and architect to make the necessary adjustment to the plans to accommodate the changes in the liturgy that were being promulgated at that time. These changes, along with a severe winter, delayed the finishing of the church. In April 1965, the cornerstone was laid, and the church was finally completed in October. Cardinal Flahiff solemnly blessed the new church in May 1966. Many dignitaries were in attendance, including Manitoba Premier Duff Roblin, Winnipeg Mayor Steve Juba, and representatives of other churches.

Oliver continued as pastor until 1972, when Joseph V. Driscoll, S.J., was appointed the fourth pastor after an outstanding success as Rector of St. Paul's High School. His major parish accomplishment was the construction of St. Marie House, which accommodated the living quarters for the Jesuit staff, parish offices, the school staff, and easier access to and from the church and the school. Before it was completed, Driscoll was appointed Rector of St. Paul's College at the University of Manitoba; it would be nine years before he could spend his first night in the house. The next pastor, Terence G. Walsh, S.J., was responsible for the completion of St. Marie House and the reorganization of the parish finances when interest rates were at their highest. His term lasted only two years. In 1982, he was replaced by Joseph Johnson, S.J., who continued for ten years, the sixth and last Jesuit pastor of the parish. Unexpectedly, the announcement came that the Jesuits would leave the parish on 29 July 1992. Although many were shocked by the news, it had been talked about, and the parishioners had been warned. In preparation for the Jesuits' departure, the parish celebrated the positive contributions the Jesuits had made over thirty-seven years, and a plaque was installed near the church entrance commemorating their work. As Johnson and his assistant, John (Jack) J. Murray, S.J., waved goodbye on 29 July, the Reverend John Currie, the new diocesan pastor and a graduate of St. Paul's High School, moved in. This ended the permanent presence of the Jesuits at St. John Brebeuf Parish.

St. Pius X Parish, St. John's, Newfoundland

In 1962, the Jesuits arrived in St. John's, Newfoundland, where they were to take over Gonzaga Regional High School and St. Pius X Parish. A mission chapel had been started in 1955 to serve the Churchill Park area of St. John's. It was the first religious institution in the archdiocese to be named after St. Pius X, a former Pope who had been canonized by Pope Pius XII in 1954. Originally called St. Pius X Chapel, it was served by the basilica's parish staff. The Reverend Charles Greene of the archdiocese was the first administrator. It consisted of the ground floor chapel area and the elementary school, directed by the Sisters of Mercy, who occupied the upper floor. This configuration was to continue until 1976, when a new church was built and the area of the original chapel became the parish hall, but between 1976 and 1999, the area was used as a gymnasium for the elementary school as well.

The Archive of the Jesuits in Canada / Archives des jésuites au Canada

John Milway Filion, s.j. (1878–1962), Provincial Superior of the Province of Canada (1918–1924), and first Provincial Superior of the Vice Province of Upper Canada (1924–1928). He promoted the beatification and canonization of the Jesuit Canadian Martyrs, and constructed Martyrs' Shrine, Midland, Ontario.

Nicolas Point, s.j. / The Archive of the Jesuits in Canada / Archives des jésuites au Canada

Holy Cross Church, Wikwemikong, Ontario, by Nicolas Point, s.j. (1799–1868). While Superior there (1847–1854), he designed and constructed the church.

Courtesy of Xavier High School, New York

A native of northern England, John Larkin became a Sulpician in Paris and was ordained a priest in Baltimore in August 1827 before being appointed to the Grand Séminaire in Montreal. He became a Jesuit in October 1840. His influence was an important one in Bishop Ignace Bourget's decision to appeal for the return of the Jesuits in 1842.

W.J. Bell / The Archive of the Jesuits in Canada / Archives des jésuites au Canada

When Dominque du Ranquet, s.j. (1813–1900), died in Wikwemikong, he was considered to have been one of the most important Canadian missionaries of the nineteenth century. He was among the first Jesuits to return to Montreal in 1842, and was the first to go directly to the Native people. The Ojibway called him Waiassahkang ("The Enlightener").

Jesuit Sources / Courtesy of Anishinabe Spiritual Centre

When he died in 1954 at the age of 100 years and four months, Joseph Richard, s.j., was the oldest living Jesuit in the world. He held the record of sixty-seven years on the Northern Ontario Missions, most of which he had spent travelling by dog-sled.

Courtesy of Xavier High School, New York

Henri Hudon (1823–1896) was born in Rivière Ouelle, Lower Canada, in 1823. He was the second Canadian-born novice to enter the Society after the return of the Jesuits in 1842. He served for over twenty years at St. Francis College in New York, and in 1880, as Superior of the Independent Canadian Mission, he became the first Canadian-born Major Superior in the Society of Jesus.

The Archive of the Jesuits in Canada / Archives des jésuites au Canada

In 1902, the renowned author and preacher Edward J. Devine, S.J. (1860–1927), was asked to minister to the miners on the gold rush in Alaska and along the Klondike in Yukon. His books in English and French relating his adventures there became bestsellers in New York and Paris.

The Archive of the Jesuits in Canada / Archives des jésuites au Canada

Richard Baxter, S.J. (1821–1904), entered the Jesuit novitiate in 1845, the first anglophone candidate to the Canadian mission. He founded the parish of St. Andrew, Port Arthur, in 1875, and spent thirty-three years on the mission in Northern Ontario. In addition, he was responsible for the construction of St. Patrick's Church, Fort William (Thunder Bay), Ontario.

The Archive of the Jesuits in Canada / Archives des jésuites au Canada

The sanctuary of St. Andrew's Church, Port Arthur (Thunder Bay), Ontario, founded by Richard Baxter, S.J., at Port Arthur's Landing, 1875.

The Archive of the Jesuits in Canada / Archives des jésuites au Canada

William ("Bill") P. Maurice, S.J. (1916–2008), spent over sixty-six years among the Native people, mostly at Spanish and Fort William, Ontario. He was a captivating storyteller to young teenagers. He became the leading genealogist of the Ojibway, and his records have been entrusted to the diocese of Thunder Bay, Ontario, where they are available for consultation.

The Archive of the Jesuits in Canada / Archives des jésuites au Canada

John A. Veltri, S.J. (1933–2008), keeps score during sports championship activities at the Spanish Residential School, Spanish, Ontario, in 1959.

Loyola High School Archives

A formal picture taken of a typical high school class to help promote the campaign to raise $300,000.00 launched by Fr. William H. Hingston in 1918.

The Archive of the Jesuits in Canada / Archives des jésuites au Canada

Collège Sainte-Marie / St. Mary's College

This building, designed and built by Fr. Félix Martin and opened on April 28, 1850, saw the origin, in 1851, of the School of law, which became the "Succursale Laval" in 1876. It in turn evolved into the Université de Montréal in 1921. Also, Loyola College grew out of it in 1896, Collège Saint-Ignace in 1927 and Collège Jean-de-Brébeuf in 1928.

Regiopolis College, Kingston, Ontario, 1960s. It was established in 1837; the Jesuits taught at and administered the college from 1931 to 1971.

St. Paul's College, Ellice and Vaughan, Winnipeg, 1950s. The college opened on Selkirk Avenue in 1926, and moved to Ellice and Vaughan in 1931. The Jesuits assumed responsibility for the college in 1933.

Don Doll, S.J.

Interior view of the Canadian Martyrs' Shrine, Midland, Ontario, which opened in 1926.

Moussa Faddoul

The Martyrs' Shrine, Midland, was solemnly inaugurated on 17 June 1926 by seven Canadian bishops led by Archbishop Neil McNeil of Toronto and a congregation of some 13,000 pilgrims.

Budd Watson, Watson Studios, Midland

Dr. Wilfrid Jury, of the department of archaeology at the University of Western Ontario, began a four-year dig at Sainte-Marie in 1949. His extensive discoveries form the basis of the scholarly conclusions that now guide our understanding of the mission at Sainte-Marie.

National Film Board of Canada

The archaeologist Denis A. Hegarty, S.J. (1907–1996), discovered the graves of saints Jean de Brébeuf and Gabriel Lalemant on 16 August 1954, nine years before the decision to restore Fort Sainte-Marie, Midland. He is seen here by the tombstone donated by the Knights of Columbus to cover the site.

Photo by Erica Zlomislic

In 1937, the old Stanley House Hotel on Lake Joseph in the Muskoka Lakes region of Ontario had become the summer "villa" for the Scholastics at the Jesuit Seminary, Toronto. Later, in 1971, it became Camp Ekon, named after St. Jean de Brébeuf, as a Jesuit summer training camp for boys.

St. Kateri Tekakwitha, a young Mohawk woman who became a Christian in 1676, was revered as a saint in her lifetime. In 2012, she was canonized by Pope Benedict XVI. Her statue adorns a Native prayer-garden on the grounds of Martyrs' Shrine, Midland.

Staff of Martyrs' Shrine

Ashley and Crippen Photographers

Martin J. Royackers, S.J. (1959–2001), is unique in the history of the English-speaking Canadian Jesuits in that he is the only one among them to be assassinated because of the ministry he had espoused. On 20 June 2001 he was shot at point-blank range outside his church in Annotto Bay, Jamaica.

Budd Watson, Watson Studios, Midland

2 May 1967. Pedro Arrupe, Superior General of the Society of Jesus, accompanied by the three Canadian Provincial Superiors (Montreal, Quebec, Upper Canada), his Vicar General, also a Canadian, and other assistants, guided by Denis A. Hegarty, S.J., prays at St. Ignace, Huronia, on the site of the deaths of the Jesuit saints Jean de Brébeuf and Gabriel Lalemant.

Attributed to Pat Sharp, S.J. / The Archive of the Jesuits in Canada / Archives des jésuites au Canada

During August 1967, two dozen Jesuit Scholastics from the three Canadian Provinces (Montreal, Quebec, Upper Canada) commemorated the historic canoe route between Quebec and Sainte-Marie among the Hurons by paddling some 925 kilometres from Sainte-Marie to the Christian Pavilion at Expo 67, Montreal. On his own historic visit to Canada that year, the Superior General of the Jesuits, Pedro Arrupe, while wishing to encourage them, helped beach their canoe!

The Jesuits had been invited by Archbishop Patrick J. Skinner, C.J.M., who appointed J. Frederick Lynch, S.J., as the first pastor. Lynch was also the Superior for the twelve-man Jesuit Community. In the following letter addressed to Gordon George, the Provincial Superior, we get a taste of what it was like when Lynch arrived to establish the Jesuit presence in St. John's:

> Here I am, having arrived yesterday at 10:20 a.m.; met at the airport by Monsignor Summers, who seemed jubilant; then met Archbishop here & he was happy to see me. I have been made welcome by all the priests whom I have met. This morning His Grace called me for a reasurring [sic] chat. Then Monsignor Summers discussed business with me for about two hours. There is no question of Ours being most welcome. You & Fr. Crusoe left a lasting impression on all. I haven't called on the Brothers but shall do so soon. Buildings. The school is enclosed & is assured for August. … The residence to be built … Monsignor Summers thinks we should begin by September to have building done for 1963. … Residence for this year (Assumption Convent). I have seen the building only from the outside. … [T]his convent will not be ready for occupation by us until August 15. So would you please have Fr. Devlin notify all those assigned coming here not to plan to come before Aug. 20, let us say. … Monsignor Summers & I think that Fr. Kevin McKenna should come as soon as convenient to make plans, etc … So Father Kevin can come & stay with me here at the palace. … The parish, as of Dec. 31, 1962, had 490 families and about 2,000 souls.[78]

To commemorate the Jesuit presence and the official start of a parish, Archbishop Skinner officially opened the parish on 2 September 1962 at the 10:30 a.m. Mass. When the Jesuits arrived, their residence had not been completed, so they lived at 50 St. Bonaventure Avenue until June 1963, when they moved into the newly completed Jesuit residence.

---

78 J. Frederick Lynch, S.J., letter to Provincial, 1 June 1962, AJC, Box F-631.

The parish boundaries were carved out of the basilica parish, and became one of the most desirable areas in the city in which to reside. In fact, when a house went up for sale, it was not uncommon to see the advertisement include the description "in St. Pius X Parish". Lynch encouraged the formation of the Ladies' and Men's Associations, both of which worked hard to find the funding to run an active, growing parish as well as an expanding school population. Mary Skinner was the first president of the Ladies' Association and Hubert Kelly the first president of the Men's. In 1967, the St. Pius X Boys' School, situated along Elizabeth Avenue, was opened, and its administration was given to the Christian Brothers, with Br. John G. Buckingham, C.F.C., as its first principal. The original elementary school was then designated as the St. Pius X Girls' School. In 1970, Lynch was reassigned to work among the First Nations people in northern Ontario; he was replaced by Leonard J. Fischer, S.J., who had been the Novice Master in Guelph for many Jesuits. The highlight of his tenure in St. John's was the building, opening, and blessing of the new church. Although planning for the new church began in 1968 under Lynch's leadership, it was Fischer who brought it to completion in 1976.

The church was designed by architect Angus Campbell and included a number of features based on the liturgical renewal following the Second Vatican Council. It was comprised of the main church, which placed the pews on an incline towards the main altar, a smaller chapel all on the same level for everyday worship, a sacristy, offices, washrooms, and a library. It was so designed that it could be adapted for a variety of uses, such as parish meetings, school concerts, recitals, and audio-visual presentations. This was accomplished by having a movable divider so that the main church could be separated from the chapel, where the Blessed Sacrament was reserved. The official opening and blessing of the new church took place on 1 December 1976 in the presence of Archbishop Skinner of St. John's, Bishop Richard Thomas McGrath of St. George's, and Bishop Alphonsus Penney of Grand Falls. The old 1955 chapel area was renovated, and a large kitchen, washrooms, and other facilities were incorporated into the space so that it could be used as a school gym as well as a parish hall for various parish activities and meetings. Fischer was also responsible for the establishment in 1970 of the parish's first formal finance committee and the parish council. Over the years, the finance committee took on more responsibility for the financial affairs, freeing the pastor to focus his attention on the spiritual needs of the parish. The Catholic Women's League was introduced into Newfoundland in May 1974, and when the charter was granted to St. Pius X Parish, Mary Goss was the first president of the parish chapter.

Fischer continued as pastor until 1982, when he was assigned to the First Nations ministry in northern Ontario, following in Lynch's footsteps again. At a Eucharistic Celebration on 28 July 1982, Archbishop Alphonsus Penney dedicated the parish library to Fischer, honouring his many years of ministry at the parish. William J. Browne, S.J., replaced Fischer. Browne was a native son of Newfoundland, the son of the well-known "Billy" Browne, a politician and judge. It was during Browne's time as pastor that Pope John Paul II visited St. John's on 11 and 12 September 1984, and commemorated the 200th anniversary of the establishment of the Catholic Church in Newfoundland. Three years later, the twenty-fifth anniversary of the canonical founding of St. Pius X Parish was marked by a variety of events: a special Mass of thanksgiving with Archbishop Penney, the publication of a parish directory that included listings of parish staff, organizations, committees, and photos of family groups along with a listing of parishioners, and a new pipe organ by Casavant Frères. The latter was controversial and almost divided the parish, as some thought it was an unnecessary expense since it involved renovations to the choir area of the main church. The inaugural organ recital was given by Patricia Fowler on 25 October 1987.

St. Pius X Parish has been, and continues to be, heavily involved in the social issues of St. John's as well as in needs around the world. Regarding the latter, it has given much assistance to Canadian Jesuit missions in Darjeeling, India, and an archdiocesan mission in Peru, as well as sponsoring a Vietnamese refugee family in 1979. In response to the terrorist attacks on the United States on 11 September 2001, the church and hall were opened to receive passengers from flights diverted from American airspace. During Browne's term as pastor, the parish assumed responsibility for Mount Scio-Nagel's Hill when the church in the area, Our Lady of Lourdes, was closed. A major development was the building of a community centre, Brophy Place, now known as MacMorran Community Centre, which became the focal point of the parish's commitment to the area. Browne was the first Jesuit to move into the neighbourhood, and was followed by Brother James McSheffrey, S.J., who resided there until his tragic death in 1999. Also tied into this outreach was the Assistance to the Neighbourhood (ATTN) committee, founded in 1976, which had taken on the commitment to provide material assistance, food, and clothing to families in need. With the addition of Mount Scio to the parish boundaries, much of the committee's efforts were now directed to this area through the generous support of parishioners. In 1988, the Catholic Women's League presented a statue of Our Lady to the parish. It was placed in an attractive setting near the entrance to the chapel. The Knights of Columbus assisted with the installation of the statue. This addition helped to make more attractive the area around the side of the church, which was dominated by the parking lot that was used by both parish and schools.

From the beginning, the parish was involved with education supporting the elementary school when it was divided into the Boys' and Girls' schools. They also were open to allow Gonzaga Regional High School to use the parish facilities for school Masses and for special days such as the Ocean Ranger Oil Rig Disaster Memorial. The Sisters of Mercy continued administering the Girls' School until 1978, and the Christian Brothers the Boys' School until 1982, when the shortage of vocations meant that both groups had to withdraw their commitment. It was after this that the elementary schools were combined into one co-educational institution: one for elementary students and one for junior high students. After two bitterly fought referenda in the late 1990s, the schools were confiscated by the Tobin government, and a secular public board was established in 1998. This ended the parish's involvement in these schools. The Jesuits withdrew from Gonzaga Regional High School the same year, since they could no longer conduct a Catholic school. The original school building was returned to the parish, but the building along Elizabeth Avenue was kept by the school board and continued as a school. Its name, however, was changed from St. Pius X to Rennies River School.

The loss of Catholic schools meant that religious education was now the responsibility of the parents. The small religious education programme that St. Pius X Parish had developed under Donald F. Beaudois, S.J., the pastor from 1988 to 1992, was expanded under Wayne J. Bolton, S.J., into a programme that educated over 300 students each Sunday. It was directed by Maria Kelsey. All of the teachers were volunteer parents who, along with other parents, took their responsibility to heart and shared their time and energy to offer a religious programme for the children. One of the outstanding areas at St. Pius X has been liturgical music. In the early years, the choir directors were Dr. Norman Brown and Dr. Ignatius Rumboldt, while in more recent times, graduates of the School of Music at Memorial University have continued the high standards. The Jesuit pastors who followed Beaudois were John D. Lynch, Wayne Bolton, Michael J. O'Donnell and, for a second time around, Bolton. Over the years, twenty-four Jesuit priests have served in the parish.

Our Lady of Lourdes Parish, Toronto

In March of 1969, after the death of Michael J. Hawkins, S.J., at Waubaushene, the Provincial Superior, Angus J. Macdougall, asked Edward Dowling, his Socius or Assistant, to speak to Bishop Fulton, the personnel director for the archdiocese of Toronto, about naming a new pastor for Waubaushene and Christian Island. Dowling was also to discuss further ways in which the Jesuits could collaborate in the pastoral work of the archdiocese. A further conversation took place on 14 June 1969, at which time the archdiocese proposed Our Lady of Lourdes, one of Toronto's oldest parishes, to be the parish administered by the Jesuits. Although a number of other parishes were considered, it was felt that "the particular apostolic opportunities of 'Lourdes' would be best undertaken by a religious community—a number of hospitals, including the Princess Margaret, and the new St. James Town housing project (a complex of high rise apartments which, when completed, will provide accommodation for nearly 20,000 persons)."[79]

79 Edward F. Sheridan, S.J., letter to Philip F. Pocock, 17 September 1969, AJC, Box F-629. Although Sheridan followed Macdougall as Provincial Superior, that change did not take place until 26 September 1969. Also in this same archival box can be found the agreement between the archdiocese and the Jesuits, signed by Sheridan on 26 September 1969.

With the approval of his Consultors, the Provincial Superior accepted the offer on 30 June, but it was not until 17 September that Archbishop Philip F. Pocock was informed of the decision. The latter came in a letter from Edward F. Sheridan, S.J., who was writing on behalf of Macdougall.[80] Clarence P. Hinphy, S.J., was named pastor, with Joseph L. Clarke, S.J., who had been appointed port chaplain in 1968, and Ernest C. Tyler, S.J., as assistants.

The Church of Our Lady of Lourdes, which was also known from 1958 onwards as the Shrine of Our Lady of Lourdes, was located on Sherbourne Street in Toronto. The church had a long and distinguished history before the Jesuits arrived. It had begun as a parish in 1886; the original church was planned by Frederick Charles Law, a commander in the Royal Navy and secretary of the lieutenant governor. It had been designed to hold 300 people at a cost of $40,000.00, an amount covered by the priests of the diocese to commemorate John J. Lynch's twenty-fifth anniversary as bishop; he was also the city's first archbishop. The first pastor had been Joseph F. McBride, the archbishop's secretary, a tradition that continued for a number of years. The church was modelled after the church of Santa Maria del Populo in Rome. Later, James Cardinal McGuigan of Toronto was to have that Roman church as his titular church, an interesting coincidence. The church was expanded in 1910, when the nave was added by the Reverend Hugh Canning, who worked with architect James P. Hynes.

Hinphy arrived in the parish only in mid October. He proved to be an experienced pastor and a good organizer, setting a solid foundation for the Jesuits who followed him. He had been in Vancouver as pastor, waiting for John "Jack" F. McCaffrey, S.J., to arrive from the Martyrs' Shrine in Midland so Hinphy could induct him into the parish before departing for Toronto. Tyler had arrived at Our Lady of Lourdes in September to start work there. The Jesuits were hardly in the parish before Sheridan, now Provincial Superior, began musing on whether the parish might be a good site for a house of studies for Jesuit Scholastics:

80 Ibid., 53.

> The thought struck me, that there might be a possibility (I would hardly make it a probability) of using the land and the location of O. L. of L. Parish church & rectory for the location of a new residence for our scholastics if it became advisable to move downtown. It might not be impossible to erect a ten story apt. bldg. or residence bldg, which would house our scholastics,—perhaps some diocesan and other students of theology for the ministry … I say this confidentially—talk about it would start a rare spate of rumours.[81]

Observing the agreement with the archdiocese, Sheridan wrote the following to the archbishop in December 1971:

> At the last meeting with my Board of Province consultors, we reviewed our acceptance (on trial and for a triennium) of responsibility for Our Lady of Lourdes Parish. I am glad to report that there was unanimity in favour of continuing this ministry, if this be satisfactory to Your Grace, and this indefinitely, the matter to be reviewed triennially.

In 1973, Joseph C. Johnson, S.J., became the pastor, and began a series of renovations to bring the church closer to those proposed by the Second Vatican Council. Nine years later, Terence G. Walsh, S.J., was appointed pastor. It was he who presided over the centennial celebrations in 1986. Earlier, in a letter dated 26 January 1976 to the Jesuit Superior General, Pedro Arrupe, Walsh, who was then Provincial Superior, had given his analysis of the situation of the parish:

> The parish is located in an area where there are many Catholics—no one has ever been able to find out just how many, since a good number do not attend Mass regularly, large numbers are in apartments and tend to move about a good deal, a great many are immigrants to Canada from the Philippines, India, Pakistan, West Indies and Latin America and it is not in their tradition to be numbered!
>
> The apostolate is traditional since there is a need for the old and the traditional for this group of parishioners. While we would like to do something new and daring, we know the

81 Edward F. Sheridan, S.J., letter to Clarence Hinphy, S.J., 29 January 1970, AJC, Box F-629.

> approach has to be gradual lest the new Canadians be alienated from the faith they have known and loved in their own countries… . So the real problem for Ours is to help these people assimilate Canadian ways without substituting materialistic values for their own more simple and more Christian ones.[82]

Walsh's analysis of the situation at Lourdes laid the groundwork for his contribution to the parish. He was replaced by Patrick Byrne, S.J., who focused on hospital and charismatic ministry. The parish not only had the Wellesley and Princess Margaret hospitals within its boundaries, but also the Grace Hospital, as well as two publicly supported parochial schools. Some Jesuit Scholastics became involved in the parish, both working and living there, but not quite in the way Sheridan had mused in his letter of 1970. For the academic year 1977–1978, for instance, Bolton, on staff at the parish, wrote to Walsh that the Scholastics were involved in baptismal preparation, music, adult education, and visitations in the parish and schools.[83]

In 1991, Robert "Bert" G. Foliot, S.J., became pastor, and once more, renovations were under way in the church. That was not, however, Foliot's only focus, as he was responsible for the growth in social ministry and the development of the food bank. The number of parishioners volunteering in the parish grew during this period, reflecting the growth of parish outreach programmes. Eight years later, William M. Addley, S.J., became pastor. He was responsible for the renovation of the parish halls, which was a great addition to the needs and work of the parish. In the new millennium, the number of volunteers reached 1,500 working in a variety of areas in the parish. Some 300 parishioners now attend daily Mass, and over ten times that number on the weekends. Addley's death on 21 January 2012 while in office was deeply felt in the parish, as witnessed by the large number of parishioners who attended the wake and funeral. Michael A. Coutts, S.J., became the acting pastor until the new pastor, John A. Sullivan, S.J., could take office a few months later.

---

82 Terence G. Walsh, S.J., letter to Pedro Arrupe, s.j., 26 January 1976, ibid.

83 Wayne Bolton, S.J., report to Terence G. Walsh, S.J., ibid.

A unique situation developed in the parish, whereby some in the Hindu community have adopted Our Lady of Lourdes for visits and petition offerings, especially for a pregnancy or a safe birth. Although not Catholic, they identify with Mary who gave birth in difficult circumstances, thus becoming a special patron for them. Today, Our Lady of Lourdes is truly a vibrant, active, and welcoming parish. Besides the regular parish staff assigned to it, a number of Jesuits, both those living in residence and in other Jesuit communities, help out. At various times, such as confessions during Advent and Lent, there are as many as twelve to fifteen Jesuit confessors available.

Holy Rosary Parish, Guelph, Ontario

The penultimate parish to be taken on by the Jesuits was Holy Rosary Parish in Guelph, Ontario. The parish was originally founded in 1956 by Bishop Joseph Francis Ryan of Hamilton, and had been placed under the direction of the Holy Spirit (Ghost) Fathers, also known as the Spiritans. The first pastor was Thomas Clarkin, C.S.Sp. In the beginning, Mass was held in the Assembly Hall of John F. Ross Collegiate, and then, in 1957, in the newly opened parish hall. In 1964, the new church and rectory were officially opened. The parish grew from 300 families in 1956 to 1,500 families in 1981, the twenty-fifth anniversary of its inception. The establishment of Holy Rosary School in 1955 preceded the founding of the parish itself. The school began with 200 students housed in six classrooms; by 1964, it consisted of 558 students in fourteen classrooms. In 1968, a second school, St. Patrick, was established to help accommodate the growing number of students. The Spiritans administered the parish until June 1999, after which it was administered for a year by the Reverend William Trusz of the diocese of Hamilton. In 2000, the Jesuits were assigned the parish, with Bernard F. Carroll, S.J., as the first Jesuit pastor. He was replaced by Vernon P. Boyd, S.J., in 2010. Since the arrival of the Jesuits, six other Jesuits have served or been in residence in the parish: Christopher Rupert, Daryl Miranda, Joseph A. Brzezicki, Leonard J. Fischer, John W. McCarthy, and Roger A. Yaworski.

Under Jesuit administration, the parish has been involved in adult faith development, leadership training programmes, the Spiritual

Exercises of St. Ignatius Loyola, social outreach, and global justice issues. In 2002, the Catholic Women's League of the parish celebrated its fortieth anniversary, and in 2003, the Catechesis of the Good Shepherd programme for children was established. The parish marked its fiftieth anniversary in 2006, by which point it served 3,500 people (or 1,200 families) and had thirty-four active committees representing many needs of the parish and wider community. Though they reside in the parish rectory next to the church, the Jesuits in the parish are part of the Guelph Jesuit Community, centred at the old Ignatius College site on Highway 6.

St. Peter's, Thunder Bay, Ontario

The most recent parish to be taken on by the Jesuits in English Canada was St. Peter's Parish in Thunder Bay, Ontario. Their involvement continued the long tradition of the Jesuits working in that area of the country. Though founded in 1906 under its first pastor, François Maynard, s.j. (1907–1914), who had been assistant at St. Patrick's Church in Fort William, he was soon appointed by Bishop David J. Scollard to St. Peter's to serve Slovaks who had immigrated to work on the railway. An interesting story in its ninetieth-anniversary booklet, entitled *St. Peter's Church / Farnost' Sv. Petra, 1908–1998,* recounts how Maynard helped a parishioner, Peter Bela, who was alone in Canada and in desperate need after both of his legs were amputated after a railway accident. Maynard welcomed Bela into the rectory, arranged for him to obtain artificial limbs, and had him retrained as a tailor. On 23 June 1917, Bela entered the Jesuits as a Brother, and was at St. Stanislaus Novitiate on 7 June 1918 during the infamous Guelph raid.[84] He was thoroughly interrogated by the military, and had to report regularly to the Guelph police since he was considered to be an enemy alien during the Great War.

Maynard was the only Jesuit to administer the parish until 2005, when Gerald McDougall, S.J., arrived to be pastor; the parish rectory became a Jesuit Community for the immediate area. In between Maynard and McDougall, the parish had been under the direction of

84 Horatio P. Phelan, S.J., "The Guelph Novitiate Raid" in AJC, Montreal.

diocesan clergy until 1934, when the Benedictines had taken it over. The latter administered it until 1950, when it reverted to the diocesan clergy. After serving as pastor for two years, McDougall was replaced in 2007 by Wayne Bolton, S.J., who remained until 2010, when he was reassigned as pastor at St. Pius X Parish in St. John's. With no Jesuits to replace Bolton at St. Peter's, the administration of the parish once again returned to the diocesan clergy.

*

As mentioned at the beginning, this chapter has dealt only with those parishes that were listed in the annual Jesuit catalogues and that were considered to be a corporate responsibility of the Jesuit Mission, Vice Province, or Province. Not included are many parishes that were mission stations but dependent upon a central Jesuit parish or Community, such as the many mission stations in the territory around Guelph that were serviced by the Jesuits associated with St. Bartholomew's Parish and, later, with the Church of Our Lady Immaculate. This same configuration is evident, too, at the parishes in Sandwich, Sault Ste. Marie, and again in Fort William. As well, due to constraints of space, not included are those parishes that individual Jesuits undertook to administer but were discontinued when that individual Jesuit was no longer available to serve there. Also not included are those parishes where Jesuits helped out on the weekends, coming from the schools and colleges to "supply" in one parish or another when help was requested.

What is clearly evident in this chapter is the extent of the work of the Jesuits in parish ministry across Canada, literally from coast to coast. Many of those parishes acted as a base for other apostolic work, demonstrated by the multitude of activities in the parishes, a methodology that also was accomplished through the schools and colleges. Saint Ignatius Loyola, the founder of the Jesuits, wanted his men to be available for the Church's most urgent tasks, and thus to do so, the Jesuit must be able to move to take up the new task. For this reason, the history of each Jesuit parish is unique. Its duration could be short, as in the case of St. Peter's in Thunder Bay where, after five years, it was handed over to the diocese, or it could have a long Jesuit association, such as the parish in Winnipeg, which has been under Jesuit administration since 1908. Today, at the writing of this chapter, only four of the twenty-one Jesuit parishes whose history has been recounted remain a Jesuit responsibility. The other seventeen have been handed over to the local diocesan administration, thus fulfilling the vision of Saint Ignatius in Canada, which allows the Jesuits to move continually to new fields of labour in the vineyard of the Lord.

IV

"Do Justice. Love Kindness": A Faith that Does Justice: Jesuit Social Apostolate in English Canada, 1842–2014[1]

Dr. Peter Baltutis

The social apostolate—bringing the Gospel message to society—has always been an integral part of the mission of the Society of Jesus. According to Saint Ignatius Loyola (1491–1556) in *The Formula of the Institute*, the charter for establishing the Society, a Jesuit "should show himself ready to reconcile the estranged, compassionately assist and serve those who are in prisons or hospitals, and indeed, to perform any other works of charity, according to what will seem expedient for the glory of God and the common good."[2]

1 The author wishes to thank Matthew Livingstone, S.J., and John Perry, S.J., who conducted initial research into this topic and prepared earlier drafts of this chapter. The author would also like to express his gratitude to William Ryan, S.J., who was interviewed throughout the research and writing of this piece.

2 "The Formula of the Institute", in *The Constitutions of the Society of Jesus and Their Complementary Norms*, ed. John W. Padberg (St. Louis: Institute of Jesuit Sources, 1996), no. 1.

This emphasis on working with "the estranged" for "the common good of society" would form an essential characteristic of Jesuit ministry. In 1975, "Decree 4" of the Thirty-Second General Congregation of the Society of Jesus (GC 32) famously declared "the service of faith, of which the promotion of justice is an absolute requirement", to be the priority among Jesuit ministries. It thus made social concern the major focus of all Jesuit ministry.[3] In the intervening centuries between Ignatius and GC 32, Catholic social teaching experienced significant development and evolution.

This chapter chronicles how the Jesuits engaged in social ministry in English Canada from the time of their return in 1842 to the present. Utilizing records from the Archives of the Jesuits in Canada, this chapter demonstrates that the Jesuit social apostolate in English Canada moved through three distinct stages. First, throughout the nineteenth and early twentieth centuries, the Canadian Jesuits operated on a model of "charity" that was concerned with helping individual persons through the traditional corporal acts of mercy. Recipients of this charity included thousands of Irish Catholics escaping famine in 1847, the Depression-era poor of Montreal, and Europeans rebuilding after the Second World War. Second, inspired by the papal encyclicals *Rerum Novarum* (1891) and *Quadragesimo Anno* (1931), which called upon Catholics to reconstruct the social order (a task clearly beyond the scope of private piety or the personal exercise of charity), the Jesuits established a Catholic Labour School in Toronto that sought to reform society through workers' education and the spreading of Catholic social teaching. Third, influenced by Vatican II and subsequent post-conciliar documents, Decree 4 of GC 32 shifted Jesuit ministry beyond reforming society to transforming social structures to bring about the spiritual and material liberation of their fellow human beings. The urgency to address social injustice in 1975 led the Canadian Jesuits into a deeper commitment to justice, new thinking about the social apostolate, and new forms of social action.

3 "General Congregation 32; Section 1; Decree 4: Our Mission Today: The Service of Faith and the Promotion of Justice", in *Jesuit Life & Mission Today: The Decrees & Accompanying Documents of the 31st–35th General Congregations of the Society of Jesus*, ed. John W. Padberg (St. Louis: Institute of Jesuit Sources, 2009), no. 2.

In identifying key moments and individuals in the history of the Jesuit social apostolate, some important limits must be placed on the scope of this investigation. This chapter will focus on the social ministry of the Jesuits to English-speaking Canadians; thus, Jesuit work with the francophone population is excluded. Furthermore, while a number of Jesuits from English Canada have been involved in important social justice ministries throughout Latin America, Africa, and Asia, this chapter will be limited to work done on Canadian soil. Finally, an important component of the Jesuit social apostolate is working with those people who have been marginalized from society, which often includes aboriginal peoples. The Jesuits have a long relationship with the First Nations of Canada. Due to the unique nature of this apostolate, the Jesuit ministry to native people has been given its own chapter.

Early Jesuit Social Ministries in Montreal and Beyond (1842–1950)

In 1842, the Society of Jesus returned to Canada at the invitation of Bishop Ignace Bourget of Montreal. According to Bishop Bourget's *Appel aux Jésuites* of 2 July 1841, the Jesuits were summoned for the purpose of resuming two historical ministries for which their predecessors in New France had become famous: education and native ministries.[4] Father Jan Roothaan, S.J., the Superior General of the Society of Jesus in Rome, approved Bishop Bourget's request and dispatched six priests and three brothers—under the supervision of Father Pierre Chazelle, S.J. (1789–1845)—to Montreal.[5] This early Jesuit community would succeed in fulfilling its original mandate of creating a school (the bilingual Collège Sainte-Marie in Montreal in 1848) and working with aboriginal peoples throughout Canada East and Canada West. (Upon the invitation of Bishop Michael Power of the newly erected diocese of Toronto, several Jesuits also travelled to Walpole Island, near Windsor, Wikwemikong on Manitoulin Island,

4 Gilles Chaussé, « Les Jésuites et le projet de société de Mgr. Bourget, » *Sessions d'étude – Société d'histoire de l'Église catholique,* vol. 53 (1986) : 45–46.

5 "Chazelle, Pierre" in DJB, vol. 1, 57–58.

and Sault Ste. Marie.)[6] Over the next forty-five years, 109 Jesuit priests and brothers from ten nations served in the Canadian missions, building churches, schools, and hospitals to minister to European settlers and native peoples.[7]

During this period, the ministries of the Jesuits regularly moved beyond the "spiritual" concerns of Catholics into ministries that could be described as "social." These social apostolates, however, operated with a "charity" mentality of reactively providing direct assistance to the material and physical needs of individual poor persons through the corporal acts of mercy (inspired by Matt. 25:31-46).[8] For example, the early Jesuit community in Montreal encountered an unexpected humanitarian crisis when, from 1845 to 1850, tens of thousands of Irish Catholics arrived in Montreal, escaping mass starvation and disease caused by the infamous potato famine. During the high point of the exodus in 1847, known popularly as "Black '47", approximately 104,000 Irish migrated to the major port cities of Canada, with most of the famine migrants—approximately 80,000—disembarking in Quebec.[9] These Irish, who were predominantly Catholic, were shunned by the population of Montreal because they carried with them the deadly diseases of typhoid and cholera. At Grosse Île (a quarantine station located 48 kilometres from Quebec City), Dr. George Douglas, the chief medical officer, estimated that in 1847 alone, 5,424 migrants died from typhoid while in quarantine.[10] Due to the long incubation period of the disease, those who were released from quarantine quickly spread the communicable disease throughout the growing Irish community of Montreal. For those Irish Catholics who survived the epidemic, many were denied work or discriminated against because they were a "double minority": a religious minority in (mainly

---

6 "du Ranquet, Dominique Chardon" in DJB, vol. 1, 101–102.

7 Terence J. Fay, *A History of Canadian Catholics: Gallicanism, Romanism, and Canadianism* (Montreal & Kingston: McGill-Queen's University Press, 2002), 79.

8 The corporal acts of mercy include feeding the hungry, sheltering the homeless, clothing the naked, visiting the sick and imprisoned, burying the dead, and giving alms to the poor. *Catechism of the Catholic Church* #2447.

9 Mark G. McGowan, "Irish Catholics", in *The Encyclopedia of Canada's Peoples*, ed. Robert Paul Magocsi (Toronto: University of Toronto Press, 1999), 743.

10 Ibid., 744.

Protestant) English-speaking Canada, and a linguistic minority in the (mainly French-speaking) Catholic Church.[11]

The Jesuits were among the first responders to the sick and dying Irish population in Montreal. Two Jesuit priests, Henri du Ranquet, S.J., and Paul Mignard, S.J. (who were sent from New York to the missions of Canada East), were especially active in ministering to the Irish directly in the fever sheds.[12] Overwhelmed by the epidemic, local Jesuit superior Félix Martin, S.J. (1804–1886), secured four additional Jesuits from the community in Fordham (New York City) to help minister (temporarily) to the burgeoning Irish population.[13] These priests were particularly valuable because they were fluent in English. After the plague had subsided, many of the children of these new Irish immigrants were enrolled in the newly opened Collège Sainte-Marie. In keeping with the tradition of the Jesuit *Ratio Studiorum* of 1599, no student was deprived of the opportunity to receive an education because of an inability to afford tuition. Thus, many of these Irish-Canadian students received a free education. Education represented a means of freeing themselves from poverty by offering them an opportunity for greater involvement in the Canadian social, political, and cultural life.[14]

Several other Jesuit ministries during the late nineteenth and early twentieth centuries also incorporated a "social" dimension. In 1898, Father Edward J. Devine, S.J. (1860–1927), organized young Catholic women into the "Loyola Literary and Art Club of Montreal" for social purposes, but also to perform charitable services. One of the pressing needs of the time that this group responded to was ministering to patients who were discharged from hospitals, but had no place to fully

---

11 John S. Moir, "The Problem of Double Minority: Some Reflections on the Development of the English-speaking Catholic Church in Canada in the Nineteenth Century", *Histoire sociale/ Social History* 7 (1971): 53–67. See also J.R. Miller, "Anti-Catholicism in Canada: From the British Conquest to the Great War", in *Creed and Culture: The Place of English-Speaking Catholics in Canadian Society, 1750–1930*, eds. Terrence Murphy and Gerald Stortz (Montreal and Kingston: McGill-Queen's University Press, 1993), 25–48.

12 T. P. Slattery, *Loyola and Montreal* (Montreal: Palm Publishers, 1962), 24.

13 Ibid., 25–26.

14 Paul Desjardins, *Le Collège Sainte-Marie de Montréal*, vol. 1 (Montreal: Collège Sainte-Marie, 1940), 31–33.

recover and heal.[15] This humble ministry of the Loyola Club to these "out-patients" eventually led to the creation of a twelve-bed Loyola Convalescent Home in 1914. Quickly outgrowing its original space, in 1929 the Home moved to a larger location (33 beds) that cared for 380 patients annually.[16] In 1933, this ministry secured private and civic funding, moved into a 104-bed pavilion, and was renamed the Montreal Convalescent Hospital.[17]

Another Jesuit involved in the social apostolate in Montreal was Father Joseph Fallon, S.J. (1894–1964). In 1923, during his years of studies in philosophy and theology at the Collège de l'Immaculée-Conception in Montreal, Fallon was asked by Coadjutor Archbishop Georges Gauthier of Montreal to organize a committee to provide aid for the unemployed.[18] Following the Wall Street stock market crash of 1929, in 1930 Father Fallon assisted in founding Montreal's Federation of Catholic Charities (FCC, later known as the Federation of Catholic Community Services) to care for the needs of the English-speaking Catholic community. The FCC was responsible for an annual fundraising campaign that gave financial help to a variety of volunteer associations that provided family welfare services, child care, employment, and an unemployed relief committee.[19] At the same time, Father Fallon helped establish Montreal's Catholic Men's Hostel and St. Martha's Home for destitute women and children.[20] The Men's Hostel and St. Martha's ensured emergency shelter for the unemployed or working Catholic men and women who were unable to afford accommodation. Food and clothing were supplied and, where possible, employment was found. In 1935, St. Martha's housed 170 women and thirty-seven babies.[21] By 1946, St. Martha's Home was caring for 676 adults and babies.[22]

---

15 "Devine, Edward J." in DJB, vol. 1, 85.

16 *Catholic Times*, Montreal, October 1989.

17 Ibid. In 1997, the Montreal Convalescent Hospital was renamed the Lindsay Rehabilitation Hospital. In 2008 it merged with the Institut de réadaptation de Montréal to form the Institut de réadaptation Gingras-Lindsay-de-Montréal (IRGLM).

18 "Fallon, Joseph" in DJB, vol. 1, 107.

19 *Catholic Times*, Montreal, October 1989.

20 Slattery, 254–255.

21 *Catholic Times*, Montreal, October 1989.

22 Ibid. In 1970, the government absorbed many of the family and childcare services. In 1974,

A final example of Jesuits responding to social problems during this early period was the creation of the Jesuit European Relief Appeal (JERA) in 1945 to help alleviate the widespread poverty in Europe in the wake of the Second World War. JERA began as the initiative of Jesuit scholastic Clarence Hinphy, S.J. (1913–1984),[23] in 1945—and was later administered by James Farrell, S.J. (1918–1996)[24]—as a response to the numerous appeals for food and clothing from wartorn Europe. Hinphy received permission to establish a Jesuit relief bureau at the Jesuit Seminary in Toronto that would collect, pack, and ship non-perishable foods, medicine, and clothing to centres at or near Jesuit institutions in Europe. Other Jesuit institutions from across English-speaking Canada provided assistance in collecting resources and raising funds: Campion College in Regina, St. Paul's College in Winnipeg, Regiopolis College in Kingston, Loyola College in Montreal, many Jesuit parishes throughout the country, and the Martyrs' Shrine in Midland, Ontario. *The Canadian Messenger of the Sacred Heart* carried advertisements appealing for Canadian Catholic laity to donate both resources and prayers for JERA. Sending out packages every two weeks, by 1949 JERA had shipped "215 tons of relief goods valued at $269,309.42. Shipments went to every country, from France to Poland and Greece, from Italy to England. Some small shipments found their way to Lebanon, Japan and South Africa."[25] The impressive work of JERA, on behalf of English-speaking Catholic Canadians, further illustrates the "charity" mentality of reacting to social problems by providing direct assistance to meet the immediate material needs of individual poor persons (in this case, providing emergency clothing and food to those affected by the Second World War).

Centraide assumed the role of principal fundraiser for numerous community groups; as a result, the Federation of Catholic Community Services Inc. divided its operation into the Catholic Community Services (CCS) and the Foundation of Catholic Community Services Inc. (FCCS). Today, CCS sponsors services to the elderly; family life services to parents, children, divorced and separated; youth programs and camps; and a referral service.

23 "Hinphy, Clarence P." in DJB, vol. 1, 141–142.

24 "Farrell, James J." in *Dictionary of Jesuit Biography: Ministry to English Canada, Volume II (1988–2006)* (Toronto: Canadian Institute of Jesuit Studies, 2007), 102.

25 "Europeans Grateful for Jesuit Relief, But Needs of Continent Still Great", *Ensign*, 26 March 1949, 14.

Early Catholic Social Teaching and the Jesuit Social Apostolate: Reforming the Social Order (1891–1962)

While Catholic concern for the poor has its roots in Scripture, in the teaching of the early Church Fathers, and in the political and social philosophy of medieval theologians, Pope Leo XIII's 1891 encyclical *Rerum Novarum* (*The Condition of Labour*) marked the beginning of official Catholic social teaching. In this landmark papal letter that addressed the inhumane situation of the poor and workers during the industrialization of Europe, Leo XIII outlined the guiding principles for the proper relationship among the state, employers, and workers. He insisted that the Church had a duty to intervene in social matters and that the state had a responsibility to intervene to defend those who suffered the most from the economic system.[26] Most importantly, the Pope pointed out that the structures and institutions of industry were themselves responsible for the wrongs in society, and hence had to change before justice could be attained for the working and poorer classes.[27] This signals a major shift in how the Church approached social problems. No longer were Catholics called to help the oppressed through individual acts of charity. Rather, *Rerum Novarum* challenged Catholics to reconstruct society altogether (a task that would have to engage people at all levels of society beyond their personal acts of piety or works of mercy).[28] Instead of focusing exclusively on the effects of social problems such as hunger and homelessness, Catholic "social justice" now promoted collective action to address the root causes of structural injustice (a flawed socio-economic system).

In 1931, Pope Pius XI commemorated the fortieth anniversary of *Rerum Novarum* by releasing *Quadragesimo Anno* (*On the Reconstructing of the Social Order*, sometimes called *After Forty*

---

26 Pope Leo XIII, "*Rerum Novarum: The Condition of Labour*", in *Catholic Social Thought: The Documentary Heritage*, eds. David J. O'Brien and Thomas A. Shannon (Maryknoll, NY: Orbis Books, 1992), #19–27.

27 E. F. Sheridan, *Love Kindness! The Social Teaching of the Canadian Catholic Bishops (1958–1989), A Second Collection* (Sherbrooke and Toronto: Éditions Paulines and Jesuit Centre for Social Faith and Justice, 1991), 17–18.

28 Thomas A. Shannon, "Commentary on *Rerum novarum (The Condition of Labour)*", in *Modern Catholic Social Teaching: Commentaries and Interpretations*, ed. Kenneth R. Himes (Washington, DC: Georgetown University Press, 2005), 134–146.

Years). Issued in the midst of the Great Depression, *Quadragesimo Anno* continued the attack on structural injustice begun by Leo XIII and confirmed the Church's solidarity with the cause of workers and the poor. The main concern for Pius XI was to eliminate conflict between workers and employers (a sharp distinction between Catholic social teaching and communism). To promote harmony between classes, Pius proposed an organic social order based on vocational groups (analogous to medieval guilds) that would organize workers and employers according to their function in society.[29] Also, it was in *Quadragesimo Anno* that Pius XI introduced the term "social justice", which referred to the set of conditions wherein each member of society is contributing, and enjoying, all that is necessary for the common good (rather than an individual's personal gain).[30] Articulated in traditional scholastic language, social justice was presented as a set of principles: the right to work; the right to own property; the right to join unions; the right to be paid a just family wage for work done; the duty of governments to work for the common good of all citizens; the obligation of the rich to help workers and the poor; etc.[31] While Pius XI went further than Leo XIII by being more insistent on the need for major structural change, he reaffirmed Leo's teachings on the organic unity of society and emphasized that collaboration, rather than class conflict, was the proper path for social renewal.[32]

It was not until the Twenty-Eighth General Congregation of the Society of Jesus (GC 28) in 1938 that the major legislative body of the Jesuits made "social justice"—as understood in *Rerum Novarum* and *Quadragesimo Anno*—fully part of the ministry of the Society. Its Decree 29 declared that social apostolic work should be commended to all, promoted everywhere, and considered among the most important ministries. To achieve this objective, GC 28 recommended that "centres for social action" (staffed by full-time Jesuits) should be

29 Pope Pius XI, "*Quadragesimo Anno*: After Forty Years", in *Catholic Social Thought: The Documentary Heritage*, eds. O'Brien and Shannon, #76–98.

30 Ibid., #88 and 137. The term "social justice" was first introduced by Luigi Taparelli d'Angelio, S.J., in the early 1840s.

31 Christine Firer Hinze, "Commentary on *Quadragesimo anno*", in *Modern Catholic Social Teaching: Commentaries and Interpretations*, ed. Himes, 167–168.

32 Joseph B. Gavin, S.J., "Catholic Social Teaching: 1891–1975", in *Promotio Iustitiae* 66 (February 1997): 7.

established to give spiritual help to workers and employers, explain the social teachings of the Church, and promote social groups and organizations.[33] The call for each province to establish a "centre for social action and research" was renewed in the Twenty-Ninth General Congregation (GC 29) in 1946.[34] Furthermore, since the Second World War prevented many provinces from implementing the calls of the previous two Congregations, the Jesuits' Superior General, Jean-Baptiste Janssens, S.J., sent a letter to the whole Society on 10 October 1949 renewing the call to set up centres of social action that would "teach the theoretical and practical social doctrine to others … by publishing books, by periodicals and various writings, by conferences, lectures, conventions, and the like, and it will strive to apply that doctrine to the needs of particular regions."[35] In his address, Janssens envisioned this orientation towards justice as being central to Jesuit ministry. "Therefore, before all else Ours [Jesuits] must be trained to that sincere active charity which is today called 'a social attitude' or 'social-mindedness.'"[36] The directives from the General Congregations and Father Janssens to promote social justice (as opposed to charity) would transform how the Jesuits of English-speaking Canada would respond to social problems.

In 1950, just a few months after the Instruction from Father Janssens, the Jesuits of Upper Canada created their first centre for social action. Father John L. Swain, S.J., the Provincial Superior, appointed Father Charles E. McGuire, S.J. (1905–1982), to be the founding Director of the Catholic Labour (Relations) School, which was located in the industrial city of Toronto. Recruiting speakers from the labour movement, senior management, government officials, clergy, and academia, Father McGuire developed a programme of courses that were offered during the evenings at St. Michael's Cathedral Choir School. The purpose of the School was to teach Catholic social doc-

33 GC 28 (1938), D.29 "On Ministries", no. 1–16, reprinted in *Promotio Iustitiae* 66 (February 1997): 18–21.

34 GC 29 (1946), D.29 "On the Social Apostolate", no. 1–5, reprinted in *Promotio Iustitiae* 66 (February 1997): 21–22.

35 "Instructions on the Social Apostolate" by Rev. Father General John Baptist Janssens, S.J., to all Provincials, 10 October 1949, no. 13, reprinted in *Promotio Iustitiae* 66 (February 1997): 31.

36 Ibid., no. 8.

trine and to prepare leaders who would have the confidence and social commitment to influence others.[37]

The curriculum of the Catholic Labour School was based on the principles found in *Rerum Novarum* and *Quadragesimo Anno*, and was intended to steer workers away from the dangers of communism. Father McGuire vigorously rejected communism's promotion of inevitable class warfare as the solution to the labour problems. Instead of violent conflict, McGuire argued that "labour and management must realize fully that they are in the same boat, though their short-run interest may differ. If both don't try to keep the boat afloat, it will sink."[38] Echoing the teachings of Leo XIII and Pius XI, McGuire's programme emphasized that fundamental co-operation (not antagonism) between labour and management was to be the basis for a new society.[39] While the first meeting had only eight people, attendance would fluctuate from 35 to 120 each semester (roughly half of the registered participants were from union locals, and the other half came from management).[40] In addition to the Labour School, Father McGuire gave many presentations at national labour conventions, made regular radio and television appearances, and often published editorials on labour relations.[41] After two decades of operation, the Catholic Labour School would close in 1970. By this date, Catholic social teaching, as articulated by Leo XIII and Pius XI and taught by Father McGuire—emphasizing the organic unity of society, cooperation, and shared values—had developed in new directions.

---

37 "McGuire, Charles E." in DJB, vol. 1, 228.

38 "Boss, Worker in the Same Boat: How Father McGuire Competes with Ed Sullivan", in *Financial Post*, February 1957, in AJC, B280 "McGuire, Charles 1905–1982".

39 "Catholic Labour School Changes Main Sessions to Monday Evening: How to Counter Communism Stressed on Encyclical Anniversary", in *Canadian Register*, 19 October 1957 in AJC-CDA, B280 "McGuire, Charles 1905–1982".

40 "Catholic Labour School, 1950–1970", in AJC, B280 "McGuire, Charles 1905–1982".

41 "Labour School Director Trans-Canada Speaker" in *Canadian Register*, 23 February 1957 and "Labour School Priest on Radio" in *Canadian Register*, 12 May 1956, in AJC, B280 "McGuire, Charles 1905–1982".

Vatican II and Post-Conciliar Catholic Social Teaching: Faith that Does Justice (1961–Present)

Catholic social teaching as expressed by Pope John XXIII, the Second Vatican Council, and Pope Paul VI brought forth a new understanding of social justice. John XXIII's *Mater et Magistra* (*Christianity and Social Progress*) in 1961 and *Pacem in Terris* (*Peace on Earth*) in 1963 expanded the scope of the Church's social concern from being limited exclusively to the problems of industrialization to a discussion of social problems that affected the whole human race (such as world peace, poverty, and political oppression).[42] He called on committed Christians and all people of goodwill to work together to address the severe imbalance between rich and poor nations and to promote world peace. Both of these encyclicals emphasized that justice must protect basic human rights.[43]

During the Second Vatican Council (1962–1965), the bishops of the world shifted Catholic social teaching away from the natural law tradition that understood justice as a list of rights and duties towards a biblically informed approach to social justice.[44] In *Gaudium et Spes* (*The Church in the Modern World*), the Church stressed that its mission in the world is to promote human life with dignity, to build up the solidarity of the human community, and to promote justice by seeking more humane and just conditions for human activity and work.[45] *Gaudium et Spes* called for greater sharing of resources among peoples, especially to provide poorer individuals and nations with

---

42 Pope John XXIII, "*Mater et Magistra: Christianity and Social Progress*", in *Catholic Social Thought: The Documentary Heritage*, eds. O'Brien and Shannon, #123–203, and Pope John XXIII, "*Pacem in Terris: Peace on Earth*", in *Catholic Social Thought: The Documentary Heritage*, eds. O'Brien and Shannon, #98–119.

43 Marvin L. Mich, "Commentary on *Mater et Magistra (Christianity and Social Progress)*" in *Modern Catholic Social Teaching: Commentaries and Interpretations*, ed. Himes, 205–11, and Drew Christiansen, "Commentary on *Pacem in Terris (Peace on Earth)*", in *Modern Catholic Social Teaching: Commentaries and Interpretations*, ed. Himes, 225–238.

44 Charles E. Curran, *Catholic Social Teaching, 1891–Present: A Historical, Theological, and Ethical Analysis* (Washington, DC: Georgetown University Press, 2002), 21–52.

45 Vatican Council II, "Pastoral Constitution on the Church in the Modern World" *(Gaudium et Spes)*, in *Vatican Council II: The Basic Sixteen Documents: A Completely Revised Translation in Inclusive Language*, ed. Austin Flannery, O.P. (New York: Costello Publishing Company, 1996), #11–45.

the means to help and develop themselves. Only in this way would humanity be led to a more just and peaceful society.[46]

The post-conciliar Church pushed social justice towards a "liberationist" position. In his 1967 encyclical *Populorum Progressio* (*On the Development of Peoples*), Pope Paul VI addressed the challenge of developing nations. He stated that justice for these poor was not limited to economic growth, but included the freedom to reach their true potential.[47] Picking up this theme, the Latin American Bishops (CELAM) who met in Medellín, Colombia, in 1968 expressed the theological concept that is now known as the "preferential option for the poor."[48] These bishops not only adopted the perspective of the poor in observing socio-economic situations, but also took on an "activist dimension" that called upon the Church to support the poor and oppressed in their struggle for freedom and justice. Terms such as "justice" and "liberation" began to replace "development", and "grass-root participation" was seen as essential to any genuine process of growth. Thus, justice now meant liberating people from any social, political, or economic structures that would prevent them from achieving their God-given dignity.[49] This same liberationist perspective informed the 1971 Statement of the Synod of Bishops, *Justitia in Mundo* (*Justice in the World*). Embracing the preferential option for the poor, the world's bishops emphasized that preaching the Gospel required a dedication to the liberation of humanity in this world.[50] This document contained the often-quoted sentence "action on behalf of justice and participation in the transformation of the world fully appear to us as a constitutive dimension of the

46 David Hollenbach, "Commentary on *Gaudium et Spes* (*Pastoral Constitution on the Church in the Modern World*)", in *Modern Catholic Social Teaching: Commentaries and Interpretations* ed. Himes, 276–282.

47 Pope Paul VI, "*Populorum Progressio: On the Development of Peoples*", in *Catholic Social Thought: The Documentary Heritage*, eds. O'Brien and Shannon, #6–21.

48 Official English translations of the four Medellín Documents are reprinted in [Latin American Episcopal Council (CELAM)], "Medellín Documents: Justice, Peace, Family and Demography, and Poverty of the Church", in *The Gospel of Peace and Justice: Catholic Social Teaching Since Pope John*, 445–476.

49 Allan Figueroa Deck, "Commentary on *Populorum Progressio (On the Development of Peoples)*", in *Modern Catholic Social Teaching: Commentaries and Interpretations*, ed. Himes, 305–308.

50 Synod of Bishops, 1971, "Justice in the World" in *Catholic Social Thought: The Documentary Heritage*, eds. O'Brien and Shannon, 2.1–2.2 (#29–35).

preaching of the Gospel, or, in other words, of the Church's mission for the redemption of the human race and its liberation from every oppressive situation."[51] Here the Catholic Church clearly expressed that its mission was concerned not simply with personal conversion, but with the social transformation of the world.[52]

During this rich period of Catholic social thought, the Society of Jesus gathered in 1965 and 1966 for the Thirty-First General Congregation (GC 31), which elected Pedro Arrupe, S.J., as Superior General. Under Arrupe's tireless leadership, the Society of Jesus made social justice a fundamental component of all its apostolic work.[53] After attending the 1971 Synod on *Justice in the World*, Arrupe told American Provincial Superiors, "We cannot remain silent, in certain countries, before regimes which constitute without any doubt a sort of institutionalized violence."[54] At the Thirty-Second General Congregation (GC 32) in 1974–1975, the Jesuits adopted Arrupe's vision that justice should be present in all of their ministries. GC 32's "Decree 4" formally committed the order "to promote justice and to enter into solidarity with the voiceless and the powerless" as a constitutive part of its mission to proclaim the Gospel.[55] Equally important, GC 32 insisted that the promotion of justice is not one apostolate among many, reserved for a few specialized experts. Rather, the social apostolate "should be the concern of our whole life and a dimension of all our apostolic endeavours. Similarly, solidarity with men and women who live a life of hardship and who are victims of oppression cannot be the choice of a few Jesuits only. It should be a characteristic of our communities and institutions as well."[56] Emerging from GC 32, the Jesuits were radically committed to the promotion of justice in

51 Ibid., introduction (#6).

52 Kenneth R. Himes, OFM, "Commentary on *Justitia in Mundo (Justice in the World)*", in *Modern Catholic Social Teaching: Commentaries and Interpretations*, ed. Himes, 333.

53 Michael Campbell-Johnston, S.J., "A Brief History", in *Promotio Iustitiae* 66 (February 1997): 11–12.

54 Quoted in Mary Ann Hinsdale, "Jesuit Theological Discourse Since Vatican II", in *The Cambridge Companion to The Jesuits*, edited by Thomas Worcester (Cambridge: Cambridge University Press, 2008), 301.

55 "General Congregation 32; Section 1; Decree 4: Our Mission Today: The Service of Faith and the Promotion of Justice", in *Jesuit Life & Mission Today*, no. 42.

56 Ibid., no. 47–48.

solidarity with the poor. Furthermore, they sought structural changes in the socio-economic order with the hope of building of a new and more just society for all.

According to Jean-Yves Calvez, general counsellor to Father Arrupe from 1971 to 1983 and a delegate to GC 32, the "most active editors of the Decree [4] came from North America and Canada."[57] All four members of the English Canadian delegation distinguished themselves in the formulation of Decree 4, but none more so than William F. Ryan, S.J.[58] According to Maryland Provincial Jim Connor, who attended GC 32, "Bill Ryan played a major role."[59] From making public interventions in the plenary sessions to working behind the scenes with the multiple commissions to drafting decrees, Father Ryan worked tirelessly to ensure that "the promotion of justice" was made "a criterion of our [Jesuit] life and apostolate."[60] As a scholar and animator, Bill Ryan has been involved extensively and for many years in the social and ethical dimensions of development in Canada and throughout the world.

After earning a Ph.D. in economics at Harvard University, Bill Ryan served as co-director of the Social Action office of the newly invigorated Canadian Catholic Conference (later renamed Canadian Conference of Catholic Bishops, or CCCB) in Ottawa from 1964 to 1970. Upon the conclusion of Vatican II, Ryan (and his co-director, Father Jack Shea) travelled across the country facilitating workshops that educated priests, religious congregations, and parish groups throughout English Canada on the importance of social justice, as articulated in *Gaudium et Spes*.[61] During these years, Ryan also drafted

---

57 Jean-Yves Calvez, *Faith and Justice: The Social Dimension of Evangelization* (St. Louis: Institute of Jesuit Sources, 1991), 36.

58 The Canadian delegation consisted of Terence Walsh, S.J. (English Canadian Provincial Superior), who attended *ex officio*, and Patrick G. Malone, S.J. and William F. Ryan, S.J. (who were both elected). Canadian Edward F. Sheridan, S.J., also attended GC 32, as he was already in Rome serving as the English Regional Assistant to Pedro Arrupe, the Superior General.

59 Quoted in Bob Chodos and Jamie Swift, *Faith and Freedom: The Life and Times of Bill Ryan, SJ* (Ottawa: Novalis, 2002), 131.

60 Bill Ryan, "Jesuits and Justice at CG 32", public lecture given by Ryan at Loretto College, Toronto, on 16 February 2012 (text given by Ryan to the author).

61 Joe Gunn and Monica Lambton, *Calling out the Prophetic Tradition: A Jubilee of Social Teaching from the Canadian Conference of Catholic Bishops* (Ottawa: Canadian Conference of Catholic Bishops, 1999), 15.

many of the Canadian bishops' public statements, interventions, and publications (including the annual Labour Day Statements).[62] Beginning in 1966 (the first Labour Day Statement authored by Ryan), these public teachings by the Canadian bishops moved away from understanding injustice as the result of religious and spiritual causes. According to Canadian Jesuit moral theologian Edward F. Sheridan, S.J., these post-conciliar documents from the CCCB articulated "the growing insight that it is the dominant ideology and the economic mechanisms of Canadian and world orders which create and maintain injustice under which a majority of mankind labours."[63]

Perhaps the most significant initiative of Ryan during his years at the social action desk was to conceive and organize a major conference in Montreal in 1968 on "Poverty at Home and Abroad."[64] Supported by twelve Christian denominations, this national conference was the first major ecumenical effort on poverty in Canada. Attended by 500 people, the conference brought together well-known international speakers (such as Barbara Ward and Archbishop Helder Camara of Recife, Brazil), academics, social workers, activists, and an outspoken contingent of Montreal's poor. Out of this widely acclaimed public conference emerged numerous ecumenical coalitions to study, educate, and exert political pressure to promote the New International Economic Order, human rights at home and abroad, corporate responsibility, and respect for refugees.[65]

Between 1970 and 1978, Bill Ryan founded and served as the first executive director of the Center for Concern in Washington, D. C., an international centre that studied issues relating to development, justice, and peace from a Christian perspective. While technically

62 Quoted in Chodos and Smith, 75–86.

63 E. F. Sheridan, *Do Justice! The Social Teaching of the Canadian Catholic Bishops (1945–1986)* (Sherbrooke and Toronto: Éditions Paulines and Jesuit Centre for Social Faith and Justice, 1987), 37.

64 Chodos and Swift, 87–89.

65 William F. Ryan, S.J., "Personal Reflections on the Implementation of the Second Vatican Council by the Canadian Conference of Catholic Bishops (1964–1990)", *CCHA Historical Studies* 73 (2007): 52. The history of these movements are contained in Christopher Lind and Joseph Mihevc, eds., *Coalitions for Justice: The Story of Canada's Inter-church Coalitions* (Ottawa: Novalis, 1994).

he was living abroad, Ryan's work for social justice would continue to affect the Canadian Church. In 1971, he served as a *peritus* (theological advisor) to the Canadian bishops during the International Synod of Bishops in Rome, which produced the landmark *Justice in the World.* At the synod, Ryan wrote public interventions for the Canadian bishops, including Cardinal George Flahiff's influential presentation that called upon the Church to make its social teachings more than theoretical academic knowledge.[66] "The Church cannot be content to think of the world theoretically; it must transform it. Only if the Church commits itself wholeheartedly to the task of forming Christians through practice and solidarity will it be credible."[67] Ryan also penned Bishop Alexander Carter's memorable intervention that warned the bishops that corporate power was eclipsing the power of nation-states. These multi-national corporations were "structurally inadequate and even inimical to the building of a just world community."[68] After the 1971 Synod, the Canadian bishops returned to Canada convinced that advocacy of social justice was part of their evangelizing office, of their preaching of the Gospel of justice and love. *Justice in the World* set their episcopal agenda for the next decade.[69]

In 1978, Bill Ryan returned to Canada to serve for six years as Provincial of the Jesuits of Upper Canada (English-speaking Canada). In late December 1982, the Social Affairs Commission of the Canadian Conference of Catholic Bishops released a sharply worded statement entitled "Ethical Reflections on the Economic Crisis" that addressed the high rate of unemployment in Canada (approximately 1.5 million Canadians, representing 13 percent of the work force).[70] This document attracted an unprecedented amount of attention from the media, because Cardinal Emmett Carter of Toronto publicly distanced

66 Chodos and Swift, 100.

67 George Bernard Cardinal Flahiff, "Christian Formation for Justice", presentation to the International Synod of Bishops, Rome, 20 October 1971 in *Do Justice!* ed. Sheridan, 221.

68 Bishop Alexander Carter, "Super States and Multi-National Corporations in a Developing World Community", presentation to the International Synod of Bishops, Rome, 20 October 1971 in *Do Justice!* ed. Sheridan, 224.

69 Sheridan, *Do Justice!* 28; Gunn and Lambton, 20–27.

70 Episcopal Commission for Social Affairs, "Ethical Reflections on the Economic Crisis", 22 December 1982, in *Do Justice!* ed. Sheridan, 399–410.

himself from the statement. Cardinal Carter argued that the proper consultation process had not been followed in the preparation of the document, and he questioned the overtly radical content of its economic and ethical analysis (which directly criticized the economic policies of Prime Minister Pierre Trudeau for not living out the Gospel principle of the "preferential option of the poor").[71] Finding himself at the centre of an unwanted controversy, Cardinal Carter reached out to Bill Ryan. They agreed that the archdiocese of Toronto would sponsor a high-profile panel to study the issues raised by "Ethical Reflections." Ryan organized the event, which was chaired by the distinguished Canadian diplomat and Chancellor of the University of Toronto, Dr. George Ignatieff (Ryan himself served as vice-chair and as the expert on Catholic social teaching).[72] From the over 100 individuals and organizations that made written submissions, the panel selected a small representative cross-sample—including politicians, church groups, business organizations, trade unions, non-governmental organizations, and representatives from the unemployed—to appear at the public hearings in Toronto. The bulk of the testimony, and the subsequent published report, *Canada's Unemployed: The Crisis of Our Times*, confirmed the general thrust of the bishops' original statement that such a high level of unemployment was, indeed, an unjust situation.[73] Ultimately, the well-publicized hearings made a positive contribution to the socio-political situation in Canada, both in terms of the substance of the final report and the process of listening to all stakeholders in the dialogue between Church and society in Canada.

Also during his tenure as provincial, Bill Ryan launched the Jesuit Centre for Social Faith and Justice in 1979. The Centre's mandate was not to start new social programs. Rather, according to its first director, Father Michael Czerny, S.J., the Centre was "a focused Jesuit effort to collaborate with ecumenical and other social action

71 Michael W. Higgins and Douglas R. Letson, *My Father's Business: A Biography of His Eminence G. Emmett Cardinal Carter* (Toronto: MacMillan of Canada, 1990), 213–219, and Tony Clarke, *Behind the Mitre: Moral Leadership Crisis in the Canadian Catholic Church* (Toronto: HarperCollins, 1995), 61–64.

72 Chodos and Swift, 178–179.

73 *Canada's Unemployed: The Crisis of Our Times*. Report on the Hearing Panel on "Ethical Reflections on the Economic Crisis" (Toronto: Archdiocese of Toronto Mission Press, 1983).

groups in witnessing to justice and furthering social change."[74] The Jesuit Centre was to research and analyze social issues at the local, national, and international levels, and then to shed a theological light on these pressing issues. Succinctly stated, the principal task was to link faith and justice (hence the title of the Centre).[75] Given its young and energetic staff of four Jesuit priests, the Jesuit Centre for Social Faith and Justice quickly established itself as a headquarters for not only social analysis, but social action as well.

Father Jim Webb, S.J. (1944–2012), who had long been active in social issues in the industrial neighbourhood of South Riverdale (where the Centre was located), focused on the local community that had a large working-class population. Father Webb was instrumental in the development of a 150-unit co-op housing program, in the founding and operation of the South Riverdale Community Health Centre, and in work with local citizens' groups concerned with environmental health hazards in the district's industrial areas.[76] In addition, Webb was chair of the Taskforce on Churches and Corporate Responsibility (TCCR) that monitored the overseas activities of Canadian-based multi-national corporations that contributed to social injustice, violations of human rights, increased militarism, or ecological abuse. For example, TCCR mobilized public pressure against Canadian banks that invested in military regimes in Latin America or in apartheid in South Africa; it lobbied for debt relief for those countries most adversely affected; and it pushed for environmental review panels for companies that operated in the Canadian North.[77] Since South Riverdale was home to many newly arrived immigrants, Jesuit Centre staff member Lois Anne Bordowitz, F.C.J., helped found the Riverdale Immigrant Women's Centre. It provided language and skills training, as well as social activities to overcome isolation and help integrate immigrants into the community.[78]

---

74 "Jesuits open Faith and Justice Centre", *Catholic Register*, 1 December 1979.

75 Michael Stogre, "Social Faith and Justice" in *The Bread of Life* 3:3 (July–August 1980), 31.

76 "Jesuits Call Canadians to Get Started: Fifth Anniversary of Faith & Justice Centre", in *Catholic New Times*, 14 October 1984, 17.

77 Renate Pratt, "The Taskforce on the Churches and Corporate Responsibility", in *Coalitions for Justice*, eds. Lind and Mihevc, 63–83.

78 Michael Czerny, S.J., *Jesuit Centre Newsletter*, May 1982, in AJC, I-0810 Social Apostolate

On the national level, the Jesuit Centre joined a campaign with other labour and social organizations to halt the erosion of Medicare (Canada's national health insurance plan) and to promote a new perspective on health for Canadians.[79] Led by Father Michael Stogre, S.J., one of the few priest-physicians in Canada, the Jesuit Centre partnered with the Ontario Federation of Labour to plan a day-long conference on Medicare issues that over 300 people attended. Out of this gathering, Father Stogre and fellow Jesuit Centre staff member Gordon F. George, S.J. (1911–1994),[80] former Jesuit Superior and director of the Jesuit Information Department in Rome, contributed to a brief entitled "Medicare in Crisis" that was submitted to the federal Commission on Medicare under Justice Emmet Hall.[81] As a physician involved in native health issues, Father Stogre also served as a medical consultant to the natives on the Rama reserve near Orillia, Ontario, as they developed a community health centre similar to the South Riverdale Community Health Centre.[82] Stogre would also represent the Jesuits on Project North, an ecumenical coalition that supported native peoples in northern Canada in the settlement of their land claims and educated Canadians about ethical issues regarding northern development.[83] Making public health a priority, in 1980 the Centre hired Dr. Rosalie Bertell, a Grey Nun of the Sacred Heart, to work on environmental and nuclear health problems (specifically, low-level nuclear radiation). Bertell served as an advisor to twenty Indian bands threatened with environmental pollution in northern Ontario and helped prepare a dossier on the ethics of a Canadian energy policy for the CCCB.[84]

U.R.#7, "Jesuit Centre For Social Faith & Justice: Brochures, Circular letters, Newspaper Clippings, Off-Prints, Publicity, etc., 1971–1984".

79 "New Jesuit Centre Promotes Unity of Faith and Justice", *Catholic New Times*, 25 November 1979, 8.

80 "George, Gordon F." in DJB, vol. 2, 111–114.

81 Gordon George and Michael Stogre, "Health Care in Canada: Growing Pains or Terminal Illness?" in *America* 142, no. 17 (3 May 1980) 379–381.

82 "Jesuits Call Canadians to Get Started: Fifth Anniversary of Faith & Justice Centre", in *Catholic New Times*, 14 October 1984, 17.

83 Peter Hamel, "The Aboriginal Rights Coalition", in *Coalitions for Justice*, eds. Lind and Mihevc, 16–36.

84 "Jesuits Call Canadians to Get Started: Fifth Anniversary of Faith & Justice Centre", in *Catholic New Times*, 14 October 1984, 17.

On the international level, Father Michael Czerny's contribution to the centre stemmed largely from his work as a member of the executive of the Inter-Church Committee on Human Rights in Latin America (ICCHRLA). Initially formed as a faith-based response by Christian churches in Canada to the human rights abuses carried out by the military junta of Augusto Pinochet in Chile in 1973, the ICCHRLA gradually expanded its scope to include advocacy work for all of Latin America. The ICCHRLA sponsored fact-finding trips into alleged human rights abuses, received visitors from Latin America, published special reports, and engaged in advocacy work with the Canadian government and international bodies (with a special concern for refugees/immigration policy).[85] Making frequent trips to Central America and regularly publishing his findings in *Central America Update* (printed bimonthly by the Jesuit Centre and the Latin American Working Group), Czerny helped to keep the Canadian public informed about social injustices in Latin America.[86]

In October 1980, Michael Czerny and Jim Webb organized a major four-day conference in Toronto entitled "Alternatives for Development: Canada and Latin America in the 1980s." Presentations were made by Cardinal Paulo Arns (Archbishop of Saõ Paulo, Brazil) as well as by Bishop Alexander Carter of Sault Ste. Marie; Bishop John Sherlock of London, Ontario; Archbishop Ted Scott, Primate of the Anglican Church; and Reverend Lois Wilson, Moderator of the United Church of Canada.[87] To augment this ministry, the Jesuit Centre hired Tim Draimin, a specialist on Canadian foreign policy towards Central America. While at the Centre, Draimin authored "From Acquiescence to Action", an important proposal for a more consistent and effective Canadian foreign policy. It was submitted to Allan MacEachen, the Secretary of State for External Affairs.[88] Under Czerny and Draimin,

85 Bill Fairbairn, "Inter-Church Committee on Human Rights in Latin America", in *Coalitions for Justice*, eds. Lind and Mihevc, 169–184.

86 Fr. Gordon F. George, S.J., *The Jesuit Bulletin*, 1981.

87 *News*, 55, no. 7 (November and December 1980), 28 in AJC, I-0810 Social Apostolate U.R.#7, "Jesuit Centre For Social Faith & Justice: Brochures, Circular letters, Newspaper Clippings, Off-Prints, Publicity, etc., 1971–1984".

88 "Jesuits Call Canadians to Get Started: Fifth Anniversary of Faith & Justice Centre", in *Catholic New Times*, 14 October 1984, 17.

the Jesuit Centre became an important channel for two-way communication, expressing Canadian solidarity with those in Latin America and bringing the voice of the powerless of Latin America to Canada.

As a complement to the existing focus on Canadian issues and Central America, in 1985 the Jesuit Centre added a third ministry and created a new Canadian Jesuit Refugee Program. The Jesuits had worked with the refugees in the past. For example, Father John R. Brown, S.J. (1913–1994), had ministered to refugees and immigrants as the chaplain at Toronto Harbour for five years in the 1960s and for twenty years in the Immigration Bureau "Pier 21" in Halifax. While Father Brown's ministry was initially in the charity model of simply responding to the immediate needs of those he encountered, he adopted the justice model of advocating for the rights of the newly arrived by carrying on extensive correspondence with members of Parliament and with Canadian bishops.[89] Respected by the latter for his work with refugees, Father Brown was appointed in 1982 as the director of immigration for the CCCB.

Father Brown's very effective years of communications with government authorities are not unreminiscent of the decades of lobbying for prison reform by Father Harold Bedford, chaplain for over thirty years at Stony Mountain Penitentiary, near Winnipeg, and trusted advisor to federal and provincial governments.

At the Jesuit Centre for Social Faith and Justice, the new Jesuit Refugee Service in Canada (JRS/Canada), under the initial direction of Father Czerny, had four interrelated aspects.[90] First, the immediate focus was to provide direct assistance to individual refugees by coordinating the financial, housing, medical, dental, and legal services necessary for sponsorship. By 1990, JRS/Canada was operating two refugee shelters that served as first homes for refugees arriving in Canada through the JRS network. From 1989 to 1990, thirty-one refugees from Sri Lanka, China, El Salvador, and South Africa used

89 "Brown, John R." in DJB, vol. 2, 22–25.

90 "Canadian Jesuit Refugee Programme, February 1985, in AJC, I-0810 Social Apostolate U.R.#7, "Jesuit Centre For Social Faith & Justice: Brochures, Circular letters, Newspaper Clippings, Off-Prints, Publicity, 1983, 1983–1997".

these two shelters.[91] Under the direction of Brother John Masterson, S.J., individuals and families received lodging, legal and resettlement help, as well as moral support.[92] A second level of response was to improve existing mechanisms of assistance for refugees as a group (such as reviewing federal policy for determining who qualifies as a refugee). In 1992, the JRS/Canada published a major review of Canada's policies and practices in removing refugee claimants, entitled "Integrity and Canada's Policy of Removing Refugees."[93] Intended for a broad audience, this report presented an alternative analysis of the challenges facing Canada as a refugee-receiving country. Furthermore, it made a series of recommendations for changes in order to meet Canada's international obligations to refugees.

The third aspect of the Jesuit Refugee Service/Canada was to protect refugees outside of Canada by ensuring that these persons had their international rights recognized (such as the right to food, shelter, and a fair hearing). To this end, the Jesuit Centre made regular financial contributions to refugee agencies in the global South. For example, in 1991, the Jesuit Centre helped fund a new JRS office in Mexico City that offered legal help, leadership training and human rights training to refugees, and national and international advocacy on behalf of the approximately 500,000 refugees dispersed throughout Mexico.[94] The fourth and most important step was to educate Canadians on the root cause of why more than 13 million people worldwide are forced to live in exile as refugees, and to explore what Canadians could do to help.[95]

To initiate structural change, in 1989 the Jesuit Centre launched *Refugee Update*, an important bulletin that provided information and analysis about Canadian and international refugee policies, and linked

91 "Annual Report 1990", Jesuit Centre for Social Faith and Justice, in AJC, I-0810 Social Apostolate U.R.#7, "Jesuit Centre For Social Faith & Justice Annual Reports, 1987–1994", 3.

92 *Sharing*: Jesuit Refugee Service/Canada Newsletter, no. 1 (February 1990), 3.

93 "Annual Report 1992", Jesuit Centre for Social Faith and Justice, in AJC, I-0810 Social Apostolate U.R.#7, "Jesuit Centre For Social Faith & Justice Annual Reports, 1987–1994", 9.

94 "Annual Report 1991", Jesuit Centre for Social Faith and Justice, in AJC, I-0810 Social Apostolate U.R.#7, "Jesuit Centre For Social Faith & Justice Annual Reports, 1987–1994", 9.

95 Letter from William M. Addley, S.J., 8 February 1985 in AJC, I-0810 Social Apostolate U.R.#7, "Jesuit Centre For Social Faith & Justice: Brochures, Circular letters, Newspaper Clippings, Off-Prints, Publicity, 1983, 1983–1997".

refugee support groups across Canada.[96] Each quarter, over 2,000 copies were sent to subscribers across Canada.[97] The Jesuit Centre also facilitated numerous organized conferences and workshops that brought together leaders of refugee communities and refugee activists from across Canada to create a united voice on refugee issues.[98] One example of these bridge-building events was on 4 April 1992, when the Jesuit Centre organized a Refugee Rights Day celebration that included presentations of theatre, music, dance, and poetry from over 150 people representing fifteen ethnic communities, as well as a series of high-profile speakers.[99] The event was attended by over a thousand people.

The Jesuit Centre inspired activity outside of Toronto as well. In St. John's, Brother James McSheffrey, S.J., a social advocate and worker, spent most of his time working with the poor and marginalized in the low-income housing project Brophy Place, of which he was a co-founder. In Regina, Father John Matheson took up prison chaplaincy and founded "Friends on the Outside" to help the rehabilitation and transition of former prisoners.

The influence of the Jesuit Centre for Social Faith and Justice reached across English Canada through its publications. To provide Canadians with the tools of analysis on social and ethical issues (including aging, ecology, women's rights, unemployment, and micro-technology), in 1984 Father Czerny, along with Jamie Swift, published *Getting Started on Social Analysis in Canada.*[100] Reflecting post-conciliar Catholic social thought, the text studied the multiple structures in Canadian society—personal, economic, political, and cultural—and clarified how people can work together to change these structures to create a more just society. Selling over 45,000 copies in fifteen years, *Getting Started* was a popular text in universities and

96 "Annual Report 1989", Jesuit Centre for Social Faith and Justice, in AJC, I-0810 Social Apostolate U.R.#7, "Jesuit Centre For Social Faith & Justice Annual Reports, 1987–1994", 8.

97 "Annual Report 1990", in AJC, 4.

98 Ibid.

99 "Annual Report 1992", in AJC, 8.

100 Michael Czerny and Jamie Swift, *Getting Started on Social Analysis in Canada* (Toronto: Between the Lines, 1984).

colleges, as well as with church-based social justice groups.[101] From 1983 to 1994, Father Edward F. Sheridan, S.J. (1912–1999), former president and professor of moral theology at Regis College in Toronto, worked at the Jesuit Centre compiling the first (and only) comprehensive collection of the significant social statements, briefs, and letters of the Canadian Conference of Catholic Bishops.[102] Published as two volumes—*Do Justice! The Social Teaching of the Canadian Catholic Bishops (1945–1956)* in 1987 and *Love Kindness! The Social Teaching of the Canadian Catholic Bishops (1958–1989)* in 1991—Sheridan's volumes serve as essential reference works for the theological and historical development of Catholic social teaching in Canada.

In early 1990, Father Czerny left the Jesuit Centre to go to El Salvador to teach philosophy at the University of Central America (UCA) in San Salvador and to assist in the formation program of theology students at the Jesuit Centre for Theological Reflection at the university.[103] A year earlier, on 16 November 1989, six Jesuits at the university, along with their housekeeper and her daughter, were murdered at night in their residence by members of the El Salvadoran military because of their vocal opposition to the human rights violations being committed by the government. Czerny and five other Jesuits from around the world volunteered to replace their slain confreres in the classroom and to continue the social apostolate of the Jesuits in Central America.[104] With Czerny's departure, the last of the "first generation" of the Jesuit Centre had left.[105] The new director was Father Edward Hyland, S.J., who had previously conducted the public education program on social analysis with the Jesuit Refugee Service. In 1995, Kevin J. Arsenault was named as director of the Centre (the first non-Jesuit to hold the post).

101 Chodos and Swift, 158.

102 "Sheridan, Edward F." in DJB, vol. 2, 301–306.

103 Patria C. Rivera, "Toronto Jesuit Replaces Slain Salvadoran Priest", in *The Catholic Register*, 3 March 1990.

104 Letter from William M. Addley, S.J., 8 December 1989 in AJC, I-0810 Social Apostolate U.R.#7, "Jesuit + Misc. Orders: News Clippings, 1989–1997".

105 Two years later, Czerny was appointed to be the Social Justice Secretary for the Society of Jesus in Rome (1992–2002). In 2002, he was appointed to be the first Co-ordinator for the African Jesuit Aids Network, centred in Nairobi, Kenya. Since 2010, Czerny has been serving as Personal Secretary of the President of the Pontifical Council for Justice and Peace; he resides in Rome.

In January 1997, the Jesuit Centre for Social Faith and Justice found itself in the midst of a controversy. The Centre published a full-colour poster entitled "Exposing the Face of Corporate Rule: Here are the Men (One Woman) who Reaped Record Profits While Slashing Jobs" that was sent to churches throughout Canada for display. The poster depicted the names, photos, and salaries of executives from Canada's 100 largest corporations, along with the firms' profits, assets, real tax rate, and number of jobs created or lost in the past five years. The average salary of these executives was almost 90 times that of the average Canadian worker ($2.65 million compared to $29,835.00).[106] The poster was especially evocative given that, in 1997, 1.5 million Canadians were out of work, many of them as a result of downsizing by these same corporations that were depicted on the poster.[107] Auxiliary Bishop John Knight of Toronto sent a letter to all the priests in the archdiocese forbidding the display of the poster on Toronto church property. He argued that it was "inappropriate to target individuals in ways which might alienate them from their communities and which may place them or their family members at risk."[108] Father Bill Ryan, chair of the Jesuit Centre's board of directors, agreed that the poster's title was not appropriate for churches, but he fundamentally supported the message of the poster, stating that the information was public, accurate, and addressed the issue of corporate accountability.[109]

A month later, in February 1997, the Jesuits in English Canada announced that they were withdrawing financial support from sixteen ministries, including the Jesuit Centre for Social Faith and Justice. Father David Nazar, S.J., the Provincial Superior in English-speaking Canada, emphasized that the decision was unrelated to the controversial poster campaign. Rather, the decision to withdraw funding from the Centre was made due to the fiscal difficulties of the Order,

106 Leslie Scrivener, "Executive Salaries Called Unfair to Workers", in *The Toronto Star*, 1 February 1997.

107 Richard Gwyn, "'Heretics Challenge Free-Market Dogma", in *The Toronto Star*, 19 January 1997.

108 Letter from Most Rev. John Stephen Knight, Auxiliary Bishop of Toronto, 29 January 1997, in AJC, I-0810 Social Apostolate U.R.#7, "Jesuit Centre, Toronto, Varia: Newspaper Clippings, etc., 1992–1997".

109 Cathy Majtenyi, "Poster Banned: Archdiocese Keeps Jesuit Centre Poster Out of Churches", in *The Catholic Register*, 10 February 1997.

specifically due to declining returns on financial investments, loss of salaries from an increasing number of Jesuit priests retiring from teaching, the increased cost of caring for elderly Jesuits (more than half of the 230 members), and abuse settlements for native people at Cape Croker First Nations reserve in Ontario.[110] Upon learning that the Centre was closing, academics from York University and labour representatives worked out a deal with Bill Ryan (acting on behalf of the province) to launch a newly configured secular Centre for Social Justice. The new Centre and its lay staff, which was affiliated with the Canadian Centre for Policy Alternatives at York University, became a progressive think tank, challenging neo-liberal economic policies and studying how the corporate sector related to the Canadian economy.[111] While the Jesuits donated office equipment and their donor list of 6,000 names, the Order was no longer associated with the new Centre.

In 1999, two years after the closing of the Jesuit Centre for Social Faith and Justice, some fifty-five Jesuits in English Canada strongly recommended that the Centre be restored.[112] The Jesuit Centre was accordingly reborn, but as an umbrella association for three Jesuits who were already involved in the social apostolate. Bill Ryan, based in Ottawa, spearheaded a program on Ethics and Politics that involved dialogue with sixty-three federal members of Parliament and fifty-five senior civil servants.[113] At Guelph in 2003, he organized an international symposium of leading academics on globalization and Catholic social teaching. The papers presented there were edited by Father Ryan and the American Jesuit Father John A. Coleman, S.J., and published as *Globalization and Catholic Social Thought*.[114] In 2007, Ryan also helped launch the Jesuit Forum for Social Faith and Justice in Toronto (the spiritual successor to the original Jesuit Centre for Social Faith and Justice that was founded in 1979).

110 Joseph Sinasac, "Money Woes Plague Jesuits", in *The Catholic Register*, 3 March 1997.

111 Cathy Majtenyi, "New Group Rises from the Ashes of the Jesuit Centre", in *The Catholic Register*, 9 June 1997.

112 Bill Ryan, interview with the author, February 2014.

113 Ibid.

114 John A. Coleman and William F. Ryan, eds., *Globalization and Catholic Social Thought: Present Crisis, Future Hope* (Ottawa: Novalis, 2005).

Now, under the direction of Anne-Marie Jackson, and with Bill Ryan serving as special advisor, the new Jesuit Forum animates communal reflection for small groups of leaders in similar fields of social responsibility for the purpose of creating possibilities for change.[115] The Jesuit Forum also facilitates workshops, seminars, and presentations on significant issues related to social justice. For example, in 2010, it prepared a workbook for the Assembly of Catholic Bishops of Ontario on *Caritas in Veritate* (*On Integral Human Development in Charity and Truth*), Pope Benedict XVI's 2009 social encyclical.[116] Furthermore, the Jesuit Forum reaches out to a wider public through *Open Space*, a newsletter that is published four times a year on significant global issues.[117]

In 1999, the ministry to refugees was restored under Father Jack Costello, S.J. Father Costello had served for many years as the chaplain to Romero House in Toronto. Founded in 1992 by Mary Jo Leddy, Romero House Community for Refugees, named in memory of the murdered Salvadoran Archbishop Oscar Romero, has provided hospitality, settlement, and advocacy services to more than 6,000 individuals and families.[118] Costello was also active in the Inter-Church Committee for Refugees (ICCR), which served as a connection point for Christian communities that sponsored refugees and sought to improve legislation (both federal and provincial) so that refugees would have improved access to permanent residency, social services, labour rights, and family reunification.[119] In 2001, ten ecumenical social justice coalitions—including ICCR, as well as the aforementioned TCCR and ICCHRLA—came together to form KAIROS: Canadian Ecumenical Justice Initiatives.[120] In 2006, Costello was appointed director of the Jesuit Refugee and Migrant Service, based in Toronto.

---

115 Jesuit Forum for Social Faith and Justice, "Our Mission", http://www.jesuitforum.ca/mission.

116 Jesuit Forum for Social Faith and Justice, "*Caritas In Veritate*: Guide for Discussion and Action" (Toronto: Assembly of Catholic Bishops of Ontario, 2010).

117 Jesuit Forum for Social Faith and Justice, "Open Space".

118 "Romero House", http://www.romerohouse.org.

119 Henriette Thompson, "The Inter-Church Committee for Refugees", in *Coalitions for Justice*, eds. Lind and Mihevc, 203–218.

120 KAIROS Canada, "Forty Years of Ecumenical Coalitions for Justice", http://www.kairoscanada.org/who-we-are/forty-years-of-ecumenical-coalitions-for-justice.

As the title of this apostolate indicates, the scope of this ministry was expanded beyond refugees to also include care for migrant workers in Canada.

The third Jesuit active in the relaunched Jesuit Centre in 1999 was Father Jim Profit, S.J. (1957–2014). Father Profit's ministry in ecology represented a new direction in Catholic social justice. Concern about the environment has been growing in the Society of Jesus for several decades. At the Thirty-Fourth General Congregation (GC 34) in 1995, "Decree 20" recommended that a study be made regarding environmental issues, how Ignatian spirituality provided an orientation for responding to them, and ways in which Jesuit communities and ministries might take action.[121] As a response, General Superior Peter-Hans Kolvenbach directed the Social Justice Secretariat to prepare the document *We Live in a Broken World: Reflections on Ecology*. This report encouraged an ever more effective ecological solidarity in the life of the Jesuits: spiritual, communal, and apostolic.[122] At the Thirty-Fifth General Congregation (GC 35) in 2008, the issue of ecology was one of the most important apostolic themes discussed. "Decree 3" on "Our Mission" incorporated this theme under the broader topic of "Reconciliation" in its three-fold dimension: reconciliation with God, with others, and with creation.[123] Thus, from this point forward, the Jesuit concern for ecology and creation was linked to their commitment to establish a just relationship with God (commitment to faith) and with other human beings (commitment to justice).

Even before the formal institutional response of the Society of Jesus to the looming environmental crisis, the Jesuits in English Canada have long been engaged in sustained reflection on the question of ecology and faith. In 1985, the Jesuit Farm Project was founded by Jesuits and their collaborators who worked at the Farm Community in Guelph, a L'Arche-inspired community that worked and lived on the 264-hectare Ignatius Farm and woodland located just north of

121 "General Congregation 34; Section IV; Decree 20: Ecology (Recommendation to Father General)" in *Jesuit Life & Mission Today,* no. 2.

122 Social Justice and Ecology Secretariat, "Healing a Broken World: Task Force on Ecology", in *Promotio Iustitiae* 106 (February 2011): 29–30.

123 "General Congregation 35; Decree 3: Challenges to Our Mission Today", in *Jesuit Life & Mission Today*, no. 18.

Guelph (formerly Ignatius College, and the Province novitiate).[124] In 1999, Father Jim Profit, S.J., and Louisa Blair founded the Ecology Project, which began to use the land to address the relationship between Christian faith and ecological spirituality. Its mandate was to further awareness and understanding of ecological issues from a Christian perspective and to integrate ecology into Jesuit ministries throughout English Canada.[125] Rooted in this deepening awareness of the apostolic nature of the land, the staff at Ignatius Jesuit Centre in Guelph—consisting of the Loyola House retreat centre, Orchard Park office complex, an ecology ministry foundation, Ignatius Farm, and community garden—developed ecology retreats, workshops, and other environmental education programs that combined science, faith, Ignatian spiritual practices, and hands-on training in ecology and spirituality.[126] Father John English, S.J. (1924–2004), a pioneer in the renewal of the Spiritual Exercises, incorporated ecological spirituality in his development of the Spiritual Exercises.[127] Father John McCarthy, S.J., who was also active in integrating ecology into Ignatian spirituality, earned a Ph.D. in boreal forest ecology from the University of British Columbia in 1994. He served for eight years as the Co-Chair of the Wilderness and Ecological Reserves Advisory Council for the government of Newfoundland and Labrador. Father McCarthy's work in forest conservation earned him the Canadian Environment Award, Gold Prize, from the Royal Geographical Society of Canada.[128]

Conclusion

The social apostolate—bringing the Gospel message to society—has long been at the heart of the Jesuit ministries in English Canada.

---

124 John McCarthy, S.J., "Mission and Ecology Commission: The Jesuits in English Canada", *EcoJesuit: Connecting Jesuits, People and Ecology*, http://www.ecojesuit.com/mission-and-ecology-commission-the-jesuits-in-english-canada/4440.

125 Marianne Karsh, "Farming as Part of Spiritual Portfolio: Ignatius Jesuit Centre of Guelph, Canada", *EcoJesuit: Connecting Jesuits, People and Ecology*, http://www.ecojesuit.com/farming-as-part-of-spiritual-portfolio-ignatius-jesuit-centre-of-guelph-canada/2143.

126 Vic Kirsch, "Local Jesuit Lobbied to Protect Retreat Centre, Help Environment", in *Guelph Mercury*, 13 January 2014.

127 "English, John J. C." in DJB, vol. 2, 90–94.

128 "Jesuit Scientists Lead Catholics in New Parish on University of British Columbia Campus", *National Jesuit News*, 20 June 2012, http://www.jesuit.org/blog/index.php/tag/jesuit-father-john-mccarthy.

During the nineteenth and early twentieth centuries, Canadian Jesuits engaged society through a model of "charity" that was concerned with the poor through the traditional corporal acts of mercy. Examples included ministering to the Irish famine immigrants in Montreal, Edward Devine's Loyola Club, which founded the Loyola Convalescent Home, and Joseph Fallon's creating Montreal's Federation of Catholic Charities. With the promulgation of *Rerum Novarum* in 1891, the Church became critical of political and economic structures in society that were unjust, and sought to reform the social order. The crucial first step that the Canadian Jesuits took towards this "justice" approach was with Charles McGuire's Catholic Labour School, which educated both labour and management in Catholic social teaching. With the adoption of Decree 4 of GC 32 in 1975—which was inspired by the Second Vatican Council and subsequent post-conciliar documents, such as *Justice in the World*—the Jesuits made the transformation of social structures a core aspect of their ministries. The Catholic Church in English Canada embraced the notion that the Catholic faith requires a firm commitment to social justice. From 1979 to 1997, the dynamic Jesuit Centre for Social Faith and Justice—through its Canadian issues team, Central America team, and Refugee team—brought the abstract principles of Catholic social teaching to the complex social realities of English-speaking Canada. Moving into the twenty-first century, the Jesuits are challenged with having to do more with fewer personnel and financial resources. Aware of these limitations, the Jesuit social apostolate is increasingly engaged in collaborative ministries—such as the Jesuit Forum for Social Faith and Justice and the Ignatius Jesuit Centre in Guelph—to empower people from all walks of life to embrace the prophetic vision of Saint Ignatius Loyola: that of ministering to the estranged from society for the greater glory of God, and for the common good of all humanity.

V

The Ministry of Communications in the Jesuit Province of English Canada, 1842–2013

JOHN D. O'BRIEN, S.J.

The Jesuits have always been at the forefront of the ministry of communications in the Catholic Church, if by that we mean paying critical attention to the transmission of ideas. The first Jesuits in Canada during the seventeenth century embodied that attention to communication. Those French missionaries to New France and Huronia sent a steady stream of letters back to their Provincial Superiors in Europe; these were published and disseminated throughout the Continent. Known as the *Jesuit Relations*, this correspondence constituted the archetypal form of Jesuit communications from the Canadian mission.[1] In the centuries that followed, Jesuits in Canada

1 *Relation de ce qui s'est passé de plus remarquables aux missions des pères de la Compagnie de Jésus en la Nouvelle France* is the title of the official annual report sent to the Jesuit Provincials in France for publication by Jesuit Superiors in Canada between 1632 and 1673. They were first collected by Félix Martin, s.j., and published in Quebec in 1858 by the Canadian government. Beginning in 1896, Reuben Gold Thwaites published them and "allied documents" in French and English in seventy-three volumes of text and indexes beginning with the year 1610 and ending with the death of the last Jesuit in Canada in 1800. In common, even scholarly, parlance,

have continued to use a variety of communications for their missions. Indeed, since its inception, the Jesuit Order has printed books and pamphlets, emphasized linguistics, rhetoric, and drama in its colleges and schools, and as teachers and preachers and lecturers, Jesuits have worked to be communicators par excellence in myriad and creative ways.

During their formative training, Jesuits were steeped in the tradition of their *Ratio Studiorum*, which emphasized the study of the classics, of ancient and modern literatures, of rhetoric and logic, and the art of debating, preaching, teaching, and public speaking. From their Novitiate days, too, young Jesuits had to practice *toni*, that is, to deliver before their peers a formulaic speech from a pulpit in the refectory, and then to be criticized for how they had delivered it; they preached sermons, and read in the refectory during meals (except breakfast). In Canada, this system of education for the training of Jesuits lasted until into the 1960s, and helped develop communicative skills that were easily applicable within a Jesuit's ministry, whether teaching or preaching, broadcasting on radio, or appearing on television. This chapter will examine the individuals and organizations within the Province of English Canada who have used communications, from print publications, radio and television broadcasting to media criticism and literacy and films, and to theories of communications as an emerging science.

Print Media

The Messenger of the Sacred Heart

There has been no Jesuit communications' ministry in Canada with greater longevity than the monthly magazine *The Messenger of the Sacred Heart*. It also holds the longest record of publication of any Catholic monthly in Canada.[2] During its many decades in print, *The Messenger* has served as the print-piece of The Apostleship of Prayer, an international Jesuit ministry that promotes prayer, the monthly intentions of the Pope, and devotion to the Sacred Heart of Jesus.

---

the term *The Jesuit Relations* is used to cover all the documents in the Thwaites edition.

2 Terence Fay, "From Catholic Piety to Ecumenical Spirituality: The Canadian Jesuit Relations in the 1960s", CCHA, *Historical Studies*, 68 (2002), 25–44.

For over 120 years, since 1891, *The Messenger* featured articles on Christian living, practical advice, fictional stories, lives of the saints, Catholic Church news, and catechetical formation. (It ceased publication in August 2014.) Distributed primarily through individual and parish subscriptions in Canada and the United States, remarkably, since 1904 the magazine had only four editors; these gave the greater part of their active priestly lives to this role. It was also a conduit for many other initiatives in communications over the decades.

The Messenger began its impressive run in January 1891 to serve the needs of Canadian members of the Apostleship of Prayer.[3] The first of many international "Jesuit Messenger" magazines, it was published first in Toulouse, France, in 1861 by Henri Ramière, s.j., who was considered the second founder of the Apostleship of Prayer.[4] Yet, even in those early days, Canada was on his mind. On 28 October 1863, Ramière wrote a letter to Bishop John Joseph Lynch of Toronto with instructions on how to promote the Apostleship of Prayer. Several decades later, in 1891, *The Canadian Messenger of the Sacred Heart* was launched with the enthusiastic endorsement of the Canadian bishops. Archbishop Joseph-Thomas Duhamel of Ottawa wrote about it: "The Canadian Messenger of the Sacred Heart should have as many subscribers as there are English-speaking Catholic families in this Canada of ours. We would wish to see it in every household of our diocese."[5]

The founding editor was John J. Connolly, S.J., who had been a preacher and confessor at the Jesuits' Church of the Gesù in Montreal.[6] He had established The League of the Sacred Heart there as a pious association of men, and in 1888 was appointed the first English-speaking

3 Founded by François-Xavier Gautrelet, s.j., at Vals in the Jesuit Province of Toulouse, France, and developed by Henri Ramière (1861–1884). See http://www.apostleshipofprayer.net/docs/THE-HISTORICAL-DEVELOPMENT-OF-THE-AP-EN.pdf.

4 When Ramière died, there were 35,000 centres, thirteen million members, and fourteen Messengers in various languages. See Peter Hans Kolvenbach, s.j., *The Historical Development of the Apostleship of Prayer*, http://www.apostleshipofprayer.net/docs/THE-HISTORICAL-DEVELOPMENT-OF-THE-AP-EN.pdf. By the year 2000, the Apostleship of Prayer had over forty million members, fifty different Messengers, and forty other periodicals.

5 To this day, Ottawa parishes are strong centres of the Apostleship of Prayer. (See "A Century of Devotion for the Messenger", *The Catholic Register*, 16 February 1991, 7.)

6 DJB, vol. 1, 63–64.

director of the Apostleship of Prayer. He worked as editor at the offices of the *Canadian Messenger* in Montreal until 1893, and then again from 1903 to 1906. Connolly was known for his keen business sense, evidenced in his founding of the Montreal Free Library several years earlier, as well as by his ability to secure funding for the Apostleship of Prayer and its magazine. In the first pages of the inaugural issue, the magazine was presented as a personified "The Messenger" to its readership. Connolly wrote: "we are sending him out and around at a considerable sacrifice, but one which, we are hopeful, will be amply rewarded by the good he will accomplish and be lessened by the zealous efforts of our promoters to obtain for him an entrance to all hearts and homes."

When Connolly returned to guide *The Messenger* again from 1903 to 1906, he reported a circulation in the "20,000s", and a staff of sixteen, "not including those in the advertising department."[7] The content continued to vary and develop. In 1903, Connolly had written an article on the "Junior League", a feature designed to help children practise the devotion to the Sacred Heart in various ways. Then, in 1904, he began to write a series of articles on the great gothic cathedrals of Europe, with full-page photos and artistic analyses. A year later he produced an article called "Fifty-Two Sundays", which emphasized the importance of attendance at Sunday Mass. Those early issues also featured a series of articles that would carry for twelve issues or more. For example, there was a series on devotion to the Sacred Heart by P. Suas, S.J., and another one by Scarboro Foreign Mission priest John Fraser, based upon his letters from China.[8] A further series, called "Fortifying the Layman", by Ernest R. Hull, S.J., outlined the principles of forming the laity for the ministry, ideas that anticipated many of the proposals of the Second Vatican Council. When he died at the age of sixty-three on 16 November 1911, Connolly was "widely considered

---

7 Frederick J. Power, S.J., "Editor's Newsletter", *The Messenger*, February 1991, 7.

8 Fraser, a diocesan priest born in Toronto, became the first North American priest to do mission work in China (1902–1949), where he remained until the Communist takeover. A year later he set out for Japan, where he remained until his death in 1962. Fraser founded the Scarborough Foreign Missions Society in Toronto, originally called "The China Mission College". See http://www.scarboromissions.ca/Learn_about_us/john_mary_fraser.php.

throughout Canada to be the founder and principal promoter of the devotion to the Sacred Heart among English-speaking Catholics."[9]

In the years between 1894 and 1902, there were a series of Jesuit editors, beginning with Arthur E. Jones, S.J., who was also a distinguished scholar, historian, and archaeologist.[10] Despite his many other commitments, *The Messenger* flourished under his tenure from 1894 to 1900. A report in 1898 described 20,000 promoters who functioned as distributors of the magazine, which was being printed in two languages; the English edition printed 14,000 while the French edition printed 11,000 copies. An estimated "500,000 readers per month" read them. The English-language magazine was compact (six and one-half inches by four inches), and contained thirty-six pages per issue. The first illustrations appeared in the December 1897 issue, accompanying a twenty-four-page story entitled "A Christmas Blossom", by an anonymous writer. Stories were often tagged with the phrase "Written for the Canadian Messenger" to indicate contributors other than the editor and the few Jesuits on staff. Editors rarely put their names to the pieces they wrote.

In the first decade of its existence, the magazine's content included poetry, prayers, and even hymns with musical notations. Early issues also printed historical documents, such as the "Aulneau Letters", a series that ran from 1892 to 1896. These were letters written by or about Jean-Pierre Aulneau, s.j., who was murdered with his companions on the Lake of the Woods in June 1736.[11] Other articles encompassed matters concerning the League of the Sacred Heart, such as news from each of the centres, the monthly totals of prayers that had been solicited by the promoters, lists of deceased members, news items from around the world, and articles on the pope's monthly intentions.

In 1900, one hundred pilgrims left Montreal for a pilgrimage to Paray-le-Monial in France, where Saint Margaret Mary Alacoque

---

9 DJB, vol. 1, 64.

10 Ibid, 157–158. Jones' history of the Huron district in Ontario was published by the Ontario government, *8endake Ehenoror or Old Ontario* (Toronto: L. K. Cameron, 1909). (*8endake* is Huron; the English equivalent is *Wendake.*) A man of ample girth, Jones led several notable, albeit precarious, archaeological expeditions to identify the sites of the first Jesuit missions before publishing his history of the area.

11 DCB, vol. II, 39–40.

had had her visions of the Sacred Heart of Jesus in the seventeenth century. These pilgrims, who represented 600,000 Canadian members of the League of the Sacred Heart, brought with them to France a red Moroccan-bound album containing the names of 150,000 Canadians who had sent to the magazine's offices in Montreal their pledged "Acts of Consecration" to the Sacred Heart. Along with a large banner of the Sacred Heart, the album was left at the international shrine as an *ex-voto* offering "to tell future generations of pilgrims, from these shores, how deeply the devotion to the Sacred Heart had penetrated Catholic Canada at the end of the nineteenth century."[12]

Among Jones' assistant editors was Lewis H. Drummond, S.J. He worked at the magazine for two years. Part of the founding editorial team of *America* magazine—a Jesuit weekly review based in New York—Drummond had also served on the editorial staff of *The Month*, a Jesuit journal published in London, England. When he died in 1929, the Canadian Press wrote in tribute, "his lucid, graceful style placed him among the leading Catholic journalists of his day."[13] Other Jesuits who worked on the Canadian *Messenger* in its early years included Isidore J. Kavanagh, S.J., a professor of science at the newly opened Loyola College on St. Catherine Street in 1896, and Louis J. Cotter, S.J.—another founding member of Loyola College—who was both assistant and acting editor from 1901 to 1904 and again from 1907 to 1909.[14]

At the beginning of the new century, in 1904, Edward J. Devine, S.J., became an assistant editor to Jean-Baptiste Nolin s.j., and then, in 1905, its editor.[15] Devine would be the first of the four long-serving twentieth-century editors—he remained editor until his death in 1927—and was a major force behind the development of the magazine. His life would be devoted to editing, printing, and writing. Earlier,

12 Frederick J. Power, S.J., "Editor's Newsletter", *The Messenger,* January 1991, 5.

13 DJB, vol. 1, 93–96. Drummond was among the first Jesuits who moved in 1885 to Collège de Saint-Boniface in Saint-Boniface, Manitoba, to assume responsibility for the college. From 1890 to 1892, he was Rector of Collège Sainte-Marie in Montreal, the only anglophone Jesuit ever to serve in that post.

14 DJB, vol. 1, 159; 71–72.

15 Ibid, 82–86, 260–261. Nolin was the director of the Apostleship of Prayer from 1887, a post he held for seventeen successive years. During that period, too, he oversaw in 1892 the birth of the *Messager du Sacré-Coeur*.

while a young Jesuit student at the Collège de l'Immaculée-Conception from 1885 to 1889 in Montreal, he acquired a printing press, trained Jesuit Brothers to be printers, and there published the first annual catalogue of the Jesuits to be printed in Canada. As a writer, he was prolific.[16] On the twenty-fifth anniversary of *The Messenger* in January 1916, he wrote a two-page editorial thanking the many promoters around Canada who had supported its growth.[17] In 1918, he published eight booklets on the Canadian Martyrs, which were promoted in the pages of the magazine. Altogether, Devine would write nine books, including a novel (*The Training of Silas*) and innumerable articles.

During the Great War, *The Messenger* was alert to the wartime needs and preoccupations of its readership. It covered items such as the damage to Rheims Cathedral by German shelling in 1914, and the fact that 400 Jesuits were serving in various roles in the French army. Those men had returned to France from exile imposed by anti-clerical laws of their day. Another article, titled "A Chaplain in the Trenches", described the experience of the difficult pastoral work on the Western Front. In 1915, there were photographs of the war and numerous letters printed from soldiers in France, which often shared stories attributing special protection to the Sacred Heart badges they wore.

At the same time, the magazine would occasionally initiate fundraising drives for various international causes. In the September 1922 issue, the editors announced a "Russian Relief Fund" for the serious food shortage in Russia, which continued for several years they received an official letter of thanks from Pope Pius XI for their efforts. The magazine also initiated prayer drives; in June 1922, the totals forwarded by members included an astonishing 10,523,128 "good works." A popular series of articles during the 1920s were

16 Before becoming editor, Devine had already lived an adventurous Jesuit life, having ministered in northern Ontario along the Canadian Pacific Railway, riding in the cabooses with the crews as he visited his "586-mile-long parish". He also worked in Nome, Alaska, between 1902 and 1904. His book *Across Widest America: Newfoundland to Alaska, with the impressions of two-years' sojourn on the Bering Coast* (New York: Benziger Bros, 1906), described those adventures. In a series of articles for *The Month* in England, he also recounted his experiences of the Canadian Pacific Railway.

17 In that year there were forty-three Messengers published in the world, in thirty different languages; by 1922 there were fifty-one with a total circulation of 1.5 million. These figures included the 375,000 circulation of the American Messenger and 300,000 of the Irish Messenger.

forty-seven episodes written by Joseph Fallon, S.J., under the pen name "Jim Wright", called "A Farmer's Letters to his Son". The series contained practical advice for a son living in the city, and it continued until 1927, when pressure from the female readership prompted its switch to "A Farmer's Letters to his Daughter." Pen names were a common practice then, partly due to the need for editors to write a broad range of original material.[18]

By the end of the second decade of the twentieth century, the magazine was printing over 45,000 copies of each issue, serving around 600,000 members in 450 centres in Canada. During those decades, and ever since the late nineteenth century, devotion to the Sacred Heart had been a main feature of Catholic piety in both English and French Canada, and pastors everywhere encouraged parishioners to subscribe to the magazine, which greatly contributed to the promoters' efforts. Copies were usually shared by many people in households and Religious Communities, which accounted for the disparity between circulation and membership.

In 1925, after the Jesuit Province of Canada had separated into the English-speaking Upper Canada Vice Province and the French-speaking Province du Bas-Canada, Devine oversaw the move of *The Messenger* from Montreal to 160 Wellesley Crescent in Toronto.[19] During that same year, the Canadian Jesuit Martyrs were beatified, an event that immensely gratified him who had written so extensively about them.[20] He would not live to see their canonization on 29 June 1930, however, for he died on 5 November 1927. An obituary penned by Anna Sadlier appeared in the January 1928 issue, poignantly memorializing "the human-hearted man we loved." Thousands of memorial cards were distributed to subscribers and others.

William H. Hingston, S.J., the son of Sir William Hales Hingston—a Montreal surgeon, former mayor of Montreal, and a

18 DJB, vol. 1, 107–108.

19 The site on Wellesley Street would later become the Wellesley Hospital. It has been replaced in recent years by condominium apartments.

20 Devine promoted the cause of the beatification of Kateri Tekakwitha, a young native girl in New France, by persuading the bishop of Albany to initiate her cause. He also "was the first to lead a pilgrimage of white people to her tomb in Caughnawaga (Kahnawake) in 1907". See DJB, vol. 1, 85. Kateri was finally canonized on 21 October 2012.

Canadian senator—was a prolific contributor to *The Messenger*.[21] Starting in November 1927, he also would serve as editor for a few months. In May 1928, however, he was appointed Provincial Superior of the Upper Canada Vice Province, at which time Joseph I. Bergin, S.J. became editor. Nonetheless, Hingston would continue to write for the magazine for many years; his contributions included a popular series on Christian Science and the Jehovah's Witnesses. These were later published as pamphlets; more than 200,000 copies were sold. In 1957, Hingston also began the well-liked instructional column "Question Box", which appeared in the weekly Catholic news publication *The Canadian Register*; his articulate and carefully reasoned replies to questions remained an admired feature of that newspaper.

When Bergin succeeded Hingston as editor in 1928, little did he know that he would fill that post for over thirty years.[22] He had begun as an assistant to Devine in 1925, when Devine himself was just completing twenty-five years as editor. Bergin proved successful in sustaining the magazine that Devine had built up. Under Bergin, *The Messenger* struck a balance between being a journal of instruction and of opinion while also serving as a channel for religious instruction that otherwise might not have reached Catholics. Since in those days Catholic publishing did not have the outreach that it would later develop, *The Messenger* was frequently the sole means for printed catechesis, for distributing the monthly papal prayer intention, as well as for presenting papal encyclicals printed in full, including the texts of Pius XI's two encyclicals published in 1931: *Casti Connubii*, on marriage, and *Quadragesimo Anno*, on socio-economic problems and their solutions. It was the only journal in Canada to do so.

Many well-known and highly regarded writers of the day contributed articles during Bergin's years as editor, including the English priest Ronald Knox; the Oxford scholar Cecil C. Martindale, S.J.; an

21 Ibid., 138–141. Hingston's mother, Lady Hingston, played a key role in organizing the campaign of *The Messenger* for soliciting nationwide donations of flowers for the International Eucharistic Congress of 1910 held in Montreal. A Catholic event, the congress was emblematic of Montreal's status as a Catholic city, with its streets and sanctuaries decorated profusely with floral arrangements of all kinds that had been sent from coast to coast.

22 Ibid, 16–17.

English moral philosopher, Joseph Rickaby, S.J.; Henry Somerville, the lay journalist and editor of *The Catholic Register* and zealous proponent of the Catholic Church's social teachings; Archbishop Alban Goodier, S.J., a profuse writer and archbishop of Bombay; the Canadian Jesuit Francis C. Smith; and the Benedictine historian and writer Dom Ernest Graf. In the late 1930s, while working as editor, Bergin would himself write stories under the pen name "O. Camesh", a name contrived from the words "Canadian" and "Messenger".[23]

Articles on the disastrous effect that Communism was having on Russia were frequent during the Stalin years, especially articles by Somerville. Several years later, the January 1948 issue would feature the first of many articles by John Hladun, a former member of the Communist Party of Canada, who wrote about the party's inner workings as well as about the secretive Lenin University in Moscow, which he had attended. The lay employee, Patrick Mulrooney, wrote many stories under the pen name "Michael Cahill", almost always two stories for adults and one for youth in each issue. These were often accompanied by brilliant ink drawings by Arthur Keelor and E. Fattori. Mulrooney would also serve as an office manager from 1918 to 1948.

During the Second World War, the Canadian bishops often wrote the articles on the papal prayer intentions, including Toronto's Archbishop (and later Cardinal) James Charles McGuigan. Richard Cardinal Cushing, archbishop of Boston, likewise contributed from time to time. *The Messenger* also continued to publish ecclesial documents. Most importantly, it promoted relief efforts that continued for a number of years after the war ended. The last editor, Frederick J. Power, S.J., remembered sorting tons of clothing and food at the Jesuit Seminary at 403 Wellington Street West in central Toronto during the early to mid 1950s. Such items would be sent by ship to Jesuits in Europe who would coordinate their distribution.[24]

During the final nine years of Bergin's editorship in the 1950s, the magazine continued its practice of having churchmen and lead-

23 The roots of this name were related by long-time editorial assistant Mary Pujolas to Frederick Power, S.J., in June 1991. Frederick J. Power, S.J., "Editor's Newsletter", *The Messenger*, October 1991, 6.

24 Ibid., 7.

ing thinkers of the day write on the papal monthly prayer intentions. During the 1950s, theologian and philosopher Bernard J. Lonergan, S.J., wrote articles entitled "Humble Acknowledgement of the Church's Teaching Authority" (January 1951), "A New Dogma" (1 November 1950), "Devotion to the Sacred Heart and the Immaculate Heart" (June 1951), and "Respect for Human Dignity" (July 1953). Other contributors were Monsignor Moses Michael Coady, the director of the world-famous Cooperative Movement at St. Francis Xavier University, Antigonish, Nova Scotia; Michael de la Bédoyère, editor of the London-based *Catholic Herald*; and Daphne D. C. Pochin Mould, the English author of books on Irish and Scots Catholics. Many Jesuits also contributed in the 1950s, including the bestselling American spiritual author Mark Link, S.J., and the English writer and retreat preacher Bernard Basset, S.J. A Canadian Jesuit, George K. McInerny, also wrote articles on religious subjects over many years, until his death in 1958.[25]

Bergin's last issue as editor was March 1959, whereupon he retired. Following that, the Provincial Superior, Gordon F. George, S.J., appointed Cecil C. Ryan, S.J., to be the national director of the Apostleship of Prayer and editor of *The Messenger*.[26] Mary Pujolas, assistant editor since 1957, became a main support of the magazine during the 1960s; she contributed, among other tasks, to the arrangement of illustrations.

Ryan would serve only until 1966. During those seven years, however, he made substantive changes to the Apostleship of Prayer and *The Messenger* by reorganizing these offices along lines inspired by the Second Vatican Council. A man with a keen understanding of people, outgoing and fully determined to update the magazine to meet not only the changes happening in the Catholic Church but also in the contemporary secular world, he set out to modernize completely its format. For the April 1959 issue, Ryan introduced the use of glossier

25 McInerny taught English literature, theology, and sacred oratory to young Jesuits in formation for many years, but suffered from a congenital foot defect, which a failed surgery in the 193●s had worsened, leaving him severely handicapped. His writing of articles for publications like *The Messenger* offered him a fruitful outlet for pastoral ministry. See DJB, vol. 1, 230.

26 Ibid., vol. 1, 312–313; vol. 2, 111–114.

paper to give the magazine a more contemporary look, and increased the number of illustrations and photographs, which, he reasoned, would attract younger readers. A year later, in June 1960, the cover went full-colour. Without the equipment on hand for printing in colour, Ryan had the issues printed by special arrangement with the staff of the American *Jesuit Messenger* in New York, which had its own printing presses. For several years afterwards, the covers would be shipped to Toronto to be joined to the rest of the magazine for binding. In 1959, Ryan also set up new offices at 226 St. George Street in Toronto. There he was assisted for one year by Alfred J. Colliard, S.J., who had been assistant to Bergin since 1957. Ryan also brought in James J. Mara, S.J., who was very successful as an advertising manager in soliciting new accounts.[27]

Several new writers contributed articles in the 1960s. David M. Stanley, S.J., the noted biblical scholar, wrote a series on the Mass, while Anna McDonald contributed a column entitled "For Women Only", beginning in March 1962, and her sister, Catherine Bolger, contributed a series, "View from a Pew", in March 1966. Bolger, who would become an international authority on pro-life issues, continued her column for twenty-two years, until retiring in 1988. From his home in the Darjeeling District of India, the Canadian Jesuit Murray Abraham wrote articles on the mission intentions during most of the 1960s. His first article centred on the "Mission Schools" (June 1961). After that, his contributions ranged widely about the mission of Darjeeling, the life and needs there, and about the Canadian Jesuits who were working there. In December 1973, Abraham wrote a reflection on Pope John XXIII's encyclical *Pacem in Terris*, which was reproduced on the editorial page of Toronto's *The Globe and Mail* on Christmas Day. The article, which discussed many social problems and their root causes, was reproduced in countless publications, both religious and secular, and most likely remains the most widely read article that ever appeared in the history of *The Messenger*. For an astonishing fifty years, he would continue writing for the magazine. His contributions

27 Ibid., vol. 2, 44–46; 199–202. Colliard would later be the first Rector in 1962 of the newly opened Brebeuf College School in Willowdale, Ontario.

ended with an article in the December 2011 issue called "Respect for Young People".[28]

At the seventy-fifth anniversary of the magazine in 1966, the editorship passed from Ryan to Power, who had worked at *The Messenger* since 1957. Power was the longest-serving editor in the magazine's history. Earlier, as a young Jesuit studying philosophy at 403 Wellington Street West from 1946 to 1949, he had written articles for the *Martyrs Shrine Message*, and had scripted dramas for radio broadcasting that were used by the St. Genesian Guild (an association of amateur Catholic actors) on a Montreal radio station. Later, during his studies in theology, he would help in the packaging and shipping of radio-discs of the Sacred Heart radio programmes.[29]

In 1967, Canada's centennial year, the magazine printed a series of articles by James S. McGivern, S.J., on the historical origins of the Catholic Church in each of the Canadian provinces.[30] During the same period, Frederick E. Crowe, S.J., a distinguished Canadian theologian, wrote a series on the changes in the Church since the Second Vatican Council.[31] In 1968, *The Messenger* gave its editorial support to the papal encyclical *Humanae Vitae*, published in July by Pope Paul VI. That same year, the magazine became international after the American *Messenger of the Sacred Heart* ceased publication. The directors of the Apostleship of Prayer in the United States unanimously voted to adopt the Canadian edition of the magazine for their use.

During the opening years of the 1970s, Power determined that there was a need for a renewed understanding of Sacred Scripture. He wrote an article entitled "Guide to Reading the Bible" for the

28 Abraham had been serving in India for sixty-three years. Power wrote at the time the following about his friend: "Father Abraham is not only an exceptionally gifted writer, your editor had the privilege of hearing him speak in practice sermons for the first six years of their seminary life together before [he] went to India. I am convinced that if he had not gone to India he would have been the 'Fulton J. Sheen' of Canada… ". (Frederick J. Power, "My 500th Visit", *The Messenger*, February 2012). Abraham's health began to deteriorate in early 2012; he died on 28 August of that year.

29 On the history of the Sacred Heart Program for radio and television, see below, page 210.

30 DJB, vol. 1, 226–227.

31 A renowned theologian, writer, and scholar of the works of Bernard J. F. Lonergan, S.J., Crowe died in the Jesuit infirmary at Pickering, Ontario, on 8 April 2012.

September 1971 issue; in subsequent months, "guides" to each book of the Bible appeared as separate articles.[32] Another important article during the 1970s was written in June 1974 by Jean Vanier, the founder of the L'Arche communities for people with developmental disabilities, titled "The Heart of Christian Love".[33]

By the early 1980s, the Jesuit Order had been undergoing many changes during the years following the Second Vatican Council and those of their own two General Congregations, the thirty-first (1965–1966) and the thirty-second (1974–1975). Like other Religious Orders of the day, the Society of Jesus was losing many members, while the involvement of some Jesuits in certain contentious issues regarding social justice became a point of concern for the Holy See.[34] *The Messenger* helped to clarify for its readers many of those issues by inviting Gordon F. George, S.J., who, carefully distinguishing fact from fiction, wrote a series of articles entitled "Would St. Ignatius Recognize His Jesuits?" The series began in June 1981 and continued until March 1983.[35] At that time, the magazine also featured an article by James E. Milord, one of the early Anglican clergymen to be received into the Catholic Church, ordained a Catholic priest, and allowed to practise as a married Catholic priest under Pope John Paul II's permitting such transitions.[36] While still an Anglican, Milord wrote an article entitled

---

32 These "guides" were eventually compiled and published as a booklet, "Guide to Reading the New Testament" in 1974 and "Guide to Reading the Old Testament" in 1975, both of which were reprinted many times. The Australian Messenger would later publish these together as one edition.

33 When Vanier wrote the article, the L'Arche movement was still new, and had fewer than thirty homes. Today there are 150 L'Arche communities in forty countries worldwide.

34 In 1981, there had developed an unusual situation in the Society of Jesus when the Superior General, Pedro Arrupe, suffered a debilitating stroke, and Paul Dezza, s.j., was appointed by Pope John Paul II as his delegate for the governance of the Society of Jesus. That was seen by many as a flashpoint for tensions between some members of the Society of Jesus and the Holy See.

35 DJB, vol. 2, 113. George was a highly respected voice among Jesuits within the Upper Canada Province. Earlier in his Jesuit life, he had been an assistant editor at *America* magazine, had been Provincial Superior from 1957 to 1963, and later, as the permanent secretary of the Canadian Conference of Catholic Bishops, had attended the final session of the Second Vatican Council (11 October 1965–8 December 1965).

36 The "Pastoral Provision" permitting married Anglican priests to be ordained Catholic priests was officially communicated in a letter of 22 July 1980 from the Congregation for the Doctrine of the Faith in Rome to the president of the National Conference of Catholic Bishops in the United States, who published it on 20 August 1980. The permission applied only to the United

"An Anglican Priest Looks at Devotion to the Sacred Heart", which Power and other Jesuits considered to be one of the finest treatments on the subject.

On the occasion of the papal visit to Canada in 1984, *The Messenger* continued its tradition of preparing spiritual bouquets for the Pope; at the time of John Paul II's visit to Martyrs' Shrine in Midland, Ontario, he was presented with one.[37] Later on that same trip, the Pope preached a homily on the Sacred Heart at the outdoor Mass at the Abbotsford Airport near Vancouver, attended by over 200,000 people. The magazine printed the text of his homily in its January 1985 issue.

During the 1980s, the magazine went through some significant transitions. Earlier, Power had overseen an increase in the magazine's size; this was reduced slightly in 1981 to obtain a better postage rate. In 1982, the staff moved to new offices at 661 Greenwood Avenue in the Danforth area of Toronto. As well, and after a long career with the magazine that had begun in 1957, the assistant editor, Mary Pujolas, retired in late 1986 due to ill health, while Alfred De Manche joined the staff after working for thirty-five years with *The Catholic Register*. His first contributions were in writing articles on the Catholic faith and in making artistic contributions to the magazine. He continued on staff until his retirement in 2007.

When in 1991 *The Messenger* celebrated its hundredth anniversary, it was a well-known and respected periodical in Canada and the United States, a familiar sight in homes and at the back of churches from coast to coast. Distributed in more than 700 churches (about 40 percent of all English-speaking parishes), it was believed to have

States, however. In Canada, such transitions were approved on a case-by-case basis. Milord was ordained a Catholic priest a few weeks before his death from cancer in Prince Albert, Saskatchewan, in the late 1980s.

37 Spiritual bouquets are prayers or devotional acts that someone offers for another, and are usually noted in a card or a letter from the donor(s) to the recipient. Such "bouquets" can consist of the offering of Masses or of Holy Communions, or of a determined number of prayers, such as the "Our Father", the "Hail Mary", and the Rosary, and of good deeds performed or to be performed. Although still a pious practice among Catholics, it has somewhat fallen out of use in recent years.

the widest circulation of any Catholic magazine in Canada.[38] It was not unusual for subscribers to write that they had been readers for forty, fifty, or sixty years, and on the occasion of its anniversary, the magazine received letters of congratulations and appreciation from Pope John Paul II, numerous bishops, laity, and a pledge of support from Jesuit Superiors both in Rome and Toronto. Its impact on the devotional and ecclesial life of the Catholic Church in Canada cannot be overestimated.

In the first decades of the third millennium, *The Messenger* continued to present the spirituality of the Apostleship of Prayer to its readers. Circulation began to decline somewhat, however, due to an increase in the age of the magazine's core readership and competition from the Internet. It was printing about 15,000 copies in 2002, compared to its peak of 55,000 in 1948; by 2012, the readership was around 30,000.[39] In 2008, the website *sacredheartcanada.com* was set up to be a point of reference for readers. Perhaps its success can best be captured in the words of Thomas B. Fulton, then bishop of St. Catharines, Ontario, who wrote: "The secret of its longevity is found in a tried and true formula. The Messenger speaks to people in a language they can understand about matters which are relevant to their lives against a background of faith and devotion. In today's terms, it is a remarkable instrument of evangelization and social communication."[40]

In 2013, and well into his eighties, Power still drove to his editorial offices every weekday morning to oversee the production of each monthly issue with the help of his associate editor, Joan Levy Earle. The February 2012 edition celebrated Power's 500th issue. In his quincentennial "Editor's Editorial", he reprised the formula that he had professed back in 1966, when he first began his work: "Really it is more a problem of expressing the ageless lessons of the love of God in language that is understood by our generation." Power added,

38 Frederick J. Power, S.J., "A Century of Devotion for the Messenger", *The Catholic Register*, 16 February 1991, 7.

39 The Canadian Messenger Archives, 661 Greenwood Avenue, Toronto, Circulation Files.

40 Thomas B. Fulton, letter, 22 August 1990.

"I trust that our present 'faithful readers' will agree that we have been true to our word these many years."[41]

The Crusader

The Eucharistic Crusade was a movement born in 1914 under the auspices of The Apostleship of Prayer, whose object was to offer a comprehensive programme of spiritual formation for elementary and high school students. By the 1950s, it was enjoying considerable success in Quebec's schools. The French-Canadian Jesuits were responsible for it, but also wanted to promote the movement in English-speaking Canada. They needed someone who could translate the bulletin of the Eucharistic Crusade into English. Marcus C. Doherty, S.J., was fluently bilingual. In 1954, therefore, he was assigned to the Jesuit Community at Loyola College, Montreal, to write the English section of the bulletin. He would serve in that position for the next five years.[42]

In 1957, Power was sent to join him, and in 1959, when Thomas Diehl, S.J., was appointed the national director of the Eucharistic Crusade in the United States, Power began to collaborate with him in producing *The Crusader* magazine. Subtitled "Canadians in the Service of Christ", *The Crusader* was designed for the formation of students in grades one to eight; Diehl and Power each would write about half the content of every issue of the magazine.[43] As of 1964, however, *The Crusader* was no longer distributed in the United States, but solely in Canada, while the movement of Eucharistic Crusade itself was dissolved in the United States in the late 1960s because of the new catechetical programmes introduced following the Second Vatican Council. However, the movement continued to grow elsewhere around the world, and by 1966 had grown to more than five million members worldwide, including around 90,000 in Canadian English-speaking schools. Power continued to write and produce *The Crusader* until 1969, when the Eucharistic Crusade was discontinued in Canadian Catholic schools. Today the Eucharistic Crusade is known

41 Frederick J. Power, S.J., "My 500th Visit", *The Messenger*, February 2012, 4.

42 DJB, vol. 1, 86–88.

43 *The Crusader* was printed at the New York presses of the American *Messenger of the Sacred Heart*.

as the Eucharistic Youth Movement (EYM); in 2012, it is present in fifty countries on five continents.

Martyrs Shrine Message

Of a different nature altogether was the *Martyrs Shrine Message*. Initially published in May 1937 as a quarterly magazine, its first editor was Thomas J. Lally, S.J., who was the director of the Martyrs' Shrine from 1928 until his death in 1953. The principal aim of the magazine was to make known to the public, as much as possible, information about the lives of the Canadian Jesuit Martyrs and of their mission to Huronia in the seventeenth century, to promote devotion to the Jesuit Martyrs, and to encourage pilgrimages to the shrine. In effect, however, the magazine also covered a wide variety of other topics, ranging from events taking place at the shrine, to the Jesuits' past and present ministry at the shrine, and to the work of the English-speaking Jesuits in Canada. Most especially, the many miraculous cures received through the Martyrs' intercession have all been recorded over the decades. The articles were written not only by the editors themselves—since 1937, there have been at least nine editors—but by Canadian Jesuit priests and Scholastics, as well as by Religious and lay men and women. The publication, which is sent free of charge to those who took out membership in the Martyrs' Shrine Mass Association, has been financed by members' fees. Although its format has changed over the years, the magazine's primary purpose still remains to make known to those who subscribe to the magazine as well as to all who visit the shrine the lives, the missions, and especially the heroic deaths of the Canadian Jesuit Martyrs.

America

Of the magazines sponsored by the Jesuits in North America, few have been as consistently important as *America* magazine. Founded in 1909 as a joint project by the Canadian and American Jesuits, it sought to be a kind of counterpart of the British Catholic publication *The Tablet*. Although from its establishment the Canadian Jesuits were involved in differing ways in the magazine's production, it was at heart an American, New York–based weekly. The first Jesuit from Canada appointed to work at the Jesuit editorial residence was Brother Hubert

Henry, S.J., in 1924. For the twenty-six following years, he acted as sacristan, handyman, and general factotum for the Jesuit Community. His task was to make sure that the building was maintained, the plumbing functioned properly, the furnaces produced heat, and that all other chores around the building were attended to. Thus the Jesuit priests could produce the weekly editions of *America* without concerns for practical household details. This Henry did with considerable success until 1950, when he returned to Canada.[44]

Two years later, the Canadian Provincial Superior, George E. Nunan, S.J., appointed Gordon F. George, S.J., for a three-year term as an associate editor of *America*, responsible for editorials and articles on health issues and on Latin America. "This was a very stimulating time", George later would write, and there was no doubt that his articles and editorials greatly reflected that. Perceptive, coherent, and written in carefully crafted prose, his writings clearly reveal his enthusiasm for addressing contemporary problems.

After the appointed three years were concluded, George returned in 1955 to his own Province. In many ways, however, this brief sojourn in New York provided a most important experience in print media for his future work. Later, from 1972 until 1975, he served as director of the Jesuit Press and Information Office at the Jesuit curial offices in Rome, and then, from 1975 to 1976, as a collaborator in the new Jesuit Secretariat of Social Communications, which also was set up at the Roman curial offices. There he helped launch Multi-Media International, an office that encouraged and provided an opportunity for Religious men and women to become actively engaged in the media. If his years in New York were "stimulating", certainly his four years in Rome were equally so. Of even greater importance was that during his time in New York, George had come to understand the necessity of Jesuits being trained in the developing area of communications. His appointment as Provincial Superior for six years, from 1957 to 1963, gave him the opportunity to encourage Jesuits to take up the study of communications.[45]

44 DJB, vol. 1, 137.

45 Ibid., vol. 2, 111–114.

Other than those Canadian Jesuits who contributed articles to the magazine over the years, the last Canadian Jesuit to live in New York at the headquarters of *America* was George E. Nunan, S.J. He was not appointed to work at its offices, but to be the Superior of the Jesuit staff of the magazine in 1959. A kindly, considerate man, he proved to be an excellent and hospitable Superior, and was greatly appreciated by the Jesuits there. After six years, at the end of his term in office, he returned to Canada.[46]

Compass

With a view to establishing a print forum for reflection on contemporary life rooted in Catholic tradition, the Canadian English-speaking Jesuits founded *Compass: A Jesuit Journal* in 1983. Although it lasted for only fourteen years, it was able in a short time to make its mark on an intellectual reading public with its wide-ranging articles and reflections on all the international and national issues of the 1980s and 1990s. Perhaps what was most remarkable about the magazine was its impressive roster of writers. Among these were Joan Chittister, O.S.B., Eric Kierans, Charles Taylor, Margaret Visser, Robertson Davies, John H. Yoder, Wilfred C. Smith, Michael Bliss, Ramsay Cook, Lawrence Kushner, Gunther Plaut, Gregory Baum, Ruth Barrows, Rosemary Haughton, Jean Vanier, Daniel Berrigan, S.J., Martin Royackers, S.J., Marc Gervais, s.j., Jacques Monet, s.j., along with a host of others—Jesuit, lay, Protestant, Catholic, and Jewish.

During its first few years, *Compass* was edited by Grant Maxwell, a layman who had worked for the Canadian Conference of Catholic Bishops; he gave the magazine its first shape. The intention was "to tell the Jesuit story", a vague and difficult task, which had its share of criticism from many English Canadian Jesuits, especially for the certain "folksy approach" it adopted. An editorial refocus took place a few years later by Michael F. Czerny, S.J., David R. Eley, S.J., and Angus J. Macdougall, S.J., who consulted publishing professionals

46 Another Canadian Jesuit who was briefly involved with *America* magazine was Neil McKenty, who worked as relief editor during the summer of 1959. As well, during 1960 to 1961, he served as an associate editor of the Jesuit periodical *The Way*, published in London, England. In 1967 he published an acclaimed biography of Ontario premier Mitch Hepburn. Cf. *Mitch Hepburn* (Toronto: McClelland and Stewart, 1967). In 1970, McKenty left the Society of Jesus.

and fashioned a more analytical style. Robert Chodos, a published author and contributing editor of *This Magazine*, was hired as editor, and served from 1987 to 1997.[47] Entire issues were dedicated to one theme, such as immigration, sexuality, free trade, and Catholic education. In 1990, the editors conceived a project of dedicating every March/April issue to "a leisurely retrospective" on each decade of the twentieth century, starting with 1900–1910. The series continued until the special issue on "The 1970s", but ended unfinished when *Compass* ceased publication in 1997.[48]

Despite *Compass* having received awards for its articles and editorials, it was unfortunate that its reading public never reached the numbers that had initially been anticipated.[49] That put a severe financial burden on the magazine. Other than through subscriptions, the magazine was for the most part supported by the English Canadian Jesuits. By the mid 1990s, it became clear that unless new financial resources were found, *Compass* would have to fold. In 1997, the Jesuits suspended their sponsorship of the magazine. Despite the editorial board's efforts to continue publication by finding new sponsors, the final issue was May/June 1997.

Catholic New Times

Although not a Jesuit newspaper, the Canadian weekly *Catholic New Times* was founded in 1976 by a group of like-minded Catholics, including James F. Webb, S.J., who were interested in the social justice questions of the day. They wanted to establish an independent Canadian Catholic voice that supported the Catholic Church's call for social justice through critical analysis. Widely recognized as a source of independent information, for the next thirty years the weekly continued to criticize, analyze, and evaluate moral, social, and religious

47 *This Magazine* remains one of Canada's longest-running "alternative journals", being founded by education activists in 1966. Chodos has written many books on Canadian business and politics, specializing in Quebec history.

48 Chodos would edit the book *Compass Points: Navigating the 20th Century* (Toronto: Between the Lines and Compass Foundation, 1999), which included the articles from the *Compass* retrospective series, as well as previously unpublished essays on the 1980s and 1990s.

49 Compass won a silver National Magazine Award in 1996 in the category of Best Editorial Package, and on several occasions was named the best Christian magazine in Canada and the best Catholic magazine in North America by the Catholic Press Association.

issues, sometimes with more than a little negative assessment of the Catholic Church's stances on contemporary moral and theological concerns. By the mid 2000s, however, with numbers of subscribers falling and a considerable amount of dissatisfaction towards the paper by many Catholics because of its liberal views, *Catholic New Times* published its final issue on 15 December 2006.

Radio and Television

The earliest Jesuit involvement in radio programming in Canada was the Sacred Heart Program, a fifteen-minute radio programme of religious instruction and sacred music produced by the Jesuits in St. Louis, Missouri, and introduced into Canada in 1943. The programme began modestly, with little publicity, under the direction of its first national director, Erle G. Bartlett, S.J. The first radio station to broadcast the programme was CFOR in Orillia. When Bartlett died only two years after his appointment, twelve stations were broadcasting the programme.[50]

His successor was Thomas J. Walsh, S.J., a witty and articulate speaker in whose capable hands the radio programme of the Sacred Heart was marketed as a free "community service programme" to managers of radio stations and programme directors across the country.[51] Walsh was never one to shy away from a challenge. A first-rate charmer, he always insisted on meeting the "top man." It usually paid off. Within two years of his becoming director, the Sacred Heart Program was being aired by over fifty stations. When the American Jesuits began production of television programming in 1956 in St. Louis, Walsh introduced the same content to Canadian television viewers. At the time, it was estimated that between radio and television, the Canadian audience numbered more than half a million.[52]

Several other Canadian Jesuits were involved over the years in the radio and television programmes. John I. Hochban, S.J., became the "voice" of the Sacred Heart Program in Canada and the United

50 DJB, vol. 1, 6–7.

51 Ibid., 339–340.

52 Ibid., 336.

States during the 1950s and 1960s, "regularly listened to by a public estimated at about one million persons."[53] For over twenty-two years, he delivered over 400 weekly talks on radio and television for the Sacred Heart Program. That meant having to take countless flights to St. Louis, Missouri. Hochban used his fine baritone voice—he was an accomplished musician—to very good effect on the radio, and his weekly programme was eagerly listened to; many came to appreciate his articulate discussions, which were always engaging, well thought out, and stimulating to the listeners. When the Sacred Heart Program began broadcasting on television, his striking good looks, rich voice, and well-groomed appearance were a perfect fit for this new medium.[54]

Beginning in 1967, and until his death in 1987, Daniel H. McLarnon, S.J., greatly involved himself at the offices of the Apostleship of Prayer. A passionate preacher and speaker, for over fifteen years he was a strong advocate of the devotion to the Sacred Heart, and he promoted across Canada radio and television programmes that featured that devotion. As the director of the Apostleship of Prayer, Frederick J. Power, S.J., also promoted the Sacred Heart Program. In the latter years of the Program, Power produced around forty episodes with Matthew Meehan, a Redemptorist priest who served as the host. The programme continued for over forty years until it closed in 2006.

A pioneer in Canadian Catholic televangelism was the charismatic and energetic Robert L. MacDougall, S.J.[55] His early life had been characterized by some dramatic events. A tail gunner during the Second World War in the Royal Canadian Air Force (RCAF), his plane was shot down in the icy waters of the North Sea near Denmark, where he was rescued by fishermen and taken prisoner by German officers.[56] Ten days later, to avoid surrendering to the advancing Russians, the Germans sought him out as the highest-ranking Western officer they could find. He was, in fact, a flying officer, the second-lowest rank in

53 Ibid., 143–144.

54 Ibid., 144.

55 Ibid., vol. 2, 175–179.

56 "The crew was with 644 Squadron and had left their base in Dorset in England at 10 p.m. on April 26, 1945". Cf. F. F. Langan, "Bob MacDougall, RCAF Flier and Priest 1924–2004", *The Globe and Mail,* 29 January 2005.

the RCAF. To his surprise, he was hailed as a liberator, and carried in triumph about the streets of Vejle, Denmark.

While swimming around the wreckage of his plane, MacDougall had promised God: "Save me from this and I'll spend my life doing good."[57] After the war, he joined the Jesuits. Following his ordination as a priest, he worked at the Toronto Catholic Rehabilitation Service and as a prison and reformatory chaplain. His hope was to be a missionary, but that was not to be. While in Uruguay, he contracted dysentery, which limited the possibility of working on the missions. Consequently, he threw himself into the difficult job of ministering to the inmates at the Stony Mountain maximum security prison near Winnipeg. Later, he worked at the Don Bosco Residence for boys in Orillia, Ontario, as a chaplain. Those were demanding jobs. In time, MacDougall fell prey to depression and a dependency upon alcohol. He was successfully treated for the latter during February 1975.

It was during that period of convalescence that MacDougall underwent a "born again" experience. One evening at the treatment centre, two friends who were priests had returned from a charismatic prayer service in central Toronto. They felt that they should pray over MacDougall: "As they prayed, he fell to the floor, felt a strange sensation in his throat, and erupted in an outpouring of nonsensical syllables known as glossolalia, the so-called 'speaking in tongues' which often accompanies this sort of conversion experience."[58] Soon afterwards, MacDougall went to the United States to meet with evangelical leaders and charismatic Christians in Solano Beach, California. His purpose was "to get a better understanding of what had happened to him, to discern what he should do about it and, as he later expressed it to a friend, to 'immerse [himself] in the Bible.'"[59] When he returned to Canada in 1975, he made contact with the Christians at Crossroads Communications, who invited him to join them in a new evangelical television channel, 100 Huntley Street, which had been launched in 1977. MacDougall was a good fit, and for the next

57 DJB, vol. 2, 176.

58 Ibid., 178.

59 Ibid.

twenty-three years he was a tireless Catholic televangelist, co-hosting and appearing on hundreds of episodes of the programme. During those years, he also preached at more than a thousand charismatic events across North America.

For two years, from 1982 to 1984, MacDougall withdrew from *100 Huntley Street* to help a friend who was the pastor of two parishes in Nova Scotia. When he returned to Toronto, he founded a Catholic television programme called *Food for Life*, which was taped in Toronto and distributed weekly throughout North America and Western Europe by satellite.[60] The show featured interviews, testimonies of personal rebirth, gospel music, and readings from the Bible. Unfamiliar with the very idea of a charismatic movement in the Catholic Church, many Catholics found the show shocking. Yet MacDougall had no doubts that it was God's will for him, as a Jesuit priest, to be a televangelist in the Catholic Church.[61]

Other Canadian Jesuits have contributed to religious broadcasting in radio and television over the years—some on occasional programmes, such as Marc Gervais, and others on a regular basis, such as Jacques Monet and John Pungente. Sometimes Jesuits have been called upon to speak before a national television audience about a specific Catholic problem or a contentious public matter; at other times, important events, such as the papal visit of 1984, have included Jesuits as presenters and commentators. Radio and television stations often contact the local Jesuit Communities across the country to seek answers about a particular religious topic or issue of the day. All in all, from the beginning, Canadian Jesuits have contributed in varying degrees and ways to advancing their ministries through the media of radio and television, and they continue to be among the Catholic Church's spokespersons to the contemporary world.

---

60 DJB, vol. 2, 175–179. See also http://www.foodforlifetvministry.org. Today the programme is largely run by the Companions of the Cross, a community of priests and seminarians based in Ottawa. See MacDougall interviewing Robert Bedard, founder of the Companions of the Cross in 1984 and 1992: http://www.youtube.com/watch?v=XaVNWIzVn9w&lr=1.

61 By the end of the 1990s, complications from the dysentery and vascular problems as a result of his plunge in the frigid waters of the North Sea were reducing his energies. He was assigned to the Jesuit infirmary in Pickering in 1999, and died there on 26 December 2004.

Jesuit Academic Programmes in Communications

The 1960s began a period of immense change in much of the world and, in Canada, at almost every level of society. At the international level, the Second Vatican Council (1962–1965) met to reassess the Catholic Church's relationship to the world. At the national level, Canada was undergoing radical changes during this time, symbolized in its becoming a social democratic nation, in its celebrations for its centennial year of 1967, and in the World's Fair in Montreal, Expo 67. Within a year of this major international event, Pierre Elliott Trudeau became prime minister of the country. Colour television was displacing the black-and-white programmes. Earlier, at the University of Toronto, Marshall McLuhan had published *Understanding Media* (1964), making media "cool" and worthy of serious study.

Yet much of the inspiration in the modern Catholic world towards communications had come from a seminal encyclical, *Miranda Prorsus* ("wonderful invention"), published on 8 September 1957 by Pope Pius XII. In it, he discussed motion pictures, television, radio, and media technologies. At the same time as he conveyed certain concerns surrounding these modern technological advances, he encouraged Catholics to involve themselves in the new technologies:

> For these new possessions and new instruments which are within almost everyone's grasp, introduce a most powerful influence into men's minds, both because they can flood them with light, raise them to nobility, adorn them with beauty, and because they can disfigure them by dimming their lustre, dishonour them by a process of corruption, and make them subject to uncontrolled passions, according as the subjects presented to the senses in these shows are praiseworthy or reprehensible.[62]

The Pope went on to say that the Catholic Church had the sacred right and duty to continue its mission of sanctifying souls by using the new media in the promotion of truth and virtue, that government

---

62 For the text, see http://www.vatican.va/holy_father/pius_xii/encyclicals/documents/hf_p-xii_enc_08091957_miranda-prorsus_en.html. Pope Pius XII was among the first of the modern popes to use the radio frequently as a means of communicating his messages to the world.

had the responsibility to spread news and teaching for the common good, and that individuals could use media to enrich their intellectual and spiritual culture. He also invited priests and Religious to enter the field of communications in the service of the Catholic Church.[63] What was also new was Pius XII's exhortation that "sincere and zealous sons of the Church, who recognize the inestimable gift of the Redemption, must exert every effort in seeing that she has the use of these technical advances to the extent that they can contribute to the sanctification of souls." For the first time, the Catholic Church was encouraging its members to enter a field that had hitherto been an almost exclusively secular one, with the one exception of Vatican Radio, which had been a leader in religious broadcasting since its founding by Guglielmo Marconi in 1931.

In the midst of all that development, a new generation of Canadian Jesuits emerged, drawn to engage the world at the level of mass communications. Of these, John (Jack) Egli O'Brien, S.J., was the first to take this up as an academic discipline.[64] He was invited by the Provincial Superior, Gordon F. George, S.J., to consider the novel path of studying for a doctorate in the then-fledgling academic field of communications. In 1959, George assigned O'Brien to begin graduate studies in communications at the University of Southern California in Los Angeles, then among the few universities in the world to offer such a degree.[65]

Four years later, in March 1964, having completed a doctoral degree, O'Brien returned to Canada. He was fortunate in having Patrick G. Malone, S.J., as Rector at Loyola College.[66] Malone had

---

63 Pope Pius wrote: "We paternally exhort Catholics, well-qualified by their learning, sound doctrine and knowledge of the arts—and in particular clerics, and members of Religious Orders and Congregations—to turn their attention to this new art and give their active cooperation, so that whatever benefits the past and true progress have contributed to the mind's development, may be also employed in full measure to the advantage of Television".

64 A native of Montreal who had attended Loyola High School, O'Brien took his baccalaureate studies at Loyola College. In 1945, he joined the Society of Jesus.

65 While he was at University of Southern California, O'Brien was elected president of Alpha Epsilon Rho, known today as the National Broadcasting Society, an association for broadcast and media students. During his tenure, he presented an award to the celebrated journalist Walter Cronkite.

66 DJB, vol. 2, 195–199.

become Rector of Loyola in 1959, and was keen to establish a programme in communications studies there. His experience as dean of arts (1952–1956) and Rector (1956–1959) at Saint Mary's University, Halifax, during the 1950s had convinced him of the importance of such a programme. Indeed, during 1953 and 1954, his intention was to improve the programme of journalism there. The university had been participating in the Halifax School of Journalism, and Malone believed that Saint Mary's programme should be a worthy partner in that school. Along with the courses in journalism leading to a diploma that the university had offered for some time, he added public relations and advertising to the curriculum.[67]

Yet Malone had further plans in mind. For some time, he pondered the establishing of courses at Saint Mary's that would lead to a diploma in communication arts. This would include studies in radio, television, newspaper and magazine production, advertising, debating, elocution, and public relations. Indeed, had the diploma been introduced at Saint Mary's as he had wanted, it would have been the first of its kind in Canada. He met stiff opposition, however, mainly from the then Provincial Superior, George E. Nunan, S.J., who, like many Catholic leaders of the day, was seriously suspicious of the newly developing technologies in television, film, and other fields of communications. Nunan was concerned that such an academic programme in communication arts would eventually lead to the secularization of Saint Mary's. He argued that it would move the university away from the traditional Jesuit role of teaching theology and philosophy along with the humanities. Malone had no such concerns. In fact, he believed the opposite: that a Catholic university could and should hold its own in the secular world. In the end, ignoring Nunan's concerns, Malone introduced a number of measures at Saint Mary's that eventually would lead to a communication arts programme.[68]

---

67 Patrick G. Malone, S.J., letter to George E. Nunan, S.J., 23 June 1953, AJC, Box F-625.

68 Patrick G. Malone, S.J., letter to George E. Nunan, S.J., 11 June 1952, ibid., Box F-264; Patrick G. Malone, S.J., letter to George E. Nunan, S.J., 23 June 1953; "Proposed Curriculum for Communications Arts", 20 February 1953; George E. Nunan, S.J., letter to Patrick G. Malone, S.J., 15 April 1954; Patrick G. Malone, S.J., letter to George E. Nunan, S.J., 10 May 1954, ibid., Box F-625.

Thus, when Malone left Saint Mary's to become Rector of Loyola College, he brought with him ideas for a communication arts programme there. Within five years, those ideas, along with the arrival of O'Brien in 1964 with his doctorate in communications studies, helped to round out Malone's wider, more ambitious plans to expand the college to the point where it could become a university. As a consequence, O'Brien was invited to develop an academic programme at the college that would reflect the increasingly important field of communication arts.

The programme began modestly. The chair of the college's English department, J. Gerald MacGuigan, S.J., invited O'Brien to teach an elective course on media and society. The problem, however, was that the academic calendar had already been printed for the year, and no more than half a dozen students were expected to register. When nearly eighty students enrolled, it became clear that contemporary communications and mass media were topics of great interest. Soon after the introduction of O'Brien's course, the college sponsored a film festival entitled "The Best of the NFB". For five successive nights, short films produced by the National Film Board of Canada were screened, with several directors and producers present as guest lecturers. The F. C. Smith Auditorium was filled to capacity.

Because of those two successful events, the college's senate, under Malone's watchful eye, invited O'Brien to submit a proposal for establishing a new department—the first of its kind in Canada—and communication arts came into being at Loyola College in the summer of 1965. Six courses were offered that first year: three cross-listed with the department of English, one with music, while the remaining two, "Introduction to Mass Media" and "The Art and Science of Communication", were the specific offerings of the new department.[69]

During this time, too, and prior to the opening of Expo 67, O'Brien, along with several others, had been invited to help design the Christian pavilion for the exposition. Constructed at the heart of the exposition's site, within the pavilion's $1.3 million interior, was a multi-media "experience" designed to provoke existential questioning

69 Ibid., Box I-312.

about life in the world.[70] In the first stage of the pavilion, visitors would experience pleasant sensations of family life, work, play, and human achievement, projected by means of sound and video. Passing to the second stage, they were bombarded with the sights and sounds of family quarrels, hunger, war, and racism. In the third stage, they entered a white room, intended for thoughtful reflection, followed by a room of mirrors and images of the good and bad in society, where the only overt Christian message was read aloud: a series of five short comments offered in several languages. The goal of the designers had been to use modern media to foster a religious experience. After *Time* magazine covered the story of the pavilion, there was an influx of applications to the communication arts programme at Loyola, including many students who already possessed advanced degrees in other academic fields.

In response to growing enrolment, during the autumn of 1967 the department created a programme for a post Bachelor of Arts diploma. Also, as a result of the Christian pavilion's "experience", two new lecturers joined the faculty: the filmmaker who helped design the pavilion, Charles Gagnon, as artist-in-residence; and Miroslav Malik, executive director of the Czechoslovakia pavilion, who, over many years, would teach courses on film, programming, and the history of communications, among others topics.

During the late 1960s and early 1970s, despite his busy schedule, O'Brien appeared regularly on television, most notably as a panellist in more than 100 episodes of the CBC television show *Would You Believe!* (1967–1973). This programme dealt with various aspects of Canadian life, including faith and justice. In 1971, he also assisted in the writing of the pastoral instruction *Communio et Progressio*, which the Second Vatican Council document *Inter Mirifica* (1963) had requested, and which emphasized the need for freedom of the press and of journalists. It also noted the positive role of the modern media in society and urged the engagement of Catholics in communications.[71]

---

70 The Christian pavilion was co-sponsored by the Catholic, United, Anglican, Presbyterian, Lutheran, Baptist, and Greek Orthodox Churches. See coverage in *Time* magazine, 25 February 1966.

71 O'Brien recalled a meeting that was taking place in Toronto on the Church and communica-

Although Loyola College would merge with Sir George Williams University in 1974 to become Concordia University, the department of communication arts would continue its national reputation for excellence. Indeed, other Canadian universities often looked to Concordia as a model for establishing similar programmes. Although the communication arts department was renamed the department of communication studies in 1977, its formula for training students in three main areas—the arts, the social sciences, and technique—continued. In the Jesuits' humanistic tradition, students had to bridge theory and practice. Media technology had to convey ideas that were thoughtful and meaningful; the message was just as important as the medium.

In 1983, O'Brien was appointed to Rome to assist the Jesuits' Superior General, Peter Hans Kolvenbach, and consequently and effectively, retired from Concordia University. During six years in Rome, he was director of the Jesuit Centre for Social Communications. From there he would visit the seventy provinces of the Society of Jesus worldwide, advising Provincial and local Superiors on communications. He also published three times a year the newsletter *JESCOM*, which was sent to every Jesuit Province in the world. Importantly for O'Brien and other Jesuits, communications studies impacted homiletics, liturgical practices, and writing. His particular concern, therefore, was primarily that Jesuits in their early formation needed training in communications, not as mere technicians, but in understanding the way concepts flow from "the head" to an audience. As well, during that period in Rome, he was a visiting professor at the Pontifical Gregorian University, and began serving as a consultor for the Pontifical Council for Social Communications, a role he would fill until 1995.[72]

At the end of his term in Rome, although he was offered a position at Lumen 2000, a large institute for Catholic broadcasting in

tions, which the great media theorist Marshall McLuhan was supposed to attend. McLuhan arrived late. He entered the room, apologized for his lateness, then said, "The Church must be counter-cultural", and promptly left. It was the only meeting of the group he ever attended.

72 Once, during a meeting on communications at Castel Gandolfo between Pope John Paul II and thirty-two Jesuits, there was a Mass at which the group of Religious was asked to sing. Unprepared, they did their best. Later, during his address to the group, the Pope affirmed how much the Catholic Church needed the efforts of the communications specialists, and that they were a tremendous gift, but, he memorably quipped, "the one gift you haven't got: you don't know how to sing!" Related in conversation by John E. O'Brien, S.J., to John D. O'Brien, S.J.

Europe, O'Brien was assigned to direct the Manresa Retreat Centre in Pickering, Ontario. During the early 2000s, he worked in and around Toronto, lecturing at St. Augustine's Seminary and directing an initiative called the Communications Desk at the Provincial Curia of the Jesuits of Upper Canada Province (English Canada). This project, which was experimental in nature, was meant to explore and coordinate the communications needs of the English-speaking Jesuit Province and to synchronize Jesuits of varied expertise for lectures and consultation—a kind of Jesuit ad-intra and ad-extra speaker's bureau.[73]

Two years after the communication arts programme was established at Loyola College, Marc Gervais, s.j., joined the department. He would become one of the experts on film for the thirty-five years that he taught there; he would also become a well-known critic and commentator about films and film studies on the world stage. Earlier, while a young Jesuit, Gervais had developed an interest in film, particularly those by Swedish director Ingmar Bergman. Once, while conversing about Bergman's film *The Seventh Seal* (1957), Gervais recalled: "I had never seen a film so religious. Not like Hollywood and *The Bells of St. Mary's*, but deeply religious, with existential questions."[74]

His first graduate degree was a Master of Arts in drama from Catholic University of America, which he received in 1963. Yet he realized then that his interests were more in film than in drama. Consequently, his Provincial Superior, Angus J. Macdougall, S.J., assigned him in 1965 to begin a doctoral degree in communications at l'Université de Paris–Sorbonne. There, as in most other universities, a doctoral programme in film had to be improvised, so new was the idea of film as an academic discipline.

While at the Sorbonne from 1965 to 1967, Gervais was named head of the Catholic Film Office (OCIC). Later, in 1968, when his

73 In 2012, O'Brien was awarded the Loyola Medal from Concordia University. During the ceremony of presentation, Dr. Frederick H. Lowry, president of Concordia University, stated that in establishing the communication arts programme, O'Brien had "created an academic discipline", and that the department had become the standard by which others in Canada were measured. The Loyola Medal was first awarded by Loyola College in 1963 to Georges-P. Vanier, governor general of Canada and an alumnus. In 1989, it was established that it would be given every two years to outstanding Canadian citizens. Recipients have included Paul-Émile Cardinal Léger, Bernard J. F. Lonergan, S.J., Oscar Peterson, and Roméo Dallaire.

74 Unpublished interview with John D. O'Brien, S.J., 6 January 2012.

office awarded its jury's prize to Pier Paolo Pasolini's homoerotic film *Teorema* at the Venice Film Festival, a storm of controversy ensued.[75] As the director of OCIC, he defended the award, stating that the film was merely about the healing power of sexuality.[76] Later, in 1973 and 1999, he published two major works: one on Pasolini, and one on Bergman. He was henceforth recognized as the leading international expert on both those directors.[77]

Although Gervais was a full-time professor during the late 1960s and the 1970s, first at Loyola College and then at Concordia University, he still had to complete his doctoral dissertation in film aesthetics for the Sorbonne. That he did in 1979. Two years later, in 1981, he was appointed a commissioner at the Canadian Radio-television and Telecommunications Commission (CRTC), a post he held until 1987. He also served as a member of the Canadian Broadcast Standards Council from 1996 to 2000.

Gervais had begun attending the Cannes Film Festival as an accredited journalist in 1965. That began a thirty-nine-year uninterrupted association with the festival. He once was invited to serve on its jury. The opening night of the first festival he attended, he was mobbed by journalists who were eager for a story about the supposed conflict between the Catholic Church and the film industry. After that, he never wore clerical garb again while in Cannes. Each year, he would send to various English and French media outlets in Montreal and elsewhere critical assessments of the films being presented during the

75 The Office Catholique International du Cinéma (OCIC) was founded in The Hague after the Catholic International Congress on Cinema in 1928 with the object of promoting the positive role of cinema in society. In November 2001, it merged with the International Catholic Association for Radio and Television (UNDA) to become SIGNIS, an International Association of the Faithful recognized by the Holy See. It continues to give jury prizes at television and film festivals including Cannes, Venice, Berlin, and Monte Carlo.

76 The film was the work of a well-known Communist atheist, and centred on a mystical figure who breathed life into a dysfunctional Italian family by seducing everyone, male and female. Defending his choice, Gervais wrote that the film was "an inquiry into the human condition. It is a work about the demands of the absolute and about the refusal to be made bourgeois that alienates all men. The fact that the OCIC has given the prize to Pasolini does not mean that 500-million Roman Catholics are obliged to see it". In later years, Gervais admitted that "I might just faint watching it today. How could we give a prize to that? It was not a film for the general public". Interview with John E. O'Brien, 6 January 2012.

77 See Marc Gervais, *Pier Paolo Pasolini* (Paris: Seghers, 1973) and *Ingmar Bergman: Magician and Prophet* (Montreal: McGill-Queen's University Press, 1999).

festival. These were highly articulate, well-reasoned judgments and general observations on the merits of each film, but most especially on the moral and religious values they espoused. In 2000, in recognition of his long-standing contribution as critic and participant at the festival, it awarded him the Festival Critics Award.[78]

In time, Gervais came to know and admire many acclaimed film directors, such as John Huston, Norman Jewison, François Truffaut, Jean-Luc Godard, John Ford, Alfred Hitchcock, and Jean Renoir. Many of them became his friends in the industry. He also came to know others, both actors and actresses and film directors, such as Jeremy Irons and Liv Ulmann. During the early 1990s, he advised Ulmann concerning mediaeval Catholic rituals for the film *Kristin Lavransdatter*. Gervais' knowledge of the ritual of the pre-tridentine Catholic Church was of immense assistance in staging the film, set in Norway during medieval times when the country was still Catholic. Indeed, having learned to celebrate the Mass in Latin as a young Jesuit, he was able to celebrate one in a Norwegian medieval-style small wooden church built for the film.[79]

Later, in 1985, he was offered an acting role in Roland Joffé's film *The Mission* (1986). He declined. Acting was not his interest, however well he could have played the part. The American Jesuit peace activist Daniel Berrigan took the part instead. However, Gervais did work as a consultant on the film *Agnes of God* (1985) by the Canadian director Norman Jewison, and on *Black Robe* (1991) by the Australian director Bruce Beresford. He also particularly admired the films of such directors as John Ford and Alfred Hitchcock, whose Catholic symbolism he enjoyed pointing out to students. In Gervais' judgment, Hitchcock,

---

78 Although on occasion Gervais attended other European film festivals than Cannes and Venice, and annually Montreal's film festival, he never would attend the Toronto International Film Festival. He argued that it was too "American", too given to attracting Hollywood stars rather than international films. On that, however, he was mistaken. Yet no amount of evidence ever convinced him or moved him from his understanding of the international quality of Toronto's annual festival.

79 Gervais related how, as part of the story, the little church had to be burned down. Because many of the actors and crew, the majority of whom were not Catholic, had come to love the church, the effect of burning it to the ground was deeply moving, indeed, for some, distressing.

Ford, and Bergman were great artists because they pointed to a deeper spiritual awareness that Gervais himself found in the world.

At Loyola College (and then Concordia University), Gervais' courses specialized in Hollywood's silent films, musicals, and Westerns, in German expressionist cinema and Italian neo-realism, and in the French New Wave. For years, in a course entitled "Film Ideas", he screened one film every week at the Cinema V in the Notre-Dame-de-Grace area of Montreal, and over the years, he would open up screenings to the general public at Concordia's F. C. Smith Auditorium. While describing the cultural, philosophical, and spiritual ethos the films were reflecting, he would examine in his lectures the sense of postmodern deconstruction that many contemporary films portrayed. In a 1996 article in the Canadian Jesuits' journal *Compass*, Gervais described a "profound cultural malaise permeating the films from the West: loss of hope, commitment, spirit, call it a postmodern whirl of meaninglessness in which film, along with 'everything else', becomes merely a game riddled with cynicism and frustration."[80] Yet, as was distinctive of Gervais, he went on to identify what he saw as the hopeful elements found in certain other films, works that were "studies of the complexity, beauty and suffering of love, ironic in their contemporary awareness, truly exploring life and expressing human aspiration while celebrating the art of film-making."[81]

Gervais took retirement from teaching in 1992. Nonetheless, he carried on lecturing at Concordia University for another eleven years in the communication arts department on a part-time basis, and during his final three years there, also in the theological studies department. At the same time, he remained a much sought-after film consultant, lecturer, and advisor for many outside the university. He continued to attend Cannes until 2004.[82]

80 Marc Gervais, "Movies Are Beginning to Breathe Again", *Compass* 14 (5), 1996.

81 Ibid.

82 Gervais was the last full-time Jesuit to teach at Concordia University. Advancing dementia necessitated his moving in 2009 to the Jesuit infirmary in Pickering. When he died on 25 March 2012, there were dozens of tributes from professionals in various fields of the communications industry. An excellent lecturer and academic advisor, he had influenced the lives and careers of many of his students, among whom were the actor and director Clark Johnson (*S.W.A.T.*, 2003, and *The Wire*, 2008), the Oscar-winning Quebec filmmaker Denys Arcand, producer Kevin Tierney (*Bon Cop, Bad Cop*, 2006), and the CBC television journalist Hannah Gartner.

Other Jesuits worked specifically in film in the early years of the communication arts department in Montreal. When Clair J. Fischer, S.J., was Rector of Saint Mary's University in Halifax, he had been very interested in the arts, was a painter himself, and saw to the establishment of an art gallery in the university. When he left Saint Mary's in 1967, he moved to Stanford University in Los Altos, California, to study communication arts. There he completed a degree in film production in 1969. He then joined the communication arts faculty at Loyola College, where he was known to be "creative in his approach and precise and clear in his assignments."[83] In the summer of 1970, Fischer, along with O'Brien and Miroslav Malik, planned a six-week summer institute on film in Europe, which twenty students from the department attended. Presenters included artists, museum curators, and filmmakers from six countries. Fischer would serve as chair of the communication studies department for three years. He retired from Concordia University in 1981.

A contemporary of Gervais, John D. Matheson, S.J., was another Jesuit film specialist; he worked in universities in western Canada. Initially, he had become especially interested in the study of film during his years of theological studies from 1962 to 1966 at Regis College, 3425 Bayview Avenue, in Willowdale, north Toronto. There, with Gervais and other Jesuits, he organized film-viewing nights for interested Jesuit Scholastics and faculty members. Such "viewings" aimed to introduce the young Jesuits to consider films not only as entertainment, but also as a form of art, a humanistic, cultural expression of the day. Thus, as well as watching a film, participants engaged in discussions afterwards about its meaning and cultural impact and significance. The Rector and the dean of the college highly distrusted such film viewing; they considered films generally to be only entertainment, unnecessary, and therefore "secular". In their minds, danger for the young Jesuits lurked in films, especially temptations against their Religious vocations. Fortunately, Matheson and Gervais were able to get around such unnecessary distrust. In doing so, they helped open a new world of art and studies to the Jesuit Scholastics.

83 *Province Newsletter*, vol. 86, no. 3, Autumn 2010, 14.

Sometimes guest speakers were invited to be present; one such was Marshall McLuhan, then at the height of his academic career, who attended and led several of the discussions.

Matheson would go on to become wholly engaged in film studies. In the late 1960s, he worked with John Veltri, S.J., a director of retreats, in designing preached retreats that used extensive audio-visual aids. Of those, Veltri recollected, "through slides we attempted to engage the imaginations of the retreatants in order that they could enter more fully into the scriptural creation stories. We used film and music to help people enter into prayer."[84] Following O'Brien's lead, Matheson later studied communication arts at the University of Southern California in Los Angeles from 1969 to 1973. Four years afterwards, he returned to Campion College, University of Regina—he had been there for a short time in the mid 1960s—where he helped found a film studies programme in 1977. There Matheson would lecture for nearly two decades, occasionally travelling to China to teach film in a university exchange programme.[85]

Of a later generation, David R. Eley, S.J., likewise received a graduate degree in communications studies. Prior to taking his doctorate at McGill University, he had completed a summer course in film studies at Columbia University, New York, in 1967. After completing his doctorate, he became a lecturer in 1976 in the department of communications at Saint Paul University in Ottawa. Two years later, the University of Ottawa, with which Saint Paul University is federated, assumed responsibility for the administration of the programme. The department of communications, therefore, transferred to the University of Ottawa; Eley was appointed its first chair.

In the years that followed, Eley would lecture at many different universities, including the Jesuits' Gregorian University in Rome. As well, he involved himself in various communications projects. One such was the Cavalletti Conferences at the Jesuits' Villa Cavalletti near Frascati outside Rome. Those annual gatherings—there were ten in

84 John Veltri, S.J., *Some Personal Reflections on the Development of the Personally Directed Retreat Movement and the Work of J. J. English, S.J. through the Guelph Centre of Spirituality.* http://www.jesuits.ca/orientations/refl_eng1.html.

85 Joseph B. Gavin, S.J., "Jesuits in Profile: Fr. John Matheson, S.J.", Jesuit Bulletin (2008), 10.

total—organized by Jesuit scholars of communications from around the world focused on seminary training and the communication arts.[86] Scholars, including lay people and Jesuit and diocesan priests, would present papers in progress, and subject them to the critique of their peers. The results were published in a series of books called *Communication, Culture and Theology*.[87] During that decade, Eley would also serve as a consulter to the Pontifical Council of Social Communications. In 2002, he was assigned to be president of Campion College and to teach film studies. In addition to his biannual course offerings at the Gregorian University, starting in 2007, he began lecturing every two years at Saint Augustine University in Mwanza, Tanzania, the largest post-secondary institution in that country.

Another Canadian Jesuit, Lloyd Baugh, has been an important voice in the area of interdisciplinary theology and communication studies at the Gregorian University for nearly thirty years. Before he joined the Society of Jesus in 1976, and while he was an undergraduate student in English literature at Loyola College at the time the communication arts programme was established, he was inspired by O'Brien to become involved in the field of communications studies. A few years later, when Baugh was teaching at Champlain College in Quebec City, he pondered whether to become a Jesuit. During that time, he met monthly over eight months with Eley, who was then living at the Loyola Jesuit Community in Montreal while pursuing his doctorate at McGill University. That greatly furthered Baugh's interest in the study of communications.

As a Jesuit Scholastic, during several courses he took with Gervais at Concordia University, Baugh was introduced to the films of Ermanno Olmi, the Italian director most acclaimed for his film *L'albero degli zoccoli* (*The Tree of the Wooden Clogs*), the winner of the Palme d'Or at the 1978 Cannes Film Festival. Later, Baugh would write both his licentiate and doctoral theses in fundamental theol-

86 The Cavalletti seminars were jointly sponsored by the Centre for Interdisciplinary Studies in Communications (CICS) and the Centre for the Study of Communication and Culture (formerly of London, then relocated to St. Louis University).

87 For example, see essay by Eley, "Beyond Necessity: Towards the Ethics of Entertainment", in *Mass Media and the Moral Imagination*, ed. Philip J. Rossi and Paul A. Soukup (Kansas City, MO: Sheed and Ward, 1994).

ogy at the Gregorian University on the work of Olmi. Because such interdisciplinary work was unknown at the time in that university, many professors there were convinced that it was an unacceptable area of studies for a pontifical university. Yet, with the encouragement of such theologians as Gerald O'Collins, an Australian Jesuit, and Rino Fisichella, an Italian diocesan priest, Baugh's interdisciplinary work helped solidify new bonds between the Interdisciplinary Centre for Social Communications (CICS) and the faculty of theology at the university.[88] It was not without difficulty, however. Opposition from the more conservative Jesuits and other professors was intense. In 1991, with the encouragement of Guiseppe Pittau, s.j., the then Rector of the university, Baugh defended his doctoral dissertation. To signal publicly his support of both Baugh and his work, Pittau took the unusual step of presiding at Baugh's thesis defence. Afterwards, Baugh was assigned to the CICS.[89]

The centre had been instituted in 1981 with the purpose of "examining the problems and opportunities which mass communication offers for proclaiming the Gospel message and in general for theological and philosophical language", and for training future church leaders in this academic field. Yet, in the minds of many at the Gregorian, the CICS remained rather peripheral to the primary academic activities of the university. After a few years of teaching film in the CICS, Baugh was invited to teach courses in the faculty of theology, which, in the long run, opened up the possibility of interdisciplinary development in theological studies. At the same time, he began to lecture in different parts of the world, often in Jesuit universities. Lectures given by Baugh, who was fluent in at least four European languages, drew large crowds, perhaps out of curiosity at first, but then with enthusiasm as they recognized the depth of theological and spiritual awareness he was able to bring to so many films. In 1997, Baugh published a pioneering

88 Fisichella later became the first president of the Pontifical Council for the New Evangelization.

89 Pittau had been Rector of Sophia University in Tokyo, as well as Provincial Superior of Japan. He was also assigned by John Paul II to assist Paul Dezza, s.j., in governing the Jesuit Order before the election of Peter Hans Kolvenbach, s.j., as Superior General in 1983. Pittau became the Secretary for the Congregation for Catholic Education, and was made an archbishop in 1998.

book, *Imaging the Divine: Jesus and Christ-Figures in Film.*[90] At the book's appearance, some Catholic quarters reacted with hostility to its principal theme. To those critics, some of Baugh's interpretation seemed far-fetched, even bordering on the blasphemous; how could he see in the sometimes unsavoury characters of films images and figures of Jesus Christ? In the end, however, his work has been well accepted as part of contemporary Catholic theological reflection, and has become a necessary inclusion on all reading lists in university courses touching on religious influences in films.

Since this book appeared, he has also published three shorter works and more than seventy articles and essays in international scholarly journals, and has given university courses and innumerable public lectures in four languages throughout Europe, Canada, the United States, the Philippines, and Madagascar. He continues his innovative approach to films in many other writings and lectures. Considered the specialist on the films of Polish director Krzysztof Kieślowski, about whom he has lectured and written extensively, Baugh is now preparing a book-length theological and spiritual analysis of Kieślowski's ten *Dekalog* films.

In 1984, Eley was lecturing in the communication studies programme at Concordia University for one year. During that time, the then Provincial Superior, William F. Ryan, S.J., was planning to establish a special communications office in Toronto, as a response to the importance placed on communications by the Society of Jesus.[91] He turned to Eley for assistance. As a result, in the autumn of 1984, Eley left Concordia University for Toronto to co-found with John Pungente, S.J., the Jesuit Communications Project (JCP). At first, the project rented offices at 10 St. Mary Street in central Toronto; the staff consisted of Eley and Pungente, a film and media literacy specialist who had received his Master of Arts degree in film from San Francisco State University in 1968. Afterwards, a United Church

90 See Lloyd Baugh, *Imaging the Divine: Jesus and Christ-Figures in Film (Communication, Culture, and Religion)* (New York: Sheed and Ward, 1997).

91 The Superior General, Pedro Arrupe, s.j., had listed "the media of mass communications" to be one of the four priorities in the ministries of the Society of Jesus, along with theological reflection, education, and social action.

minister, Desmond McCalmont, and a Catholic layman named Leo Serroule also became part of the staff there, with Adrienne Pereira as executive assistant and treasurer. The stated goal of the JCP was "for the purpose of focusing on the relationship between the faith communities in Canada and the mass media and exploring the opportunities and challenges that media offers us in a society where their influence over our lives and culture is so great."[92]

During its first four years of existence, members of the JCP researched, pursued special projects, and taught courses. They also began developing a curriculum for the Toronto School of Theology in the University of Toronto and gave classes on media studies to Jesuit novices in Guelph. Among the projects was a major one: working with the Canadian Conference of Catholic Bishops (CCCB) and the Association of Roman Catholic Communicators in Canada (ARCCC) to develop pastoral plans for social communications. The JCP would work with the CCCB for more than twenty years on various projects for the Catholic Church in Canada.

Another project was the development of media literacy curriculum for students at both the elementary and secondary school levels. To that end, JCP collaborated with the oldest media organization in Canada, the Association for Media Literacy (AML). Founded in 1978, AML is an educational initiative that aims to increase students' understanding and enjoyment of how the media work. It was the first comprehensive organization for media literacy teachers in Canada. Together, JCP and AML wrote a media literacy guide for the Ontario ministry of education; the guide went on to be translated into many languages and was used around the world. When the 1987 film *The Mission* was released, the JCP sponsored the film's premiere at a gala event in Toronto with Regis College and the Canadian Jesuit Missions Office; similar benefit nights took place across Canada sponsored by various Jesuit groups.

In 1989, however, the funding from the Jesuit Province was reduced. Eley left JCP to teach half-time at the communications studies department at Concordia University. Pungente and Pereira remained

---

92 From the first brochure of the Jesuit Communications Project.

the sole members of the JCP. Pungente decided to focus the work solely on media literacy.[93] In May 1990, the first North American Media Literacy Conference, organized by the JCP and the AML, took place at the University of Guelph, with 420 participants. It was a first for the developing field of media literacy and proved to be a particularly influential experience for Ontario English teachers, who by then were teaching media literacy as a standard part of the curriculum. That same year, Pungente produced a video, commissioned by the English-speaking Jesuits, centring on John J. C. English, S.J., a renowned Canadian director of retreats based on *The Spiritual Exercises* of Saint Ignatius Loyola. English specialized in personal discernment. The video, titled *A Heart to Understand*, followed two lay people during the course of a retreat of discernment at Ignatius College in Guelph; it became an award-winning documentary.

In 1992, a second media literacy conference was held at the University of Guelph. This time it hosted nearly 500 delegates from eighteen countries. As a result of this meeting, the Canadian Association of Media Education Organizations (CAMEO) was formed as an umbrella for provincial organizations of similar intent. CAMEO would work with the Canadian government on issues such as violence in the media and on the successful blocking of the introduction of commercial advertising in classroom programming. In 1993, a national "clearing house" for information on media violence, called the Media Awareness Network (MNET) was founded by Pungente and Joan Pennefeather, director of the National Film Board of Canada. For more than twenty years, MNET was a leading resource for information on media literacy.

Economic conditions in the province of Ontario in 1996 caused the ministry of education to end its relationship with the JCP; the

---

93 Pungente defined the goal of media literacy as helping students "develop an informed and critical understanding of mass media, the techniques used by them, and the impact of these techniques. More specifically, it is education which aims to increase students' understanding and enjoyment of how the media work, how they produce meaning, how they are organized, and how they construct reality. Media literacy also aims to provide students with the ability to create media products. Or, very simply, helping people to watch carefully and think critically about the media". (John Pungente, *Jesuit Communications Project Celebrates Twenty-Five Years*, to John D. O'Brien, 15 January 2012.)

Jesuit Provincial Superior was also forced by financial restraints to withdraw support. As a result, Pungente alone remained. He had to look for new sponsors. Eventually, the JCP became partners with The Alliance for Children and Television (ACT) and a number of commercial companies, including Toronto's CHUM Television and Warner Brothers Canada.[94]

The following year, Pungente began hosting and producing a half-hour television programme, *Scanning the Movies*, produced by Warner Brothers. It aired in Canada on the Bravo! Network. The show was a big success, and would run for ten years, from 1997 to 2007.[95] As writer and host, Pungente discussed how to "read" a movie, with the aim of fostering a broadened critical appreciation for film in general. He also produced a teaching aid for media literacy teachers called *Scanning Television* (1997). This consisted of four one-hour videocassettes and lesson plans. The kit won several major awards from international television and film festivals.

In 2000, a large conference convened in Toronto, co-sponsored by the JCP, the AML (of which Pungente was then Executive Secretary), and two other media literacy organizations. The congress, entitled "Summit 2000: Children, Youth and the Media—Beyond the Millennium", hosted 1,400 delegates from fifty-five countries, and lasted for five days, from 13 to 17 May. The conference featured 248 presentations by some 400 speakers from various fields. It had the unprecedented scope of bringing together those who teach media and those who produce it.

Pungente has written several books on media literacy during the course of his professional life. In these he has developed his basic theme of respect and acceptance of the electronic media, and offered tools for a critical discernment of content. His 1999 book, *More than*

94 The aim of the Alliance for Children and Television, founded in 1974 as the Children's Broadcast Institute, is to act as a catalyst in generating more and better television programmes, and to initiate and encourage research, develop and promote higher programming standards, analyze the needs of parents, stimulate funding for production of Canadian programming, and provide a mechanism for and recognition of excellence.

95 The press reviewed the programme favourably (see Henry Mietkiewicz, "TV's Best-Kept Secret", *Toronto Star*, 30 January 1998).

Meets the Eye: Watching Television Watching Us, was his first work, written in collaboration with writer and journalist Martin O'Malley.[96] Five years later, in 2004, he co-wrote *Finding God in the Dark: Taking the Spiritual Exercises of St. Ignatius of Loyola to the Movies* with Monty Williams, S.J., a then director of The Spiritual Exercises at Loyola House in Guelph. In this award-winning book, films were posited as carriers of spiritual experiences that mirrored, to an extent, the spiritual trajectory of The Spiritual Exercises.[97] A successful sequel was published in 2011.[98] Pungente also designed *Inside Plato's Cave*, a media literacy training curriculum for Canadian teachers that would be offered through Athabasca University in Alberta.[99] Pungente still lectures internationally and nationally and is in charge of the library of the JCP in Toronto, which contains a large collection of more than 4,000 books and periodicals.

*

In the second decade of the third millennium, with dizzying rapidity, the electronic media began converging into the Internet. Keeping up with this advance has been, and remains, challenging, although the Jesuits in English Canada have striven to involve themselves fully in this new electronic world. As well, and for some time, the English-speaking Jesuits have had a website, as has almost every major Jesuit ministry in the country. As with most individuals and groups in contemporary society, personal and even, at times, official communications between Jesuits is almost wholly by e-mail; individually and in small groups, Canadian Jesuits are also writing blogs.[100] During the celebrations in 2011 to 2012 of the 400th anniversary of the arrival of the first Jesuits in Canada (1611–2011), several projects were

96 John Pungente and Martin O'Malley, *More than Meets the Eye: Watching Television Watching Us* (Toronto: McClelland and Stewart, 1999).

97 John Pungente and Monty Williams, *Finding God in the Dark: The Spiritual Exercises of St. Ignatius of Loyola Go to the Movies* (Ottawa: Novalis, 2004). The book won first place in the Catholic Press Association Awards for soft-cover books.

98 John Pungente and Monty Williams, *Finding God in the Dark II: The Spiritual Exercises of St. Ignatius of Loyola Go to the Movies* (Ottawa: Novalis, 2011).

99 See http://jcp.proscenia.net/platoscave.htm. Note this is also the website of the JCP.

100 A blog created by some Canadian Jesuit Scholastics called "Ibo et non Redibo" received more than 1,000 hits per month during its first year, 2012.

produced, including digital videos of the re-enactment of the arrival of Pierre Biard, s.j., and Ennemond Massé, s.j., at Port Royal, Nova Scotia. Likewise, the English-speaking Jesuits Province's congress held in Midland, Ontario, in July 2012, has been produced as a DVD.[101]

Emailing, blogging, tweeting, and whatever else is now available electronically raise major challenges and concerns about social media policies, the maintaining of privacy and, for the Jesuits at least, the storing of historical records in archives. It is far easier to discard correspondence and documents from a computer than it ever was from hard copy. Yet if challenges exist, as they have in the past—albeit different ones—Jesuits in Canada still willingly embrace them. Previously, they recognized the value of communications as a tool for their ministry; they still do so today. While the number of Jesuits who enter communications studies has not been as large as it once was, and while many of the Canadian Jesuits' print, radio, and television ministries have disappeared, in the end, communications as a national and international Jesuit ministry remains, although now more in the direction of the Internet, in Church-related media productions, and in the teaching of discernment and literacy in a media-saturated world.

101 The *Catholic Register* printed a thirty-six-page special insert on the Canadian Jesuits' anniversary, thousands of which were distributed in Jesuit schools, and which was made available online. See http://www.catholicregister.org/jesuits.

CHRONOLOGY OF JESUIT EVENTS

1842 Pierre Chazelle and eight Jesuit companions arrive in Montreal from France, and settle at the parish of the Nativity of Our Lady, La Prairie, Canada East

1843 Paul Luiset, s.j., opens the first Canadian Jesuit novitiate in La Prairie on 31 July, but shortly afterwards moves it to rue Saint-Antoine, Montreal, where Auguste Régnier becomes the first Canadian novice on 9 September

Pierre Point, s.j., the first Jesuit after the restoration of the Society of Jesus in Canada, returns to Assumption Parish, Sandwich, Canada West

1844 Dominique du Ranquet, s.j., and Joseph Jennesseaux, s.j. begin the mission on Walpole Island, Canada West

Jean-Pierre Choné, s.j., arrives at Holy Cross Mission, Wikwemikong, Manitoulin Island, Canada West

Pierre Chazelle, s.j., visits the site of Sainte-Marie-among-the-Hurons, Midland, Canada West

The Sisters of the Hôtel-Dieu return documents of Jean-Joseph Casot, s.j., to the Jesuits on 25 November

1845 Clément Boulanger, s.j., makes a Visitation to the Mission

Richard Baxter from Barrie, Canada West, enters the Jesuit Novitiate in Montreal on 17 September, the first anglophone Canadian novice to enter the Canadian Jesuits

1846 Jean-Baptiste Menet, s.j., arrives at Sault Ste. Marie, Michigan, to reopen the Jesuit mission there, and founds Holy Rosary Parish

The New York–Canada Mission is established, a dependency of the Province of France

1848 Collège Sainte-Marie/St. Mary's College is founded in Montreal by Félix Martin, s.j.

Jean-Pierre Choné, s.j., founds a mission at Fort William, Canada West

John Holzer, s.j., opens a residence at Wilmot, Waterloo County, Canada West

Joseph-Urbain Hanipaux, s.j., founds a mission at Garden River, Canada West

1849 The Jesuits open a residence on rue Dauphine, Quebec City

1850 Novices from New York join the Canadian Novitiate in Montreal

The Jesuits withdraw from their mission on Walpole Island, Canada West

1851 The Jesuit Novitiate moves to Collège Sainte-Marie/St. Mary's College, Montreal

1852 John Holzer, s.j., and Gaspar Matoga, s.j., assume responsibility for St. Bartholomew's Parish, Guelph, Canada West

1853 The Jesuit Novitiate moves from Collège Sainte-Marie/St. Mary's College to Maison Saint-Joseph, Sault-au-Récollet, Montreal

1854 The Jesuits transfer the parish of the Nativity of Our Lady, La Prairie, to the diocese of Montreal

1856 The Jesuits close their residence at Wilmot, Canada West

1857 The Jesuits open a residence and assume responsibility for St. Joseph's Parish, Chatham, Canada West

1859 Pierre Point, s.j., transfers Assumption Parish, Sandwich, to the diocese of London, Canada West

Félix Sopranis, s.j., is appointed Visitor to the New York–Canada Mission, 28 November

1860 The Jesuits leave Holy Rosary Parish, Sault Ste. Marie, Michigan

1863 John Holzer, s.j., opens St. Ignatius College, Guelph, in September

The New York–Canada Mission is attached to the new Province of Champagne, France

John Holzer, s.j., proposes the building of a new and large church to replace the existing St. Bartholomew's, Guelph, but this is abandoned due to its enormity and the protests of the parishioners

1864 St. Ignatius College, Guelph, closes

The Jesuits return to Sault Ste. Marie, Michigan, to minister in St. Mary's (later Holy Name of Mary) Parish

1865 Auguste Kohler, s.j., builds two residences for missionaries, one at Garden River, Canada West, the other at Sault Ste. Marie, Canada West

The Church of the Gesù, a *chapelle publique* of Collège Sainte-Marie/St. Mary's College, opens at 1200, rue de Bleury, Montreal

1866 A Jesuit Juniorate for classical studies opens at Quebec City

1869 The New York–Canada Mission separates from the Province of Champagne to become an Independent Mission

The Jesuit Juniorate for classical studies moves from Quebec City to Sault-au-Récollet, Montreal

1874 The Jesuits transfer St. Joseph's Parish, Chatham, Ontario, to the diocese of London, Ontario

1875 St. Andrew's Parish, Port Arthur (now part of Thunder Bay), Ontario, is founded by Richard Baxter, S.J.

1876 The American novices at Sault-au-Récollet, Montreal, move to a new Novitiate at West Park, New York

1877 Pierre Hamel, s.j., begins the building of a neo-gothic church on the site of St. Bartholomew's, Guelph, under the direction of Joseph Connolly, the leading architect of several Ontario Catholic churches

1878 St. Bartholomew's Church, Guelph, is renamed the Church of Our Lady Immaculate

1879 Edward I. Purbrick, S.J., is appointed Visitor to the New York–Canada Mission on 7 August

The Mission of Canada, with 179 Jesuits, separates from New York and becomes attached to the English Province

1880 The Jesuits accept the direction of St. Dunstan's College, Charlottetown, from the diocese

The Jesuit church at Sault Ste. Marie, Ontario, becomes Sacred Heart Parish (later Precious Blood Cathedral)

1881 The Jesuits withdraw from St. Dunstan's College, Charlottetown

1882 Collège de l'Immaculée-Conception, the Jesuit theologate, is founded at Trois-Rivières, Quebec

1883 Jean-Baptiste Nolin, s.j., founds the parish of Ste-Anne-des-Pins, Sudbury, Ontario

1884 The federal government agrees to grant subsidies to the residential schools at Wikwemikong, Ontario

The Jesuit philosophate is founded at rue Dauphine, Quebec

1885 Jesuits accept the direction of Collège de Saint-Boniface/ St. Boniface College, Saint-Boniface, Manitoba

The Jesuit theologate and philosophate move to Collège de l'Immaculée-Conception,, 1855 rue Rachel Est, Montreal

1886 Jean-Baptiste Lessmann, s.j., is appointed Visitor to the Canadian Mission, 15 August until 9 November 1887

1887 The Mission of Canada separates from the English Province to become an Independent Mission

An English-language classical course programme is officially established at Collège Sainte-Marie/St. Mary's College, Montreal

1888 With the exception of its two front towers, the Church of Our Lady Immaculate, Guelph, is completed and consecrated

The Jesuits accept the administration of St. Augustine of Canterbury Parish, Brandon, Manitoba, with John A. S. MacDonald, S.J., appointed the first pastor

1889 Pope Leo XIII signs the Apostolic Constitution *Iamdudum* on 2 February, granting Collège Sainte-Marie/St. Mary's College the privileges of the *Ratio Studiorum*

In July the "Jesuit Estates Question" is settled by the Quebec legislature

The new church of Ste-Anne-des-Pins, Sudbury, opens

The Jesuits' parish church l'Immaculée-Conception opens at 1855, rue Rachel Est, Montreal

1890 The *Canadian Messenger of the Sacred Heart* is first published

1891 The Jesuits return St. Augustine of Canterbury Parish, Brandon, to the archdiocese of St. Boniface

1892 The first Mass is celebrated in St. Patrick's church, Fort William (now Thunder Bay), Ontario, by Rémi Chartier, s.j.

1893 Ludger Arpin, s.j., opens St. Patrick's parish church (later cathedral) in Thunder Bay

1896 Loyola College opens at the corner of Bleury Street and 2084 St. Catherine Street, Montreal, as a separate college from Collège Sainte-Marie

1898 Fire destroys Loyola College on 12 January, and in February the college moves to 68 Drummond Street, Montreal

1899 The Privileges of *Iamdudum* are extended to Loyola College, 5 February, by Pope Leo XIII

Loyola College is incorporated on 10 March by an act of the Quebec legislature

1900 The Jesuits officially accept the administration of St. Patrick's Parish, Fort William, and Ludger Arpin, s.j., is appointed the first pastor

1902 L'église Saint-Ignace, Steelton (now in Sault Ste. Marie), Ontario, is founded

1903 The first academic degree at Loyola College is conferred on 22 June through the charter of Université Laval

1906 The Jesuit parish of St. John the Evangelist, Waubaushene, Ontario, is founded

On 17 June, the Loyola Alumni Association, Loyola College, Montreal, is established

1907 The Canada Mission becomes the Province of Canada , 15 August

A chapel is blessed on the site of what was thought to be St. Ignace II on 15 August, a few miles west of Waubaushene, with more than two thousand pilgrims attending, a location later known as Martyrs' Hill

The Canadian Jesuits accept responsibility for the Alaska Mission

1908 Publication of *Old Huronia* by Arthur E. Jones, S.J.

St. Ignatius Parish, Winnipeg, is established, with the first Mass celebrated in a rented store at 1099 Osborne Street, Fort Rouge

The first church building for St. Ignatius Parish, Winnipeg, bought from the Baptists, is moved to the corner of McMillan and Nassau Streets

John C. Coffee, S.J., is appointed the first pastor of St. Ignatius Parish, Winnipeg

1909 St. Ignatius Parish purchases a property at Stafford, Corydon, and Jessie Streets, Winnipeg, and begins the construction of a church building

1911 Fire destroys the girls' school at Wikwemikong, Ontario

The announcement is made on 15 July that the residential schools will move to Spanish, Ontario, from Wikwemikong

1912 The Canadian Jesuits transfer the Alaska Mission to the California Province of the Society of Jesus

The first Mass is celebrated in the basement of the unfinished church of St. Ignatius, Winnipeg

1913 On 6 September, seventeen English-speaking novices move from Sault-au-Récollet, Montreal, to the newly established St. Stanislaus Novitiate in the Bedford House, Guelph

The residential schools move on 23 July from Wikwemikong to Spanish, Ontario

Collège du Sacré-Coeur (later University of Sudbury), Sudbury, is founded as a bilingual college

Collège Saint-François-Xavier (Collège des Jésuites)/(Jesuit College) is founded at 2010 28th Street, Edmonton, as a bilingual college

The Jesuits transfer Sacred Heart Parish at Sault Ste. Marie to the diocese of Sault Ste. Marie

1914 The Jesuits transfer St. Mary's (later Holy Name of Mary) Parish, Sault Ste. Marie, Michigan, to the diocese of Marquette, Wisconsin

The Juniorate programme of classical studies for young Jesuits opens in August at the Villa-on-the-Speed on the property of St. Stanislaus Novitiate, Guelph

1916 Loyola College moves from 68 Drummond Street to Sherbrooke Street West, Montreal

1917 St. Ignatius Loyola Parish, Montreal, is founded at Loyola College

William I. Power, S.J., begins a Visitation of the Province of Canada/Province du Canada from 4 April 1917 to 8 July 1918

The Catholic College of Regina (Campion College) is incorporated on 5 December by an act of the Saskatchewan legislature for the archdiocese of Regina

1918 A School of Sociology and Social Service opens at Loyola College, Montreal, the first in Canada

A military raid occurs at St. Stanislaus Novitiate, Guelph, on 7 June, searching for young men who, it was thought, should have been on the war front

Jesuits accept the direction of Campion College from the archdiocese of Regina, and Thomas J. MacMahon, the Vice Rector, opens the college at 3136 13th Avenue on 5 September

1919 Campion College moves from 13th Avenue to 1412 Argyle Street, Regina

1921 Under the direction of Eduardo de la Peza, s.j., the prefect of studies, Loyola College changes from the classical course system of education to an academic system of four years for the high school and four years for the college

1922 On 2 November, Campion College moves to the corner of Albert Street and 23rd Avenue, Regina

Fire destroys St. Boniface College on 25 November; nine students, along with Brother Frederick Stormont, S.J., perish in the conflagration

1924 On 19 January, the arena/rink (Loyola Stadium) is inaugurated at Loyola College, Montreal, by the Rt. Hon. Narcisse Pérodeau, lieutenant governor of Quebec

On 27 June, the Province of Canada is divided into the Vice Province of Upper Canada, with 137 members, and La Province du Bas-Canada, with 330 members

The Jesuits assume responsibility for the parish of the Immaculate Conception at 3851 29th Avenue West, Vancouver

The Jesuits transfer St. Patrick's Parish, Fort William (Thunder Bay), to the diocese

The first residence of the Provincial Superior of Upper Canada opens at 5 Harbord Street, Toronto

1925 On 21 June, the eight Canadian Martyrs—Jean de Brébeuf, Isaac Jogues, and their companions—are beatified in Rome

The office of the *Canadian Messenger of the Sacred Heart* moves to 160 Wellesley Crescent, Toronto

Construction begins on the Martyrs' Shrine at Midland, Ontario

John M. Filion, s.j., and Joseph Fallon, S.J., direct the first laymen's retreat in Toronto on Labour Day weekend at St. Augustine's Seminary

On 25 November, the Provincial Superior's residence moves to 160 Wellesley Crescent, Toronto

During December, the first *News Letter* of the Province of Upper Canada is published at St. Stanislaus Novitiate, Guelph

1926 The refectory building at Martyrs' Shrine, Midland, Ontario, is completed in April

The opening and consecration of Martyrs' Shrine church, Midland, takes place on 27 June

The two 61-metre front towers of the Jesuits' Church of Our Lady Immaculate, Guelph, are completed on 13 November

On 12 December, the new Immaculate Conception church opens at 3776 28th Avenue West, Vancouver

1927 The administration building and tower of Loyola College, Montreal, are completed

1929 Archbishop Arthur A. Sinnott of Winnipeg blesses the new church of St. Ignatius, Winnipeg

1930 Pope Pius XI canonizes the eight Canadian Martyrs at St. Peter's Basilica, Rome, on 29 June

Joseph Fallon, S.J., plans the first independent retreat house in English-speaking Canada in St. John, New Brunswick

Joseph Fallon, S.J., establishes the Federation of Catholic Charities, the Catholic Men's Hostel, and St. Martha's Home for destitute women and children in Montreal

The Jesuit philosophate opens in September at 403 Wellington Street West, Toronto (formerly Loretto Abbey)

Oxford University Press publishes *Gerard Manley Hopkins* by Gerald F. Lahey, S.J., the first biography of the poet

1931 The Jesuits accept the direction of Regiopolis College, Kingston, Ontario

Construction begins on the chapel and auditorium of Loyola College, Montreal

On 6 September, the Jesuits transfer the Church of Our Lady Immaculate, Guelph, to the diocese of Hamilton

1932 The Canadian Martyrs are assigned by the Superior General of the Jesuits, Wlodimir Ledóchowski, to be patron saints of the Vice Province of Upper Canada

1933 A General Secretariate for the Sodality of Our Lady at the Jesuit Seminary is established at 403 Wellington Street West, Toronto

On 2 April, the blessing and opening of the chapel at Loyola College, Montreal, takes place

Construction begins on 31 July at St. Stanislaus Novitiate, Guelph, of a Juniorate building and a tunnel between the new building and the Bedford House

The Jesuits accept the direction of St. Paul's College and High School, Winnipeg, from the archdiocese of Winnipeg on 19 August

St. Paul's College and High School, Winnipeg, moves from Selkirk Avenue into the former Manitoba College building at the corner of Ellice Avenue and Vaughan Street

The auditorium at Loyola College, Montreal, is completed during November, and is later to be named after Francis C. Smith, S.J.

1934 Regiopolis College is given federal incorporation on 4 January

On 10 January, the new Jesuit Juniorate building at Guelph opens

On 16 March, royal assent is given to a bill of the Ontario Provincial Legislature to incorporate Regiopolis College, Kingston, by amending its royal charter to "enlarging its provisions and granting it more ample powers" as "Regiopolis University"

The chapel at the Jesuit Seminary is constituted a parish for the Czecho-Slovakian residents in Toronto

1935 The Jesuit Seminary Fund (later Jesuit Seminary Association) is founded on 12 October by Erle G. Bartlett, S.J., at a bridge party attended by 400 people in Toronto

1937 Stanley House on Lake Joseph in the Muskoka Lakes Region, Ontario, is rented as a summer "villa" for Scholastics at the Jesuit Seminary, Toronto

The Jesuits depart from Sault Ste. Marie, Ontario

1939 On 12 March, the Vice Province of Upper Canada becomes the Province of Upper Canada, with 300 members

The Jesuits at Campion College, Regina, open a "villa" at Stilton, Saskatchewan, with much of the construction undertaken and carried out by John M. Filion, s.j.

James O'G. Fleming, S.J., establishes a retreat centre for men at the Jesuit Seminary, 403 Wellington Street West, Toronto

1940 On behalf of the archdiocese of Halifax, the Jesuits accept from the Christian Brothers the direction of Saint Mary's College (later University) on Windsor Street, Halifax

The Jesuits purchase the site of Sainte-Marie among the Hurons, Midland, Ontario

On 16 October, Pope Pius XII names the Canadian Jesuit Martyrs the secondary patrons of Canada after Saint Joseph

1941 Under the direction of Dr. Kenneth Kidd of the Royal Ontario Museum, archaeological excavations begin at Sainte-Marie among the Hurons

After four years of renting Stanley House on Lake Joseph in the Muskoka Lakes Region, Ontario, as a summer "villa" for the Scholastics, the Upper Canada Province purchases it for the Jesuit Seminary

1943 The faculty of theology is established at the Jesuit Seminary, 403 Wellington Street West, Toronto

The Provincial Superior's residence moves from 160 Wellesley Crescent to 2 Dale Avenue, Rosedale, Toronto

The *Sacred Heart Radio Hour* (later *Sacred Heart Program*) is founded

1944 The *Canadian Messenger of the Sacred Heart* office moves in January to 2 Dale Avenue, Toronto

Michael W. Burke-Gaffney, S.J., publishes *Kepler and the Jesuits*

1945 The Jesuit European Relief Fund is founded by the Scholastics at 403 Wellington Street West, Toronto

1946 The Canadian English-speaking Jesuits accept their first overseas mission in Darjeeling District, West Bengal, India

The retreat centre at 403 Wellington Street West, Toronto, directed by James O'G. Fleming, S.J., moves to Erindale, Ontario, and becomes Villa Manresa

Manresa Retreat House (Immaculate Heart of Mary) is established at 180 Beaconsfield Boulevard, Beaconsfield, Quebec

The Loyola Jesuit Community, Montreal, purchases from the estate of Dr. Oscar Mercier the "villa" on an island in Lac L'Achigan, in the Laurentian mountains

1947 The Jesuits' Darjeeling Mission Service (later incorporated into the Canadian Jesuit Missions) is established at 403 Wellington Street, Toronto

1948 The high school programme opens at Garnier Residential School, Spanish, Ontario

1949 The Villa Manresa retreat house moves from Erindale to Liverpool Road, Pickering, Ontario

The Jesuit Seminary Association is founded, and its first director, Wilfred T. Harris, S.J., is appointed

The Hungarian Jesuits take over the administration of St. Elizabeth of Hungary parish at Spadina and Dundas streets in central Toronto, and for a number of years, the church also serves as the winter shrine for devotion to the Canadian Martyrs

The "Salute to Canada", a pageant directed by Daniel A. Lord, S.J. (Missouri Jesuit Province), is produced at Martyrs' Shrine, Midland, on 27–31 July to commemorate the tercentenary of the deaths of the Canadian Martyrs of Huronia

1950 Bellarmine Hall, a residence for Jesuits studying at the University of Toronto, opens at 226 St. George Street

1951 Charles E. McGuire, S.J., opens the Catholic Labour School in Toronto

Publication of the *Jesuit Seminary Bulletin* begins by the Jesuit Seminary Association

Saint Mary's College and High School move from Windsor Street to 35 Robie Street, Halifax (Gorsebrook Campus), and the college is granted the status of university

1952 The Jesuits open Canadian Martyrs Parish, Halifax

1953 Loyola Retreat House, Raydor, opens at Oakville, Ontario

1954 Fire destroys the churches of Holy Cross, Wikwemikong, and St. Anthony Daniel, Kaboni, on Manitoulin Island, 24 January

On 17 August, the grave of St. Jean de Brébeuf is discovered at Sainte-Marie among the Hurons, Midland, by Denis A. Hegarty, S.J.

The Jesuit seminary formally changes its name to Collegium Christi Regis (College of Christ the King)

"The Marian Pageant", written and produced by Daniel A. Lord, S.J., is staged on the grounds of the Canadian National Exhibition, Toronto, in October to mark the Marian Year

Fire destroys the Bedford House at St. Stanislaus Novitiate, Guelph, on 18 November

1955 St. John Brebeuf Parish opens at St. George's Chapel, Winnipeg, and is serviced from St. Ignatius Parish

Clement J. Crusoe, S.J., is appointed the first dean of studies for the Upper Canada Province

1957 In May, Jesuits of Saint Mary's, Halifax, acquire property for a villa at Mason's Point, St. Margaret's Bay

Frederick J. Power, S.J., is appointed to the national secretariate of the Apostleship of Prayer

Insight: A Study in Human Understanding, by Bernard J. F. Lonergan, S.J., is published

The gymnasium auditorium opens at Campion College, and is named in memory of Francis J. Boyle, S.J., a former Rector who had begun the project

The National Jesuit Campaign, to raise $2 million to build extensions at St. Stanislaus Novitiate, Guelph, and for a new Jesuit seminary building in the Toronto area, begins

1958 Garnier Residential School in Spanish, Ontario, closes

The faculty of philosophy at the Jesuit Seminary, 403 Wellington Street West, Toronto, closes and the Jesuit students transfer to Mount St. Michael's College, Gonzaga University, Spokane, Washington State, for their philosophical studies

St. Paul's College moves from Ellice Avenue and Vaughan Street to the Fort Garry Campus, University of Manitoba, Winnipeg, into a building designed by the famed Vancouver architect Peter Thornton

In September, St. Paul's College, Winnipeg, becomes the first Canadian Jesuit institution of higher education to admit women to its undergraduate programme

St. Stanislaus Novitiate, Guelph, is incorporated as Ignatius College

1959 After reaching its goal, the National Jesuit Campaign ends

The first electronic digital computer (Royal-McBee LGP 30) in Atlantic Canada is installed at Saint Mary's University, Halifax

The first women students are admitted to Loyola College, Montreal

The *Canadian Messenger of the Sacred Heart* office moves in November to 226 St. George Street, Toronto

1960 The new wings for classrooms, chapel, and refectory open at Ignatius College, Guelph

The programme of psychological evaluation for candidates to the Society of Jesus is initiated in the Upper Canada Province

Due to the ill health of the Superior General, Jean-Baptiste Janssens, s.j., John L. Swain, S.J., is appointed Vicar General of the Society of Jesus on 22 April

St. John Brebeuf church opens at 605 Renfrew Avenue, Winnipeg

1961 The Jesuit Seminary moves on 21 March to 3425 Bayview Avenue, Toronto (Willowdale), to the building designed by the noted architect Peter Dickinson, and assumes a new name: Regis College

The McNally Building opens at Saint Mary's University at 923 Robie Street, Halifax

A Jesuit residence opens for the first time in Ottawa at 175 Stewart Street

The laying of the cornerstone takes place at Loyola College, Montreal, on 28 October for a science building designed by Peter Dickinson and named after Lewis H. Drummond, S.J.

The Czech Jesuits in exile open the Czech Mission House at 4605 West Broadway Avenue, Montreal

J. Raymond Oliver, S.J., is appointed the first director of the Mission Band

A Jesuit residence opens at St. John Brebeuf church, 570 Renfrew Street, Winnipeg

1962 In St. John's, Gonzaga High School is founded at 16 Smithfield Crescent, and a Jesuit residence opens at 50 Bonaventure Avenue

The Science Wing at St. Paul's College, Winnipeg, opens in September

W. A. Royden Devlin, S.J., is appointed the first director for vocations in the Upper Canada Province

The Jesuits accept the direction of St. Pius X Parish, 16 Smithfield Crescent, St. John's

1963 An agreement is signed between the Upper Canada Province and the Government of Ontario for the rebuilding and management of Sainte-Marie among the Hurons, Midland

Saint Mary's University High School, Halifax, closes

Hingston Hall, a men's residence at Loyola College, Montreal, opens on 18 April, and is named in honour of William H. Hingston, S.J., Rector of Loyola from 1918 to 1925

The Jesuits open Brebeuf College School, 211 Steeles Avenue East, Toronto (Willowdale)

1964 Campion College becomes a federated college of the University of Saskatchewan (Regina Campus)

Gonzaga Jesuits move from 50 Bonaventure Avenue to 16 Smithfield Crescent, St. John's

Manresa Retreat House (Immaculate Heart of Mary) moves from Beaconsfield to 2305 Bord du Lac, Île-Bizard, Quebec

St. Paul's High School, Winnipeg, moves from Ellice Avenue and Vaughan Street to 2200 Grant Avenue, Tuxedo, in south Winnipeg

Loyola Retreat House, Raydor, moves from Oakville to Ignatius College, Guelph, and Clifford N. Rushman, S.J., is appointed director

A student cafeteria wing and the Jesuit Residence opens at St. Paul's College, Winnipeg

The Provincial Superior's residence moves from 2 Dale Avenue to 2 Hawthorn Gardens, Toronto

Bellarmine Hall at 226 St. George Street is sold and moves to 2 Dale Avenue, Toronto, to continue as a residence for Jesuits studying at the University of Toronto

The Jesuit Seminary Association moves from 226 St. George Street to 27 Eglinton Avenue East, Toronto

The Canadian Jesuits from Darjeeling District, India, arrive in Kanglum, Bhutan

On 27 October, Governor General Georges-P. Vanier opens the Georges P. Vanier Library of Loyola College, Montreal

A new "villa" is constructed on the farm at Guelph for the Juniors and novices

Loyola College High School is incorporated separately from Loyola College, Montreal

The *Canadian Messenger of the Sacred Heart* office moves from 226 St. George Street to 68 Broadview Avenue, Toronto

1965 The department of communications, the first in Canada, is established at Loyola College, Montreal, under the direction of John E. O'Brien, S.J.

The library building at Gorsebrook Campus, Saint Mary's University, Halifax, opens

1966 The church of St. Ignatius Parish, 4455 West Broadway Avenue, Montreal, opens

St. John Brebeuf, Winnipeg, opens a new church at 570 Lanark Street

The new Campion College building, designed by Peter Thornton, opens on the campus of the University of Saskatchewan (Regina Campus, and later University of Regina)

The first retreat is given for women at Manresa Retreat House, Pickering

The Bryan Building of Loyola College, Montreal, opens to house the department of communications

1967 Pedro Arrupe, s.j., makes the first visit to Canada by a Superior General of the Society of Jesus

Two dozen young Jesuits from both Canadian Provinces join to retrace the three-week canoe journey of the early Jesuit missionaries from Sainte-Marie among the Hurons to Montreal, arriving at Expo 67 on 4 September—the first inter-Provincial Jesuit activity since the separating of the Province of Canada in 1924

Manresa Retreat House (Immaculate Heart of Mary) at 2305 Bord du Lac, Île-Bizard, Montreal, closes

During the summer, the O'Donnell-Hennessey Student Centre opens at Saint Mary's University, Halifax

The Athletics Complex opens at Loyola College, Montreal

Regiopolis College and Notre Dame Convent School, Kingston, Ontario, unite to form Regiopolis–Notre Dame Catholic Secondary School

The Biology-Chemistry Building opens at Saint Mary's University, Halifax

The programme in classical studies (the Juniorate) at Ignatius College, Guelph, closes and the Jesuit students attend University of Guelph

1968 The first Canadian Jesuits arrive in Zambia to join the Mission there

The Campion Jesuits' "villa" at Silton is torn down, and a new one is constructed under the management of Brother Maurice H. Kline, S.J.

A ceremony takes place to mark the official restoration of Sainte-Marie among the Hurons

The first "intentional small community" of the Upper Canada Province opens on Bleeker Street, Toronto, as a "satellite" Jesuit house for Scholastics of Regis College, Willowdale

1969 The new Loyola Jesuit Residence, Montreal, opens in February on the campus of Loyola College

The buildings at the former Garnier Residential School, Spanish, Ontario, are sold

Jesuits accept the direction of Our Lady of Lourdes Parish, 41 Earl Street, Toronto, from the archdiocese of Toronto

A house on Lake Winnipeg, named "Tarsus Villa" by John J. Murray, S.J., is purchased by the St. Paul's High School Community

Regis College becomes a founding member of the Toronto School of Theology at the University of Toronto, an ecumenical federation of seven theological faculties and colleges

1970 The Jesuit Infirmary opens at Regis College, Toronto (Willowdale)

Huskies Stadium opens at Saint Mary's University, Halifax

Canadian Martyrs Parish, Halifax, moves from Saint Mary's University chapel to temporary quarters on Inglis Street

Jesuits formally incorporate Saint Mary's University, Halifax, under the "Acts of Incorporation" with a Board of Governors and an Academic Senate

1971 Jesuits withdraw from Regiopolis College (Regiopolis-Notre Dame), Kingston

For his scholarly contributions, Bernard J. F. Lonergan, S.J., is invested by Governor General Roland Michener as a Companion of the Order of Canada on 31 March 1971

Camp Ekon begins at Stanley House on Lake Joseph, Muskoka Lakes Region, Ontario

In May, Saint Mary's University, Halifax, opens both the students' highrise Loyola Residence and Vanier House

Jesuits transfer Campion High School to the Catholic Separate School Board of Regina, and withdraw from the high school

The new church of Canadian Martyrs Parish opens at 5900 Inglis Street, Halifax

1972 Bernard J. F. Lonergan, S.J., publishes *Method in Theology*

A library building opens at St. Paul's College, Winnipeg, and is later named after Harold J. Drake, S.J.

Michael M. Murray, S.J., is appointed the first director of the Indian Lay Deacons Program

A "satellite, experimental" house opens at 6124 South Street, Halifax, consisting of three Jesuits from the Saint Mary's Community

An observatory opens at Saint Mary's University, Halifax, and is named after Michael W. Burke-Gaffney, S.J.

1973 A congress of all the members of the Upper Canada Province is held at Regis College, Toronto, from 19 to 24 August, with Pedro Arrupe, s.j., Superior General of the Society of Jesus, in attendance

The *Canadian Messenger of the Sacred Heart* office moves to 833 Broadview Avenue, Toronto

A Jesuit residence opens at 67 West Avenue, Toronto, with four members as a "satellite" house to the Pickering Jesuit Community

1974 Loyola College merges on 22 August with Sir George Williams University to form the new Concordia University, Montreal

The collegiate programme at Ignatius College, Guelph, ends, and the Jesuit students move to St. Michael's Institute, Gonzaga University, Spokane, Washington State, for their university studies

Jesuits transfer the administration of Saint Mary's University to the archdiocese of Halifax

The former Campion College and High School building on Albert Street and 23rd Avenue, Regina, is sold to the Catholic Separate School Board

1975 Ogilvie Residence, 175 Stewart Street, Ottawa, closes and is sold along with the "villa" (Ogilvie Point) at Larrimac, Quebec

The Upper Canada Province transfers the assets, including the royal charter, and the administration of Regiopolis College, Kingston, to the archdiocese of Kingston

The "satellite, experimental" house at 6124 South Street, Halifax, closes

A building is purchased at 15 St. Mary Street, Toronto, adjacent to the campus of the University of Toronto, as a new home for Regis College

The Upper Canada Province accepts the offer by the Ontario Bible College and Wahumith Enterprises Limited to buy the property of Regis College at 3425 Bayview Avenue, Willowdale

1976 On 27 January, the Jesuit Infirmary moves from Regis College, Willowdale, to 398 Vine Street, St. Catharines, Ontario

The residence and offices of the Provincial Superior move from 2 Hawthorn Gardens to 67–69 Marmaduke Street, Toronto

Regis College moves from 3425 Bayview Avenue to 15 St. Mary Street, and the Jesuits move into eleven houses in central Toronto

A Native Prayer Garden opens at Martyrs Shrine, Midland, on 29 August

The Ignatian Spirituality Centre opens at 4567 West Broadway Avenue, Montreal

1977 The Red House apostolate is founded at Ignatius College, Guelph

St. John Brebeuf Parish, Winnipeg, is officially established as an independent parish

1978 The Regis College Act of the Ontario legislature receives royal assent on 24 November, giving the college full legal status on a par with other Ontario universities and colleges

The Indian Lay Deacon Program is established along with the Ojibway Theological Centre at Spanish, Ontario, by Michael M. Murray, SJ

The new gymnasium of Loyola High School, Montreal, opens on 2 December

1979 The Jesuit Centre for Social Faith and Justice opens in Toronto

Regis College becomes a federated college of the University of Toronto

The first Provincial communal discernment takes place at Guelph under the direction of John J. C. English, S.J.

The Upper Canada Province establishes the Jesuit Companions

Lonergan University College on Loyola Campus, Concordia University, Montreal, and named after Bernard J. F. Lonergan, S.J., is founded and receives its first students in September

1980 Hévey Residence is established at 512 Jarvis Street for Jesuits visiting Toronto

The Jesuit Infirmary moves from St. Catharines to the grounds of Manresa Retreat House, 2315 Liverpool Road, Pickering

Frederick E. Crowe, S.J., is appointed the first director of the Lonergan Centre (later renamed Lonergan Research Institute), Regis College, Toronto

Bellarmine Hall (now Residence) moves from 2 Dale Avenue to 94 Kendal Avenue, Toronto

The Red House is named the Ignatius Farm Community, Guelph

1981 On 28 February, the Jesuits move from their residence at Saint Mary's University, 923 Robie Street, to a renovated apartment building at 1061 Wellington Street, Halifax

Elliott MacGuigan Hall opens at 67 St. Nicholas Street, Toronto, as part of Regis College

1982 Jesuits transfer St. Ignatius Parish to the archdiocese of Montreal

Provincial offices move to 1709 Bloor Street West, Toronto

The *Canadian Messenger of the Sacred Heart* office moves to 661 Greenwood Avenue, Toronto

A residence for Regis College at 18 Dundonald Street, Toronto, is purchased and named Daniel House

1983 *Compass: A Jesuit Journal* is founded

The Jesuit residence of St. Paul's High School, Winnipeg, moves from 2200 Grant Avenue to 1044 Grosvenor Street

Tradition and Innovation: Essays by Jesuits from a Canadian Perspective is published, containing essays by thirteen Jesuits who were working in Canada

For his contribution to higher education in Saskatchewan, E. Peter W. Nash, S.J., is invested by Governor General Edward Schreyer as a Member of the Order of Canada, 5 October

	A residence for Regis College, Toronto, opens at 94 Isabella Street and is named "Pedro Arrupe House" in honour of the Jesuit Superior General
1984	Jesuits transfer Immaculate Conception Parish, 3776 West 28th Avenue, to the archdiocese of Vancouver
	Jesuits move from the residence at Campion College, University of Regina, to 2929 26th Avenue, Regina
	Anishinabe Spiritual Centre opens at Anderson Lake, Ontario, under the direction of Michael M. Murray, S.J.
	Jesuits transfer the administration of Brebeuf College School, 211 Steeles Avenue, (Willowdale) Toronto, to the Presentation Brothers
	Pope John Paul II visits Martyrs' Shrine and Sainte-Marie-among-the-Hurons, Midland
1985	The Jesuit Communications Project opens at 10 St. Mary Street, Toronto
	The Lonergan Research Institute is incorporated, and moves from Regis College to 10 St. Mary Street, Toronto
	A Jesuit residence opens at 135 Sweetland Avenue, Ottawa
	St. Elizabeth of Hungary church, Toronto, is transferred by the Hungarian Jesuits to 432 Sheppard Avenue East, Toronto
1986	The first Canadian Jesuits, James F. Webb, S.J., and Brian Massie, S.J., arrive in Jamaica to join the New England Jesuits' mission
	The Riverdale Jesuit Community at 67 West Avenue transfers to 57–59 Pape Avenue, Toronto
	Regis College's Jesuit Community residence at 316–318 St. George Street moves to 567 Huron Street, Toronto
1988	Provincial offices move from Bloor Street West to 92 Indian Grove, Toronto

The mission at Garden River is transferred to the diocese of Sault Ste. Marie

The Jesuit Refugee Program is established in Toronto

The offices of the Jesuit Centre for Social Faith and Justice move to 947 Queen Street East, Toronto

The Canadian Institute of Jesuit Studies opens in Toronto

The Jesuit Centre for Faith Development and Values opens at St. Paul's College, University of Manitoba, Winnipeg

The Loyola Jesuit Institute for Studies in International Peace (Loyola Peace Institute) is founded at Concordia University, Montreal

On 3 October, the Jesuit Community at Pickering, Ontario, is renamed the Manresa Jesuit Retreat Community, and a second community, the Manresa Jesuit Pickering Community, is canonically established, with a Superior appointed for each Community

1990 The Ottawa Jesuit Community moves from 135 Sweetland Avenue to 167–169 Sunnyside Avenue, Ottawa

A house at 505 Parkside Drive, Toronto, is purchased to serve as a centre for refugees

The Jesuit residence closes at St. Paul's College and moves to 99 Thatcher Drive, Winnipeg

A residence at 569 Huron Street, Toronto, is purchased for Regis College

1991 In February, the Jesuits' St. Andrew and the Thunder Bay District amalgamate into one Jesuit Community called the Thunder Bay District Community

The Jesuits accept the direction of St. Anne's Church (Fort William Reserve), 126 Mission Road, Thunder Bay, and of Our Lady of the Snows Parish, Armstrong, Ontario

The *Dictionary of Jesuit Biography: Ministry to English Canada, 1842–1987* is published

	The Jesuit residence at 47 Ranleigh Avenue, Toronto, closes
	A congress of all the members of the Upper Canada Province is held from 27 to 31 July on the campus of the University of Guelph
	The Jesuits close the residence at St. Theresa's Parish, Beardmore, Ontario
	La Storta residence opens on the grounds of Manresa Retreat House, 2320 Liverpool Road, Pickering
1992	The Provincial Superior's offices return to 69 Marmaduke Street, Toronto
	The Jesuits transfer the parish of St. John Brebeuf to the archdiocese of Winnipeg
	Loyola High School moves from Loyola Campus, Concordia University, to a new building at 7272 Sherbrooke Street West, Montreal
1993	Bellarmine Residence at 94 Kendal Avenue, Toronto, is sold and closes
	The Riverdale Jesuit Community at 57–59 Pape Avenue, Toronto, transfers to 23 Jones Avenue
1994	The Daniel Centre of Spirituality, 1050 Wellington Street, Halifax, opens
	A formal agreement is concluded between the Upper Canada Province and the New England Province concerning participation in the work of the Canadian Jesuits in Jamaica
	The novices of the Upper Canada Province move to St. Paul, Minnesota, on 19 August
	The Riverdale Jesuit Community at 23 Jones Avenue, Toronto, closes on 1 September
	The Regis College residence at 18 Dundonald Street, Toronto, is sold

1995 Jesuit residence at 99 Thatcher Drive closes, and a new residence opens at 155 Canora Street, Winnipeg

The Jesuit Novitiate, Guelph, closes, and the novices of the Upper Canada Province transfer to the Jesuit Novitiate at St. Paul, Minnesota

1996 Our Lady of the Snows Parish, Thunder Bay, is transferred to the diocese of Thunder Bay

The Upper Canada Province sends its Scholastics to Campion House, Creighton University, Omaha, Nebraska, for the humanities programme, and to Milltown Institute, Milltown Park, Dublin, Ireland, for philosophical studies

Kitchitwa Kateri parish opens in Thunder Bay, Ontario

1997 The Jesuit Residence at 155 Canora Street, Winnipeg, closes

The Jesuit Residence at 2929 26th Avenue, Regina, closes, and the Jesuits move to a new residence at 333 Avon Drive

The final issue of *Compass: A Jesuit Journal* is published in May

Hévey Guest House at 512 Jarvis Street, Toronto, is sold

St. Andrew's Parish is transferred to the diocese of Thunder Bay

Francis Xavier Community, British Columbia, is established for Jesuits working in the archdiocese of Vancouver and the diocese of Victoria

1998 The Jesuits' Tarsus Villa on Lake Winnipeg is sold, and a new Tarsus Villa is constructed on part of that property

The Halifax Jesuits move from 1061 Wellington Street to 1050 Wellington Street, Halifax

The Daniel Spirituality Centre, 1050 Wellington Street, Halifax, closes

The Jesuits withdraw from Gonzaga High School, St. John's

The Jesuit Centre for Catholic Studies is founded at St. Paul's College, University of Manitoba

A Jesuit Development Office is established for the Province of Upper Canada

1999 J. Winston Rye, S.J., and J. Joseph Frechette, S.J., are appointed to help establish St. Bonaventure College, St. John's

Cardoner Jesuit House of Studies is established at 122–124 Sackville Street for those studying the humanities and philosophy in Toronto

2000 The Provincial Superior's offices move from 69 Marmaduke Street to 1325 Bay Street, Toronto

The Jesuit residence at 47 Ranleigh Avenue, Toronto, is sold

The Jesuits accept responsibility for Holy Rosary Parish, 175 Emma Street, Guelph, and appoint Bernard F. Carroll, S.J., as parish priest

On 3 November, the new Angus Reid Arts and Multi-Media Centre opens at St. Paul's High School, Winnipeg

2001 On 9 January, John F. Hodgins, S.J., is awarded posthumously the Caring Canadian Award by Governor General Adrienne Clarkson in recognition of his fifty-one years of work at the Montreal Convalescent Hospital

The Provincial Superior's residence moves from 67 Marmaduke Street to 427 Parkside Drive

Martin J. Royackers, S.J., is murdered on 20 June outside his church at Annotto Bay, Jamaica, where he worked to support the poor farmers in their claim for more favourable land for farming

The Jesuits accept the direction of Kitchitwa Kateri Parish, 451 Syndicate Avenue, Thunder Bay

The Loyola Jesuit Residence and property, Montreal, is sold to Concordia University, but the Jesuit Community continues to live there until a new residence is purchased

The Ignatius Farm Community, Guelph, closes

Ignatius College (formerly St. Stanislaus Novitiate), Guelph, closes as a Jesuit residence on 4 November, and the Red House becomes the residence for the Jesuit Community

In November, the name of the Jesuit Infirmary in Pickering, Ontario, is formally changed to René Goupil House

2002 An adjacent residence at 335 Avon Drive, Regina, is purchased for the Regina Jesuit Community

The Upper Canada Province sponsors ANIA 2002, an Ignatian Pilgrimage at the Martyrs' Shrine, Midland, in association with World Youth Day 2002, Toronto

The Province Archives are renamed The Patrick Boyle Jesuit Provincial Archives on 15 November

2003 The Cardoner Jesuit House of Studies moves from 122–124 Sackville Street, Toronto, to a house at 7 Howland Avenue leased from the Redemptorist Fathers, which also serves as a house for Jesuits visiting Toronto

The Ecology Project at Guelph is founded by the Jesuits

2004 The Loyola Peace Institute at Concordia University, Montreal, closes

The Loyola Jesuit Community, Montreal, moves to two residences at 4410 Coronation Avenue and at 4605 West Broadway Avenue

2005 The Jesuits transfer Canadian Martyrs Parish to the archdiocese of Halifax

The Jesuits assume the direction of St. Peter's Church, 615 Connolly Street, Thunder Bay

A Jesuit residence and the Jesuit Centre of Ignatian Spirituality are founded at 2267 Brunswick Avenue, Halifax

The blessing of the new classroom wing, atrium, and Centre for the Performing Arts at Loyola High School, Montreal, takes place on 4 December

2006 The first joint meeting of the Provincial Superiors and Consultors of the Upper Canada and French Canadian Provinces is held at Villa Saint-Martin, Pierrefonds, Montreal

The Province of Upper Canada changes its name to Jesuits in English Canada

Martyrs Hall, an educational centre for school groups and pilgrims, opens at Martyrs' Shrine, Midland, Ontario

The Jesuit Centre for Social Faith and Justice becomes the Jesuit Forum for Social Faith and Justice, Toronto

The Regis College residence at 105 Madison Avenue, Toronto, is sold, and a house is purchased at 565 Huron Street, Toronto

The Jesuit residence at 1050 Wellington Street, Halifax, closes

On 31 July, the Jesuits purchase 7 Howland Avenue, Toronto, to continue as the Cardoner Jesuit House of Studies and as a guest house for Jesuits who visit Toronto

The North American Martyrs Novitiate at St. Paul, Minnesota, becomes a tri-Province house (Upper Canada, Missouri, and Wisconsin)

The building housing the Provincial Superior's offices at 1325 Bay Street, Toronto, is sold

Construction begins on a new chapel wing at René Goupil House, Pickering

On 7 October, the Lonergan Research Institute moves from 10 St. Mary Street to Regis College, 15 St. Mary Street

2007 A Catholic Studies programme is established at Campion College

The *Dictionary of Jesuit Biography: Ministry to English Canada, 1988–2006* is published

2008 The Jesuit Community of St. Paul's High School, Winnipeg, purchases a residence at 714 Park Boulevard South

The Jesuit residence of St. Paul's High School at 1044 Grosvenor Street, Winnipeg, is sold

With Bernard Carrière, s.j., as Superior and Erik Oland, S.J. as novice director, the novices from the Jesuits of English Canada and the French Canadian Jesuits move in August into a joint Novitiate at 5611, avenue Gatineau, Montréal

On 27 September, the Provincial Superior's offices move from 1325 Bay Street, Toronto, to 43 Queen's Park Crescent East, Toronto

2009 In October, Regis College moves from 15 St. Mary Street, Toronto, to 100 Wellesley Street West, Toronto

Jean-Marc Laporte, s.j., is appointed sacramental minister of St. Patrick's Parish, Halifax

The joint archive of the two Canadian Jesuit Provinces opens on 29 September at Maison Bellarmin, 25 rue Jarry Ouest, Montréal

2010 After 104 years of administering the parish of St. John the Evangelist, Waubaushene, Ontario, the Jesuits transfer it to the archdiocese of Toronto

The Jesuit Centre of Spirituality opens at 2287 Brunswick Street, Halifax

Jean-Marc Laporte, s.j., is appointed priest-in-charge of St. Patrick's Parish, Halifax

The ministry of The Spiritual Exercises begins in Vancouver

2011 The celebration by the two Canadian Jesuit Provinces at Port Royal, Nova Scotia, for the 400th anniversary of the arrival of the first Jesuits in Canada is held on 22 May

A Congress of the English-speaking Jesuit Province takes place from 27 to 31 July in Midland, Ontario, with the Superior General, Adolfo Nicolás, s.j., present, along with representatives from the French Canadian Province and with lay assistants from both Provinces

A plaque is unveiled at Canso, Nova Scotia, on 16 August commemorating the first recorded Mass in Canada on 5 May 1611 by the first Jesuits, Ennemond Massé and Pierre Biard, on nearby Grassy Island Fort National Historical Site

Jesuits transfer the parish of St. Peter, Thunder Bay, to the diocese of Thunder Bay

The Jesuit Spiritual Exercises Ministry is formally established in Vancouver

2012 The closing celebrations by the two Canadian Jesuit Provinces of the 400th anniversary of the arrival of the first Jesuits in Canada takes place on 12 May in Sillery, Quebec

Ivon Bellavance, s.j., a member of the French Canadian Province, is appointed as a Regent to the English Jesuit Province, and teaches at the Mother Teresa Middle School (Nativity School) in Regina

Robert J. Allore, S.J., is appointed the parish priest at the new parish, St. Mark's, Vancouver

The Jesuit residence at 4410 Coronation Avenue, Montreal, is sold

The first joint catalogue of the two Canadian Jesuit Provinces is issued

Kateri Tekakwitha is canonized at St. Peter's Basilica, Rome, by Pope Benedict XVI on 21 October

2013 The first joint meeting of the Superiors of the two Canadian Jesuit Provinces is held from 1 to 2 March

John W. McCarthy, S.J., is appointed director of formation for both Canadian Jesuit Provinces

The Jesuits in English Canada celebrate the hundredth anniversary of the founding of St. Stanislaus Novitiate, Guelph

The Jesuit Community of St. Paul's High School, Winnipeg, puts up for sale the residence at 714 Park Boulevard South, and in September moves to 260 Young Street in central Winnipeg

Frederick J. Power, S.J., ends a record-breaking fifty-six-year tenure as the National Secretary of the Apostleship of Prayer, and a record-breaking forty-seven-year tenure as editor of the *Messenger of the Sacred Heart*. The magazine ceases publication.

INDEX

A

Aboriginal Rights Coalition, 69
Abraham, Murray, 200
Addley, William M., 152
Akwesasne First Nation, 59
Alaska mission, 68, 241
Albanel, Charles, 31
Alberta, 232
alcoholism, 30, 38–39, 42, 50, 212
Allouez, Claude-Jean, 31
Ambrozic, Aloysius, 120
America magazine, 91, 194, 206–8
Anglicans, 38, 130, 177, 202–3
Anishinabe Spiritual Centre, 66–67, 259
Annotto Bay, 25, 263
anti-Catholicism, 41, 114
Apostleship of Prayer, 190–92, 199, 201–5, 211, 249
Appel aux Jésuites, 82, 105–6, 159
Arns, Paulo, 177
Arpin, Alphonse, 93, 102
Arpin, Ludgar, 112–13, 240
Arrupe, Pedro, 124, 129, 151, 170–71; visit to Canada, 97, 253, 255
Arsenault, Kevin J., 181
Ashes and Tears, 69
Assiginack, Jean-Baptiste, 44–45
Association for Media Literacy (AML), 229–31
Association of Roman Catholic Communicators in Canada (ARCCC), 229
Athabasca University, 232
Augustinian Sisters, 80, 82

Aulneau, Jean-Pierre, 193
Auriesville (New York), 80, 85

B

Baillargeon, Charles-François, 84
Baltutis, Peter, 25
Baraga, Frederic, 55–57, 108
Barry, Hugh W., 62
Bartlett, Erle G., 210, 246
Baudin, Alphonse, 117
Baugh, Lloyd, 226–28
Baxter, Richard, 111–12, 236, 238
Beaudois, Donald F., 149
Beausoleil First Nation, 120
Beckx, Pieter Jan, 57, 108
Bedford, Harold, 178
Bégin, Louis-Nazaire, 86
Békési, István, 137
Bela, Peter, 154
Bélanger, Charles, 54
Bellarmine, Robert, 34
Bellarmine Hall (Toronto), 248, 252, 258, 261
Bellavance, Ivon, 69, 267
Bellemare, Albert, 59
Benedict XVI, 70, 184, 267
Benedictines, 155, 198
Bergin, Joseph I., 197–200
Berrigan, Daniel, 208, 222
Bertell, Rosalie, 176
Beschefer, Thierry, 81
Biard, Pierre, 233, 267
Blain, David, 48
Blair, Louisa, 186
Blind River (Ontario), 49
blogs, 232–33
Bolton, Wayne J., 149, 152, 155
Bond Head, Sir Francis, 36, 43, 46
Bordowitz, Lois Anne, 175
Boulanger, Clément, 56, 235
Bourdeau, Onésime E., 118
Bourget, Ignace, 27, 39, 82, 105–6, 159

Bouvrette, Stanislaus, 119–20
Boyd, Vernon, 153
Boyle, Francis, 249
Boyle, Patrick J., 133, 264
Boyle, William, 131
Bradley, George, 115
Brandon (Manitoba), 104, 118, 239
Brébeuf, Jean de, 21, 34; beatification of, 82–90, 243; canonization of, 73–74, 90–92; death of, 118, 119; grave of, 248; veneration of, 74–82, 92–102
Brebeuf College School. *See under* high schools
Bressani, Giuseppe, 83
British Columbia, University of, 186, 262
Brophy Place, 148, 180
brothers, 159, 195, 206; and native ministry, 32, 35, 45, 55, 58, 68; and parishes, 108, 114, 118, 119; and social apostolate, 148, 179, 180
Brown, Edward M., 134–35
Brown, George, 48–49
Brown, (Brother) George, 118
Brown, Jenny, 69
Brown, John R., 178
Browne, William J., 147–48
Bruchési, Paul, 87
Brzezicki, Joseph A., 153
Burka, Lelemen, 136
Burns, E. Leo, 126
Buteux, Jacques, 84
Byrne, Patrick, 152

C

Calvez, Jean-Yves, 171
Camara, Helder, 172
Campbell, Mary McMartin, 92
Campion College (Regina). *See under* colleges
Canadian Centre for Policy Alternatives, 183
Canadian Conference of Catholic Bishops (CCCB), 171–72, 176, 178, 181, 208, 229
Canadian Jesuit Missions Office, 229, 247
Canadian Martyrs: 118, 195, 245, 248; beatification of, 82–90, 243; canonization of, 73–74, 90–92, 244; death of, 118, 119; graves of, 248; veneration of, 74–82, 92–102
Canadian Pacific Railway, 59, 109, 111
Canadian Radio-television and Telecommunications Commission (CRTC), 221

Cape Croker (Ontario), 40, 120, 183
Carney, James Francis, 133–34
Carney, Robert, 39
Carrez, Louis, 45
Carrière, Joseph, 59
Carroll, Bernard F., 153, 263
Carter, Alexander, 66, 173, 177
Carter, Emmett, 173–74
Casey, Kenneth C., 129
Casey, Timothy, 130–31
Casot, Jean-Joseph, 82, 101, 235
Casti Connubii, 197
Catherine the Great, 23
Catholic Film Office, 220
Catholic Labour School, 158, 166–67, 187, 248
Catholic New Times, 209–10
Catholic Register, 198–203
Catholic social teaching, 29–30, 70, 158, 164–74, 180–87
Catholic Women's League, 148, 154
Cazeau, Charles-Félix, 45
Center for Concern (Washington, DC), 172
Central America, University of (UCA), 181
Chabanel, Noël, 75, 80, 86–87
Charbonnel, Armand de, 114
Chartier, Remi, 112, 240
Chaumonot, Pierre-Marie, 79
Chazelle, Pierre, 32–33, 39, 55, 159; as first superior of Canada mission, 28, 82, 105–7, 235
Chodos, Robert, 209
Choné, Jean-Pierre, 21, 38–39, 45–47, 52–53, 106, 235
Christian Brothers, 130, 134, 146, 148, 246
Christian Island, 79, 120, 149
Christian Life Communities, 42, 124
Clarke, Joseph L., 150
Clement XIII, 22
Clement XIV, 22, 82, 106n5
Cloran, J. Brendan, 133
Coady, Moses M., 199
Coffee, John C., 121, 241
Coleman, John A., 183

colleges: Collège de l'Immaculée-Conception (Montreal), 113, 162, 195, 238, 239; Collège de St-Boniface (St-Boniface), 113, 121, 239, 243; Collège du Sacré-Coeur (Sudbury), 241; Collège Saint-François-Xavier / Collège des Jésuites (Edmonton), 241; Collège Sainte-Marie (Montreal), 28, 57, 85, 159, 161–62, 236, 237; Campion College (Regina), 68, 69, 163, 225–26, 242; Ignatius College (Guelph), 154, 186, 230, 237, 250; Loyola College (Montreal), 58, 124–25, 215–17, 220–24, 240; Regiopolis (Kingston), 142, 163, 244, 245, 253; Regis College (Toronto), 67, 181, 229, 250, 254; St. Bonaventure College (St. John's), 263; St. Dunstan's College (Charlottetown), 238; St. Ignatius College (Guelph), 237; St. Paul's (Winnipeg), 142–44, 163, 245, 249, 251
Colliard, Alfred J., 200
Compass: A Jesuit Journal, 208–9, 223, 258, 262
Concordia University, 219–21, 223–24, 226, 228–29
Conilleau, Charles, 106, 117
Connolly, John J., 191–92
Connon, Thomas, 93
Conroy, George Michael, 115
Consalvi, Ercole, 23
Cooper, Alfred, 64
Costello, Jack, 184
Côté, Louis, 117
Cotter, Aloysius, 113
Coutts, Michael A., 152
Couture, Joseph-Marie, 54
Cranston, William, 96
Crinnon, Peter Francis, 115
Crowe, Frederick E., 201, 258
Crusader, 205–6
Currie, John, 144
Czerny, Michael, 174–75, 177–78, 180–81, 208

D

Daniel, Antoine, 21, 75, 79–80, 86–87
Darjeeling mission, 147, 200, 247, 252
Daughters of the Immaculate Heart of Mary, 52, 58
D'Azeglio, Luigi Taparelli, 30, 165n30
deacons (aboriginal), 67, 100–1, 255, 257
Debassige, Louis, 41
de La Lande, Jean, 75, 80, 86–87
de la Ronde, Charles, 47
de L'Incarnation, Marie, 80

De Smet, Pierre-Jean, 35
Devine, Edward J., 84–85, 88, 111–12, 161, 187, 194–97
Dezza, Paolo, 123, 202n34, 227n89
dictionaries (aboriginal), 50, 75
Diocesan Order of Women (Diocesan Order of Service), 67
Doherty, Marcus C., 205
Dominus ac Redemptor (1773), 22, 103
donnés, 38
Donovan, Daniel J., 113, 118
Dorion, Antoine-Aimé, 45
Dowling, Edward J., 134, 149
Dowling, Thomas Joseph, 115
Draimin, Tim, 177–78
Driscoll, Joseph V., 143–44
Drolet, Joseph, 119
Drummond, Lewis H., 118, 121, 194, 250
Dubrisson, J. Guion, 81
Dugas, Jacques, 121
Dulles, Avery, 31
Dunn, William, 115, 131
du Ranquet, Dominique, 21, 32–35, 106, 235
du Ranquet, Henri, 161

E

Ebner, Rupert, 114
ecological work, 25, 180, 185–86, 264
ecumenism, 69–70, 133, 172–74, 176, 254
El Salvadoran martyrs, 181, 184
Eley, David R., 208, 225–26, 228–29
English, John J., 25, 66, 186, 230, 257
Espanola (Ontario), 66
Eucharistic Crusade, 205–6
evangelization, 31, 53, 70–71, 111, 204
excommunication, 42
Expo 67 (Montreal world exhibition), 97, 214, 217, 253

F

Faithful Companions of Jesus, 175
Fallon, Joseph, 162, 187, 196, 243, 244
famine ministry, 158, 160, 187
Farm Community. *See* Jesuit Farm Project

Farrell, James J., 99–100, 163
Farrell, John, 114–15
Feeley, W. Ross, 133
Férard, Martin, 50–51, 106, 117
Filion, John M., 88–91, 99, 125, 129–31, 243
Filles de Marie, 53, 61
fire, destruction by, 36, 49–50, 59, 111, 119, 240
First Nations University of Canada, 69
Fischer, Clair J., 57–58, 224
Fischer, Leonard, 58, 146–47, 153
fishery disputes, 37–38, 44–47, 49
Flahiff, George Bernard, 143, 173
Florida, 47
Foliot, Robert G., 152
Fordham University, 161
Forgách, László, 136
Formula of the Institute, 157
Fort Sainte-Marie Inn, 92, 98
Fort William (Ontario), 39, 51–54, 56, 109–13, 154–55
Fox, Sherwood, 84
Fraser, John, 192
Frémiot, Nicolas, 49
French River, 40
Friends on the Outside (FOTO), 69, 180
fundraising, 22, 137, 140–41, 143, 162, 195
Fruzzini, Joseph, 114

G

Galt, John, 114
Garden River (Ontario), 51, 55–57, 109, 236–37, 260
Garden Village (Ontario), 40
Gardner, George, 67
Garnier, Charles, 75, 78, 80, 82, 86–89, 95
Garnier College (Spanish, Ontario), 61, 63–65, 247, 249, 254. *See also* St. Peter Claver Industrial School
Gaudium et Spes, 168, 171
Gauthier, Georges, 126–27, 162
Gavin, Joseph B., 24
general congregations (GC) of Society of Jesus: GC27, 89; GC28, 165; GC29, 166; GC31, 24–25, 170, 202; GC32, 24–25, 158, 170, 202; GC34, 185; GC35, 185
George, Gordon F., 145, 176, 199, 202, 207, 215

Georgetown University, 115
Gervais, Marc, 208, 213, 220–24, 226
Gésù, Church of the, 117
Gibbard, William, 44, 46–48
Gonzaga High School (St. John's). *See under* high schools
Goupil, Réne, 74, 80, 85, 87
Great Depression, 61, 122, 158, 165
Green Bay (Wisconsin), 39
Green Lake (Saskatchewan), 69
Greene, Charles, 144
Greer, Allan, 79–80
Gregorian University, 219, 225–27
Grosse Île, 160
Guelph, 25, 66, 104, 133, 183, 185–86. *See also* Juniorate; Novitiate; parishes; retreat houses
Guelph raid, 154, 242
Guelph, University of, 230

H

Halifax, 178. *See also* high schools; parishes; Saint Mary's University
Hall, Emmet, 176
Hamel, Pierre, 115, 238
Hanipaux, Joseph-Urbain, 35, 39, 42, 44, 55, 236
Hannin, Daniel J., 66–67, 68–69, 70
Harris, Wilfrid, 247
Hawkins, Michael J., 149
Hayes, James M., 136
Hegarty, Denis A., 95–97, 248
Henry, Hubert, 206–7
Heroux, Aloysius, 113
high schools: Brebeuf College School (Toronto), 120, 129, 251, 259; Campion College High School (Regina), 242, 243, 249, 255, 256; Gonzaga Regional High School (St. John's), 144, 148, 251, 262; Loyola College High School (Montreal), 124, 129, 242, 252, 257, 261; Regiopolis (Kingston), 142, 163, 244, 245, 253; St. Bonaventure College (St. John's), 263; Saint Mary's University High School (Halifax), 62, 134, 248, 251; St. Paul's High School (Winnipeg), 143, 245, 251, 254, 258, 263
Hingston, William H., 115–16, 126, 132, 196–97, 251
Hinphy, Clarence P., 104, 133, 139–42, 150, 163
Hoch, Charles, 114
Hochban, John I., 210–11

Holy Cross Mission, 35, 37, 42–43, 235, 248. *See also* Wikwemikong *and* Manitoulin Island
Holy Names of Jesus and Mary, Sisters of, 122, 141
Holzer, John E., 113–15, 236, 237
Hôtel-Dieu, Sisters of (Hospitalers), 82, 89, 235
Hudon, Théophile, 88
Hudson Bay Company, 52–54
Huron, 28, 31, 34, 75. *See also* Wendat
Huronia, 21, 28, 31, 34, 83–85, 100, 120, 206
Huronia Historical Development Council, 96
Hus, Jean-Baptiste, 116
Hyland, Edward, 181

I

Ignatieff, George, 174
Ignatius Jesuit Centre, 186–87
Immaculate Conception, Mission of, 52–55
inculturation, 43
Indian Affairs, Department of, 59, 65
Innocent X, 75
Inter-Church Committee on Human Rights in Latin America (ICCHRLA), 177
Inter-Church Committee for Refugees (ICCR), 184
Internet, 204, 232–33
Inuit, 60
Ironside, George, 49
Iroquois Confederacy, 29, 36, 77, 79, 81

J

Jackson, Anne-Marie, 184
Jaffré, Jean, 106, 116–17
Jamaica, 25, 93, 259, 261, 263
Jamot, Jean-François, 109
Janssens, Jean-Baptiste, 166, 250
Jennessaux, Joseph, 21, 32, 34, 35, 41, 43
Jesuit Centre for Social Communications, 219
Jesuit Centre for Social Faith and Justice, 174–83, 187, 257, 260, 265
Jesuit Communications Project (JCP), 228–32, 259
Jesuit estates, 118, 239
Jesuit European Relief Appeal (JERA), 163, 247
Jesuit Farm Project, 25, 185–86, 258, 264
Jesuit Forum for Social Faith and Justice, 183–84, 187, 265

Jesuit Messenger, 191, 200
Jesuit Refugee and Migrant Service (JRMS), 178–79, 181, 184, 260
Jogues, Isaac, 21, 75–76, 80, 84–87, 243
John XXIII, 65, 168, 200
John Paul II, 70, 99–101, 147, 202–3, 204, 259
Johnson, Joseph, 136, 144, 151
Jones, Arthur Edward, 85–86, 102, 118, 193–94, 241
Juniorate, 238, 242, 245, 253
Jury, Wilfrid, 95, 97, 102
Justice in the World, 29, 169–70, 173, 187

K

Kahnawake (Quebec), 31
KAIROS: Canadian Ecumenical Justice Initiatives, 70, 184
Kateri Tekakwitha, St., 31, 70, 85–86, 99, 196n20, 267
Kavanagh, Isidore J., 194
Keane, Henry J., 94
Keating, Joseph A., 92
Kennedy, Raphael E., 132–33
Kentucky, 32
Kettler, William, 114
Kidd, Kenneth E., 94, 102, 246
King, Cecil, 44
Kinoshameg, 47
Knight, John, 182
Knights of Columbus, 124, 148
Knox, John D., 130
Knox, Michael L., 21
Knox, Ronald, 197
Kohler, Auguste, 35, 39, 47–49, 55–57, 109, 237
Kolvenbach, Peter-Hans, 185, 219
Kroker, Lawrence J., 55, 67

L

LaCoste, Adrien, 108
Lake Huron, 35, 55, 114
Lake Joseph, 54, 246, 255
Lake Nipissing, 40
Lake Superior, 28, 52–53, 55, 109–11
Lalemant, Gabriel, 77–82, 85–91, 93, 95, 97, 118–19
Lally, Thomas J., 92–96, 206

Lamarche, Prosper, 112
L'Ancienne-Lorette, 31, 120
Langevin, Adélard, 120–21
Langevin, Alfred, 119
La Prairie (Quebec), 24, 104–5, 235, 236
l'Arche communities, 185, 202
Latin America: lay ministry, 40, 72, 133, 163, 192, 226, 255; missions in, 21, 34, 71, 151; and social justice, 159, 169, 175, 177–78, 207
Leahy, J. Adalbert, 132, 134
Lecompte, Édouard, 121
Leddy, Mary Jo, 184
Ledóchowski, Wlodimir, 126, 130–31, 245
Le Jeune, Paul, 34, 79
Leo XIII, 164–65, 167, 239, 240
Little Current (Ontario), 39
liturgical life, 42–43, 100, 128, 133, 142–43, 146
Livingstone, Matthew W., 69
Lonc, William P., 50, 136
Lonely Island (Ontario), 46–47
Lonergan, Bernard J., 25, 30, 199, 249, 255, 257
Lonergan Research Institute, 25, 258, 259, 265
Lord, Daniel J., 96, 248
Loretto, Sisters of, 114, 116, 244
Loyola College (Montreal). *See under* colleges
Loyola Convalescent Home, 162, 187
Loyola High School (Montreal). *See under* high schools
Loyola Peace Institute, 260, 264
Loyola Retreat House. *See under* retreat houses
loyalists, 36
Luiset, Paul, 105, 235
Lynch, J. Frederick, 134, 145–47
Lynch, John D., 57, 149
Lynch, John J., 150, 191

M

MacDonald, John, 113, 118, 239
Macdougall, Angus J., 97–98, 149–50, 208–9, 220
MacDougall, Robert L., 211–13
MacEachen, Allan J., 177
MacGilvray, Roderick A., 142–43
MacGuigan, J. Gerald, 217

MacIsaac, James, 123
MacMahon, Thomas J., 242
Madagascar, 27, 228
Malone, Patrick G., 215–17
Manitoba, University of, 142, 144, 249, 260, 263
Manitoulin Island, 29, 34–40, 43–49, 51–53, 82, 159
Manitowaning, 37–38, 42, 47, 49
Manresa Retreat Centre. *See under* retreat houses
Mara, James J., 68, 200
Marckhgott, Francis, 114
Marconi, Gugliermo, 215
Margaret Mary Alacoque, St., 193
Martin, Félix, 28, 83–86, 102, 161, 236
Martindale, Cecil C., 197
Martyrs' Shrine (Midland, Ontario), 74, 87, 90–100, 102, 120, 163, 248
Martyrs' Shrine Message, 201, 206
Maryland, 171
Masterson, John, 128, 179
Massé, Ennemond, 233, 267
Mater et Magistra (1961), 168
Matheson, John D., 69, 180, 224–25
Matoga, Gaspar, 114, 236
Matthews, Carl, J., 120
Maurice, William, 70
Mayhew, Bernard A., 68
Maynard, François, 154
McCaffrey, John F., 96–97, 133, 150
McCarthy, John W., 153, 186, 267
McCrea, Charles, 91
McDonald, Joseph F., 128
McDougall, Gerald, 154–55
McDougall treaty (1862), 45
McDowell, F.W. Davey, 93, 102
McEleney, John J., 137
McGill University, 89, 225, 226
M'Chigeeng, 41
McGivern, James S., 201
McGivern, Toby, 100
McGuigan, James Charles, 137, 150, 198
McGuire, Charles, E., 166–67, 187, 248
McKague, A.H., 62

McKey, John E., 65
McLarnon, Daniel H., 211
McLuhan, Marshall, 214, 218n71, 225
McManus, Walter, 130–31
McNally, John T., 115, 134
McNeil, Neil, 91–92
McSheffrey, James, 148, 180
McWatch, Milton, 67
Medellín conference, 169
Meehan, Matthew, 211
Menet, Jean-Baptiste, 55–57, 106, 108–9, 236
Merchant, Edwin, 98–99
Mercier, Honoré, 73
Mercy, Sisters of, 144, 148
Messenger of the Sacred Heart, 88, 163, 190–205, 239, 243
Methodists, 38
Métis, 28, 69
Michigan, 36, 55, 57, 104, 107–8, 236
Mignard, Paul, 161
Miranda, Daryl, 153
missiology, 21, 34, 71
Mississagi River, 49
Mississippi River, 36
Mitchikinatoning, 39. *See also* West Bay
Mohawk, 31, 59, 85, 93
Molay, Jacques de, 23
Monahan, Peter Joseph, 113
Monet, Jacques, 208, 213
Month, The, 194
Morrison, James, 33, 35
Mother Teresa Middle School (Regina), 69, 267
Mullally, Thomas J., 120, 133
Murray, Gerald, 122–23
Murray, John J., 144, 254
Murray, Michael M., 66, 255, 257, 259

N

Nadeau, Paul, 51–52
Napoleon, 23
National Museum of Canada, 94
Nativity school. *See* Mother Teresa Middle School (Regina)

Nazar, David, 182
Neault, Olivier, 112
New York–Canada mission, 117, 236, 237, 238
Nipigon (Ontario), 53
Nolin, Jean-Baptiste, 87, 104, 117, 119, 194, 238
North Bay (Ontario), 53
Northwest Fur Company, 109
Notre Dame, School Sisters of, 68
Nova Scotia, 58, 134, 199, 213, 233, 266
Novitiates: at Guelph, 25, 146, 229, 230, 241, 242; at Sault-au-Récollet, 50, 236, 238, 241
Nunan, George E., 134, 207–8, 216

O

Oblate Fathers, 40, 54, 100, 116, 131, 140
O'Boyle, William P., 131
O'Brien, John D., 25
O'Brien, John E., 215, 217–21, 224–26, 252
O'Connell, William Henry, 91
O'Connor, Denis T., 86
O'Connor, Richard A., 110, 112
Odawa, 28, 50
O'Donnell, Michael J., 149
O'Gara, Edward, 108, 122
Ojibway: 28, 33, 50–51, 59, 93; language of, 21, 39, 50–51, 55
Oka, 21, 32
Oklahoma, 36
Oliver, J. Raymond, 61, 143, 251
Open Space, 184
Orange order, 118
orphanages, 53, 63, 111, 114
Osawanimiki, Chief, 47–49
Osceola, Chief, 47
Ottawa, University of, 225
Our Way of Proceeding in the '80s, 129, 134

P

Pacem in Terris (1963), 168, 200
Paquin, Julien, 32, 41, 47, 113
Paraguay, 35
Paray-le-Monial, 193

parish missions, 105
parishes: Assumption (Sandwich), 106–7, 235, 237; Canadian Martyrs (Halifax), 104, 134–36, 248, 254, 255, 264; Holy Rosary (Guelph), 153–54, 236, 237, 263; Immaculate Conception (Fort William), 109–11, 112; Immaculate Conception (Vancouver), 129–34, 243, 244, 259; Immaculée-Conception (Montreal), 117, 239; Kitchitwa Kateri (Thunder Bay), 55, 67, 262, 263; Nativity of Our Lady (La Prairie), 24, 104–5, 235, 236; Our Lady Immaculate (Guelph), 24, 113–16, 239; Our Lady of Lourdes (Toronto), 104, 148, 149–53, 254; Our Lady of the Snows (Armstrong), 260, 262; Precious Blood / Sacred Heart (Sault Ste. Marie), 108–9, 238, 242; St. Andrew's (Port Arthur / Thunder Bay), 110, 111–12, 238, 260, 262; St. Anne's (Thunder Bay), 55, 260; Ste-Anne-des-Pins (Sudbury), 104, 117, 238, 239; St. Augustine of Canterbury (Brandon), 118, 239; St. Bartholomew's (Guelph), 114–15, 155, 236, 237, 238; St. Elizabeth of Hungary (Toronto), 136–39, 248, 259; St-Ignace / St. Ignatius (Steelton), 57, 240; St. Ignatius (Winnipeg), 68, 120–24, 139, 142, 241; St. Ignatius Loyola (Montreal), 124–29, 242, 252, 258; St. John Brebeuf (Winnipeg), 104, 123, 139–44, 249, 250, 257; St. John the Evangelist (Waubaushene), 86, 118–20, 240, 266; St. Joseph's (Chatham), 116–17, 237, 238; St. Mary's (Sault Ste. Marie, Michigan), 55, 104, 107–8, 237, 242; St. Patrick's (Fort William), 110–11, 112–13, 154, 240, 243; St. Peter's (Thunder Bay), 154–55, 264, 267; St. Pius X (St. John's), 144–49, 155, 251
Paul VI, 168, 169, 201
Pearen, Shelley, 50
Penetanguishene (Ontario), 35, 86, 119
Penney, Alphonsus, 146–47
Pereira, Adrienne, 229
Pigeon River (Ontario), 39, 52
pilgrims, 73–74, 85–87, 90–102, 139, 193–94, 206, 240
Pinochet, Augusto, 177
Pinsonneault, Pierre-Adolphe, 107, 116–17
Piovesana, Roy, 110, 112
Pittau, Giuseppe, 227
Pius VII, 23
Pius IX, 109
Pius X, 86, 144
Pius XI, 73, 89, 90, 91, 164–65, 197
Pius XII, 94, 144, 214–15, 246
Ploughboy affair, 47–49
Pocock, Philip F., 68, 139–41, 150
Point, Nicolas, 35, 39, 106
Point, Pierre, 21, 104, 106–7, 235, 237
Pontifical Council for Social Communications, 219, 226

Populorum Progressio (1967), 169
Potawatomi, 28
Power, Frederick J., 198, 201, 203–5, 211, 249, 268
Power, Michael, 105–6, 113, 159
Pratt, E.J., 93, 102
preferential option for the poor, 169, 174
Presentation, Brothers of the, 120, 259
Presentation, Sisters of the, 91
Primeau, Albini, 113
Primeau, Joseph, 126
prison ministry, 69, 124, 157, 178, 180, 212
Profit, Jim, 185–86
Project North. *See* Aboriginal Rights Coalition
Proulx, Jean-Baptiste, 35, 37, 38, 46
Proulx, Philémon, 46–47
Province congresses, 233, 255, 261, 266
Pujolas, Mary, 199, 203
Pungente, John, 213, 228–32

Q

Quadragesimo Anno (1931), 158, 164–65, 167, 197
Quebec City, 34, 45, 47, 80–82, 89, 125, 236

R

radio, 100, 167, 190, 201, 210–11, 213–16
Ragueneau, Paul, 21, 76–79, 81, 83
railways, 54, 59, 109, 111–12, 154
Ramière, Henri, 191
Ratio Studiorum (1599), 161, 190, 239
Reddin, A. Earland, 122
Redemptorists, 130, 211, 264
reductions, 21, 32, 34, 35
refugees, ministry among, 124, 137–38, 147, 177–81, 184–85, 187
Regina, 62, 68–69, 163, 180, 242
Regina, University of, 69, 225, 253, 259
Regis College (Toronto), 67, 181, 224, 229, 248, 250, 254
Regnault, Christophe, 77
Regnouard, Marie, 81
Relations, 51, 74–75, 79–80, 83–85, 189
relics, 77–78, 80–82, 89, 91, 96, 100–1
Rerum Novarum (1891), 158, 164–65, 167, 187

residential schools, 40, 42, 53, 58–61, 63, 70, 239. *See also* Garnier College, St. Joseph's School, St. Peter Claver Industrial School
Restoration (of Society of Jesus), 23, 82, 235
retreat houses: Loyola House, 25, 186, 187, 248, 252; Manresa, 220, 247, 251, 253, 258
Ricci, Lorenzo, 23
Richard, Joseph-Richard, 51
Rickaby, Joseph, 198
rites (Chinese and Malabar), 21
Riverdale Immigrant Women's Centre, 175
Robarts, John, 96
Robichaud, Marie, 91, 98
Robillard, Joseph, 118
Robillard, Ruth, 69
Romero, Oscar, 184
Romero House, 184
Roothaan, Jan P., 27, 82, 105, 107, 159
Roque, Ferdinand, 38
Rouleau, Raymond-Marie, 73–74
Royackers, Martin, 25, 208, 263
Royal Ontario Museum, 94
Ruel, Alexdrine, 91
Rupert, Christopher, 153
Ryan, Cecil C., 199–201
Ryan, Joseph Francis, 153
Ryan, William F., 123, 133–34, 171–74, 182–84, 228
Rye, J. Winston, 24, 98, 263

S

Sacred Heart devotion, 190, 192–95, 199, 203, 211
Sacred Heart, League of the, 191–92
Sacred Heart, Sisters of, 41, 130–31, 133, 176
Sacred Rites, Congregation of, 87, 89, 90–91
St. Ann, Sisters of, 132
St. Augustine's Seminary, 220, 243
St. Francis Xavier University, 199
St. Ignace II (village of), 77, 85, 87, 93–94, 97, 118, 240
St. Ignatius College (Guelph). *See under* colleges
St. Ignatius Loyola, 106, 134, 142, 155–56, 157–58, 187
St. Joseph, Sisters of, 53, 58, 111, 113, 114
St. Joseph's School, 60, 64–65
St. Laurent, Louis, 96

St. Mark's College (Vancouver), 267
St. Mary's Academy (Winnipeg), 122
St. Mary's College (Montreal). *See under* colleges
Saint Mary's University (Halifax), 58, 128, 216, 224, 246
Saint Paul University (Ottawa), 225
St. Paul's College (Winnipeg). *See under* colleges
St. Peter Claver Industrial School, 60–61
Sainte-Marie among the Hurons, 31, 34, 76–78, 82, 96–98, 100, 235
Sandwich (Windsor), 21, 24, 33, 104, 106–7, 155, 235, 237
Santerre, François Xavier, 117
Saskatchewan, 69, 242, 246, 251, 253, 258
Saul, John Ralston, 28–29
Sault-au-Récollet. *See under* Novitiates
Sault-Ste-Marie (Michigan), 107–8
Sault-Ste-Marie (Ontario), 28, 39–40, 47–48, 55–58, 108–9, 236
Scarboro Foreign Mission Society, 192
School Sisters of Notre Dame, 68
Schreyer, Edward, 99, 258
Scollard, David Joseph, 111, 154
Scott, Ted, 177
Seasons, Harvey D., 133
Seminole, 47
Shanahan, David, 62–64
Sheguiandah, 39
Sheridan, Edward, 128, 136, 150–52, 172, 181
Sherlock, John, 177
Sheshegwaning, 39
Sillery (Quebec), 34, 267
Sinnett, John C., 115
Sinnott, Alfred Arthur, 122–23, 244
Sir George Williams University, 219, 256
Skinner, Patrick J., 145–46
slavery, 34
Smithsonian Institute, 50–51
societas perfecta, 34, 65
sodalities, 23, 42–43, 89, 132, 245
Sollicitudo Omnium Ecclesiarum (1814), 103
Somerville, Henry, 198
South Bay (Ontario), 39
Spanish (Ontario), 40, 58, 60–65, 241, 247, 249. *See also* Garnier Residential School
Spanish influenza, 60
Spanish River, 60

Spencer, Henry, 120
Spiritual Exercises (of St. Ignatius Loyola), 25, 123, 186, 230, 232, 266, 267
sports, 62
Stakum, Thomas, 118
Stanley, David M., 200
Steelton (Ontario), 57, 240
Stoeklin, Martin, 35
Stogre, Michael J., 70, 176
Stony Mountain penitentiary, 178, 212
Sudbury (Ontario), 104, 117, 119, 238, 239, 241
Sudbury, University of, 239, 241
Sullivan, John A., 152
Sulpicians, 33
Suppression (of Society of Jesus), 22–23, 31, 82, 103, 106n5
Swain, John L., 97, 166, 250
Sweeney, James, 35
Swift, Jamie, 180

T

Tablet, The, 206
Taché, Alexandre-Antonin, 118
Talbot, Francis-Xavier, 95, 102
Taschereau, Elzéar-Alexandre, 86
Taskforce on Churches and Corporate Responsibility (TCCR), 175
Tecumseh, Chief, 29, 45
television, 100, 167, 190, 210–16, 221, 231–33
Tellier, Rémi-Joseph, 105, 117
temperance societies, 42, 105. *See also* alcoholism
Three Fires Confederacy, 28–29, 31
Thunder Bay, 40–41, 55, 67–68, 104, 110, 154–55, 238
Thwaites, Reuben Gold, 85, 189n1
Toronto, University of, 94, 174, 229, 248, 252, 254, 256
Toronto School of Theology, 25, 229, 254
treaties (with First Nations), 34, 37, 44–46, 52
Trudeau, Pierre E., 174, 214
tuberculosis, 60
Tyler, Ernest C., 150

U

Urban VIII, 84
urban native ministry, 55, 67–69, 180, 262–63, 267
Ursulines, 80, 89, 108, 117

YUKON
NORTHWEST TERRITORIES
NUNAVUT
BRITISH COLUMBIA
ALBERTA
Edmonton
SASK-ATCHE-WAN
MANITOBA
Vancouver
Regina
Winnipeg
ONT
Spanish